HOW TO START
A HOME-BASED
RESUME SERVICE

D1378945

DATE DUE

JUN 20 2011		

Also by Jan Melnik

How to Start a Home-Based
Secretarial Services Business

HOW TO START A HOME-BASED

RESUME SERVICE

2nd edition

by Jan Melnik, CPRW

The Globe Pequot Press

Old Saybrook, Connecticut

Cover and text design by Nancy Freeborn

Library of Congress Cataloging-in-Publication Data is available.

ISBN 0-7627-0068-8

Manufactured in the United States of America
Second Edition/First Printing

To my three bright rays
of sunshine—Westy, Danny, and Stephen—
and to Bobby (after 35 years, it was about time!)
I love you all so very much.

CONTENTS

ACKNOWLEDGMENTS

I am privileged to count among my friends, colleagues, and clients some very special individuals who not only are incredibly talented and respected in their chosen professions but are especially forthcoming. They were willing to share their expertise and valuable insight with me as I wrote this text.

I'm especially grateful to George Eames and Bob Francis for letting me lean on our friendship and for giving me so much of their personal time; thanks, Kit and Fran, for sharing your insights, impressions, and the much-appreciated boost of confidence.

I would be remiss not to acknowledge the contributions of the other professionals and colleagues with whom I've had the pleasure to work over the past few months in some instances and over many, many years in other cases.

Peter Ferris, Walt Truscinski, Don McCarthy, Bill Breck, Chuck Embree—I've enjoyed and grown from our collegial, professional, and personal friendships over the years and I am very appreciative of your contributions to this project.

Cindy Cannon, Bob Esposito, Bob Wolfe—I'm very grateful to you all for your time, knowledge, and support. Dave Denino, Susan Rietano, Theresa Bachhuber, Wendy Pease, Patricia Frechtman, June Walker—I am enriched to have learned so much from you all in the months spanning this project. Thank you for your generous assistance. And to Cathy Moore, thanks for facilitating a number of key contacts.

Within my own industry I've enjoyed the camaraderie and support of some very talented professionals and dear friends. I thank every professional resume writer who responded to my in-depth survey and willingly shared details and experiences with me, including my colleagues on the Internet. I'm especially appreciative of the contributions of three cherished friends in this group: Louise Kursmark, Carla Culp, and Dawn LaFontaine. Lou, thank you for the invaluable "sanity checks" and, as always, for your deep friendship and support. I am also appreciative of the detailed industry background and cutting-edge focus provided by the executive director of the Professional Association of Resume Writers, Frank Fox. Marty Weitzman, whom I consider a colleague and personal friend, is the president of the National Resume Writers' Association. He was helpful in providing information about the newest professional association serving our industry—a true "grassroots" effort to deliver to resume-writing members what they need and want in a professional organization to excel. In addition, I owe a debt of gratitude to two Internet "wizards" in the resume field: Lisa Freeman and René Hart. Thank you both for your invaluable contributions.

Elizabeth Richards, my editorial associate, was instrumental in expertly organizing and analyzing the results of detailed questionnaires submitted by successful resume writers and colleagues from all over the country. Shana Murphy, my editorial assistant, provided lots of behind-the-scenes assistance and support, for which I am grateful.

It takes the talents and efforts of many to bring a project like this to fruition. It almost goes without saying that I could not have completed this book without the objective and skillful assistance of my editor, Mace Lewis, whom I treasure as a dear friend as well.

To Laura (Francis), thanks for the champagne, laughs, and celebrations every step of the way! To my folks, Matt and Jane LaFountain, thanks for all the things you do. To Stephen, Westy and Danny—thank you for once again sharing Mom with the outside world and greeting me each day with your beautiful smiles. And, Bobby, I now know what it feels like to have the true support and love of the man in my life: *absolutely wonderful!* Thank you so much for everything.

INTRODUCTION

Nothing great was ever achieved without enthusiasm.
—Ralph Waldo Emerson, *Essays: First Series. Circles* (1841)

While this page opens the book, I reserved writing it until the very end of the project. I basically planned all along to use it as my "fencepost" for spouting a few key nuggets that I hoped would incite the reader with my enthusiasm for the resume-writing field and the myriad possibilities for building a lucrative and highly rewarding business in this industry. With the benefit of knowing what follows, I'm more excited than I could possibly have imagined about inspiring others to enter this field. I could not have anticipated the personal and professional growth I would experience in the process of interviewing, researching, and writing the material in this text. And that's what is so thrilling: that even after owning my business for fourteen years, I'm still energized and learning. The significant revisions *and* additions to this, the second edition of this book, reflect the continuing changes in this exciting industry!

Another motivating factor is the excitement and energy every resume writer I surveyed expressed about this field—and their synergistic optimism about the future of our industry. These "veterans" range from those who have owned their businesses only a few years to those who started out more than twenty years ago! The enthusiasm they conveyed speaks volumes to the prospective entrepreneur who is contemplating a start in the field.

Let's get busy!

*Man, unlike any other thing organic or inorganic in
the universe, grows beyond his work, walks up the stairs
of his concepts, emerges ahead of his accomplishments.*
—John Steinbeck, *The Grapes of Wrath* (1939)

Sample Bio (my own!)

JAN MELNIK, CPRW
P.O. Box 718
Durham, CT 06422
(860) 349–0256 ● fax (860) 349–1343

Professional Highlights

- Author, ***How to Start a Home-Based Resume Service*** (Globe Pequot [2nd ed.], published summer 1997)—every facet of starting and running a successful resume service, the ideal business for the 90s and beyond! Jan has consulted with 5,500+ clients, surveyed more than 250 professional resume writers, and interviewed scores of industry professionals in human resources and executive recruitment as well as hiring managers in researching this book. Available from booksellers nationwide.

- Author, ***How to Start a Home-Based Secretarial Services Business*** (Globe Pequot [2nd ed.], published fall 1996)—called the "industry Bible" and available from booksellers nationwide.

- Editor/Publisher ***The Word Advantage***—a quarterly newsletter distributed nationwide by subscription; designed for those who work with words (writers, graphic designers, desktop publishers, and owners of resume, word-processing, secretarial, and office support services).

- President, Absolute Advantage/division, Comprehensive Services Plus of Durham, CT (1983–Present) Highly successful home-based business; provides professional desktop publishing, business consulting, resume/career search, and office support services to clients throughout the country.

- Contributing Editor, ***NASS Newsletter, Keyboard Connection, MASS·NASS Newsletter, Bootstrappin' Entrepreneur, S-O-S Quarterly.***

- Invited Guest Speaker, Paul and Sarah Edwards's national business radio program, *Vera's Voice* and *Money Radio* programs, America Online and numerous other radio and television programs.

- Business/Marketing Consultant to small businesses, universities, hospitals, medical/psychological practices.

- Training Consultant/Lecturer and National Keynote Speaker—address various associations on all aspects of operating a successful home-based business.

- Formerly held management, training, and administrative positions (12 years) at John Hancock Mutual Life Insurance Co. (Boston, MA), Digital Equipment Corp. (Burlington, MA, and Meriden, CT), Parker-Hannifin Corp. (Middletown, CT), Two Ems, Inc. (Madison, CT), and Bunting & Lyon Publishers (Wallingford, CT).

- Graduate, Bay Path College (Longmeadow, MA); cum laude.

Professional Memberships

- Professional Association of Resume Writers (PARW); Certified Professional Resume Writers (CPRW); National Resume Writers' Association (NRWA).

- National Association of Secretarial Services (NASS); Middlesex County Chamber of Commerce.

Civic Involvement

- Founder/President/Treasurer, Middlesex County Mothers of Twins Club 1/89–Present

- Durham Planning and Zoning Commission, Commissioner/Recording Secretary 4/90–Present

- Classroom Volunteer and Room Mother, Brewster and Korn Schools 9/93–Present

CHAPTER ONE

WHAT IS A RESUME SERVICE?

THE SERVICES OF A RESUME BUSINESS

What services does a professional resume business provide? Obviously, resumes are the chief product of such a firm. These can be anything from basic retypes (professional typesetting) of a resume already written by a client to complete development of a resume "from scratch" (typically developed from material gleaned during extensive consultation)—and everything in between. Many clients who seek professional resume services already have a resume but need to have it brought up to date. Because of limitations on time, lack of editorial expertise, or inadequate word-processing and computer equipment, many prospective resume service clients feel unable or unqualified to write or update their own resumes. Hence, they seek the services of a professional dedicated to this field.

Nine times out of ten, the client who thinks he or she has a resume that just needs to be typed will benefit from the services of a professional resume writer in fine-tuning, expanding, or editing the existing materials. Many prospective resume clients do not give consideration to presenting a well-developed summary of qualifications or a concise listing of distinguishing attributes in their resumes. With the exception of those who work in sales, most clients do not consider the impact of quantifying key accomplishments by listing numeric results on their resumes. These are all areas in which a resume writer can use his or her expertise to prepare

QUOTABLE INSPIRATION

"Helping people find employment has always been a great source of satisfaction to me. I love to see my clients really enthused about their credentials when they take a look at their new, professionally prepared resume."—*Vivian Belen, CPRW, The Job Search Specialist (Fair Lawn, New Jersey)*

the client for the competitive job search process.

In addition to traditional resume preparation services, most professionals in the field also write cover letters for their resume clients. This can expand to include the preparation of mass mailings, targeted direct mail campaigns, and tailored weekly responses to newspaper advertisements. Few clients recognize the value of a carefully written and individually tailored cover letter. As recommendations from hiring managers presented later in this book attest, cover letters are just as important to the hiring process as well-written resumes. Many resume professionals provide leave-behind materials for their resume clients to present during job interviews. And a number also develop and promote interview follow-up correspondence. For individuals who so require, most resume professionals offer curriculum vitae (CV) development as well.

Beyond the paperwork associated with conventional job searches, a growing number of resume writers have advanced into such career preparation services as career counseling, interview training, job-search-technique skill building, aptitude and skills testing, and style analysis. For those resume services also offering secretarial services, typing of applications (for graduate school, private employment, and government SF-171 preparation) is a sideline. (SF-171 is the standard form required of prospective employees of state and federal government.) In some instances, consulting with clients to develop the responses to these applications is a profit center. Some resume services offer research services to their clients— from conducting in-depth library or on-line searches for hiring contacts to phoning companies in a particular geographic area to learn contact names.

Resumes are required for nearly every position for which an opening may or does exist. From undergraduate students seeking summer or midyear internship placements, new graduates investigating graduate school admission, and college graduates seeking first-time employment to individuals who are changing careers, seeking promotions, or recovering from corporate "reengineering" or "downsizing" (read: layoffs), there are literally millions of potential clients for resume services. In addition to traditional job search requirements, people need professionally written resumes for community or civic purposes, when developing business plans or serving as public speakers, and so on. Even individuals pursuing volunteer positions with such institutions as hospitals or elderly care facilities are well served to have professional resumes in hand at the time of the interview.

Because of technological advances, a professional resume writer today is able to conduct much business by telephone. This affords a unique home business opportunity without geographic limitations. If desired, a home-based resume writer may opt never to meet with clients but, rather, to provide all services by telephone (chapter 3 details how Wendy Enelow, CPRW, has developed a highly profitable business devoted exclusively to serving high-end resume clientele by phone).

A resume service is ideally suited for development as a home-based business. The owner's ability to meet with clients in hours beyond the traditional 9-to-5 window provides a competitive edge over downtown businesses in this field. And the home business owner's availability to meet with clients before or after hours is a convenience, not only to clients but to the proprietor as well. A resume business lends itself perfectly to flexible scheduling because client meetings can be scheduled on an appointment-only basis (more about this in chapter 7). This allows the service owner to work precisely those days, and hours, desired. The ability to offer Saturday appointments to clients employed during "regular" weekday hours can be a significant plus for a business. Such meetings are often confined to Saturday mornings. In exchange, a resume service operator might opt for "Fridays off"—or instead use the time for productive writing without interruptions by client appointments.

Resume services operated from retail storefronts, commercial offices, or executive suites typically must be "open" during the 9-to-5 hours and, frequently, may not offer client hours outside of this schedule. They must assume large overhead costs in maintaining these spaces. And they nearly always must have at least one employee in addition to the owner to provide walk-in coverage and telephone answering support. The home-based resume service provider incurs far fewer costs in establishing the business—and can closely monitor the growth of the operation to assess the appropriate times for hiring staff if desired. For those resume services operated from homes in which there are other residents "after hours," there are greater securities afforded them as compared with the sole proprietor in executive suite space meeting alone with a client after hours.

Whether operated from a home office or commercial space, resume services in the nineties are expected to provide clients with the highest-quality printed materials. Laser-printed original resumes on quality paper are standard in the industry. Flexible word-processing capability is *de rigueur*. Clients will expect at least a minimal period of access to their materials for subsequent updating (specifics regarding storage of client materials on disk are discussed in detail later). Inherent in the resume service business is the axiom "once a client, *always* a client." If you have satisfied the needs of your clients, they will return to you countless times in the years (and decades!) ahead for updating of their professional materials. And if a satisfied client is a middle-aged parent, in all likelihood you will be asked to prepare the resumes of his or her children as they graduate from college. Similarly, if you type resumes for an about-to-graduate college student, you may end up being asked to prepare career search materials for that individual's parents, siblings, or roommates.

Probably more than any other service business, the resume field has the greatest potential for repeat and referral business. These are areas in which the savvy entrepreneur is well advised to maximize—and this book will provide many concrete examples showing how to capitalize on these two phenomena. Resume services also enjoy incredible "staying power" (stability, that is), regardless of economic times. In areas of the country where there are regionalized pockets of continuing recession or slow growth, prospective clients especially need to have a competitive edge with their resume and cover letter materials. During booming economic times and periods of great growth, prospective clients will be scurrying for up-to-date resumes as they continue advancing up the career ladder. New college graduates need expert help in preparing distinctive resumes to help them compete effectively in the shifting job marketplace. Military personnel reentering the civilian workplace require resumes that accurately portray their accomplishments in lay terms. If you provide top-quality career materials, deliver excellent service, and generate client satisfaction, the amount of success—and money—you generate as a home-based resume service provider is limited only by the number of hours you choose to work.

WHAT YOU'LL NEED

It's relatively easy to open and operate a resume business at home. A discussion of skills and training will follow, but here's what you need, at minimum, in order to be able to offer resume services:

THE BASICS

☑ A good word processor with a reasonable selection of fonts (in addition to the standard fonts provided with most systems and printers, adding perhaps five to ten additional fonts appropriate for resumes is adequate)

☑ A laser printer with a minimum resolution of 300 dpi (dots per inch, the gauge for printing quality—the higher the number, or resolution, the sharper the image)

☑ A telephone (standard business or home business line preferred)

☑ A telephone answering machine or voice mail system

☑ Professional business cards (lots—you want to give these out freely and begin to cultivate referrals)

☑ A selection of at least three or four quality papers with matching envelopes (more details later)

☑ A business checking account

☑ Appropriate licenses and permits from your city or town

☑ A sales and use tax permit (if required in your state for collecting sales tax)

- ✔ A space designed for client meetings (a separate office area in your home is ideal; this can be a basement room, a spare bedroom, an unused dining or living room, a den, or an actual office space)
- ✔ Appropriate furniture (a desk, at least two chairs, a table, a file cabinet, and a bookcase)
- ✔ Adequate lighting

Beyond this bare-bones listing, the successful resume service owner should consider investing in the following "options" (some of these could be considered nearly mandatory; most will enhance your profitability):

OPTIONS

- ✔ A fax machine (for quickly transmitting resumes to executive recruiters on clients' behalf) or fax modem
- ✔ Merchant account status (ability to accept major credit cards; absolutely mandatory for long-distance dealings with clients outside your area, this allows you to market higher-end services to all clientele)
- ✔ An electronic or electric typewriter (for preparing oversize envelopes for clients' mail-merge mailings)
- ✔ A photocopier (useful in preparing work order copies and receipts for clients, copying clients' completed applications for your files, providing duplicate letters of recommendation to clients, and so on)
- ✔ A professional brochure for your business
- ✔ A regular newsletter or similar device for communicating with your clients regularly
- ✔ A professional library with materials to consult when preparing resumes and to loan to clients—or perhaps "rent" for a small fee with deposit (the Appendix includes recommended resources for the library of a professional resume writer)

If you already possess the furniture and lighting for your office and have a computer or word processor, you're more than halfway there with regard to equipment. You can probably invest between $500 and $1,000 additionally and be in business. Even if you lack every item on the bare-bones "basics" list, careful and creative purchasing techniques (tag sales, auctions, secondhand office furniture outlets, and so on) will enable you to open shop for under $3,000. If you wish to purchase top-of-the-line office furniture, a state-of-the-art Macintosh computer, color monitor, and 600 dpi printer with color capability, and so forth, you can easily invest $10,000 or $15,000.

My recommendation? Hold on to your money. As long as you create a professional office space in which to meet with your clients and have good equipment that produces professional-looking documents, there are numerous areas in which you can cut a few start-up-cost corners. Save some of those "ego dollars" (those that you may wish to spend on the trappings to make you feel or look good); invest them, instead, in Yellow Pages advertising and client cultivation efforts (you'll read more about these ideas later on).

EASING INTO THE BUSINESS

Many full-time resume service operators begin on a part-time or abbreviated basis, oftentimes moonlighting during the evening and weekend hours while maintaining a regular job on a part- or full-time basis during the day. Workers employed on the second shift might begin by tending to their resume service during the traditional daytime work hours, which allows them to go to their evening jobs after closing their resume office doors at 5:00 P.M.

With massive cutbacks still occurring across a wide range of industries nationwide, more and more individuals are seeking alternative forms of employment, not the least of which is self-employment. Among those who have been terminated by their "regular" employer, there is clearly a trend to launch their resume business full-scale on a full-time basis. I regularly consult by telephone and through on-line services with folks around the country who are entering the professional resume-writing business, and I see nearly every example of getting into the field successfully. Certainly for those with the security of a regular daytime position and the ability (and energy level) to start on a part-time, evening-and-weekend basis, the risk factor is significantly reduced. While open for debate, this can be considered the "easy" way to do it—it's the way I began my business.

Always knowing that I wanted to run my own company someday, I started providing resumes (as well as typing term papers) to clients from a basement office in my home. Because I worked away from my home from 8:00 A.M. until 5:30 or 6:00 P.M. five days a week, I had to rely on an answering machine to accept calls throughout the day during my absence. I never alerted clients that I was "working" during the day; my message simply indicated that I was unavailable (presumably with a client) and would return the call as quickly as possible. By offering my clients the advantage of an appointment during the evening or on a Saturday (or even Sunday), I quickly defined a niche for my business. Of course, in the words of my father, this frequently required "burning the candle at both ends." And while this was a financially comfortable way to begin my business, I can say firsthand that it rarely was easy.

But the rewards were clear from the beginning: Clients began to beat the proverbial path to my door and referrals began to occur in earnest. There was a magical point somewhere between twelve and eighteen months (heavily coincident with the publication of the local telephone directory carrying those invaluable Yellow Pages advertisements about which I'll preach later in this text) when repeat business began to establish itself, referral business became automatic, and new business occurred regularly. I liken this threshold to the one a dedicated runner achieves at the point that near-daily runs are an automatic part of the routine—when warming up, stretching out, and, later, cooling off happen almost without thinking, and the 4- or 5-mile run is as conditioned as it is therapeutic: It just seems to happen.

QUOTABLE INSPIRATION

"For years, I have always wanted to have my own business. I could never think of what business to start. I finally asked myself, 'What am I really good at that others want?' It dawned on me that with my experience and educational background, and the fact that I have been doing resumes for friends and relatives for years, a resume business was just the thing!"

—*Penni D. Schratz, Resume Composition &Design (Traverse City, Michigan)*

THE POTENTIAL FOR IMMEDIATE CASH FLOW

Before concluding the discussion of why a resume service represents an ideal home business enterprise, a preliminary look at how the numbers can work in this industry is important—both for inspiring the novice entrepreneur in the field and for bolstering the professional about to cross over from a related profession (executive recruiter, desktop publisher, or secretarial service operator, for example).

Let's suppose that you open for business on June 1 and that you have followed a later recommendation in this book to make your business opening coincide with publication of your area's updated Yellow Pages telephone directory. As a conservative beginning, we will project only one or two telephone calls from prospects per day (during "traditional" office hours). We'll also assume that you are 60 percent successful in "closing" business (in convincing callers to schedule appointments, that is). By the way, my objective throughout this text is to up the odds on your closure rate significantly by sharing detailed information from industry experts. We'll spread things out evenly across a week: With five to seven calls per week during normal hours and 60 percent closure, you will book about four appointments a week.

Let's presume one involves a basic retype for which you charge $30 (for purposes of this exercise, numbers provided are hypothetical; pricing details appear in chapter 5). Another appointment is for your complete consultation and top-end resume package ($200), and the other two are miniconsultations—one for a two-page format ($50, plus a total of 1.5 hours of consulting and writing at $50 an hour, for a grand total of $125) and one for a one-pager ($30, plus 1 hour of consulting and writing at $50 an hour, or $80 in all). You've grossed $435 for the week. Keep in mind several other factors: The longer you are in operation, the more business you can expect to occur from *repeat clientele* ("Susan, that resume you did for me a few months ago? I need twenty more originals." . . . "David, I'd like to change the summary on the resume we did last month." . . . "Dana, can we create cover letters now to go with the resume you did for me?" . . . "Gayle, I'd like to schedule time to meet with you regarding my interviewing techniques.") and from *referral clientele* ("Ed, Jane Smith told me you did a super resume for her last week. I'd like to meet with you regarding an update." . . . "Ann, I understand you worked with my father

Key Assumptions:

. . . 5 to 7 calls per week (based on publication of small, in-column ad in the "Resume Service" section of the Yellow Pages of phone directory)

. . . business owner able to directly answer the phone nearly 100 percent of the time between 9:00 A.M. and 5:00 P.M.

. . . 60 percent closure rate (that is, the ability to "book" 60 percent of the new callers per week into actual appointments)

Type of Call/Booked Business	Running Income Total
■ *Booked Call #1* Basic One-Page Resume Retype . . . flat fee: $30	$30
■ *Booked Call #2* Complete Consultation (top-end resume package) . . . $200	$230
■ *Booked Call #3* Miniconsultation and Editorial Services . . . 1.5 hours @ $50 . . . $75 Two-page Resume Retype . . . flat fee: $50 . . . TOTAL $125	$355
■ *Booked Call #4* Miniconsultation and Editorial Services . . . 1 hour @ $50 . . . $50 One-page Resume Retype . . . flat fee: $30 . . . TOTAL $80	$435
Total Gross Income for Week:	**$435**

Note: *Again, this scenario does not take into account the significant amount of referral and repeat business inherent with a resume service. After fourteen years in business, my typical week includes more than a dozen appointments with repeat clients—some for only additional copies of their recently prepared resume, others for extensive updates of their now-dated resume (easily can cost $150–$200 if a number of years have passed).*

on his resume a month ago. I will be graduating this May from the university and need some help." . . . and so it goes!).

It really takes very little time in this business to begin to build these all-important channels to continuing business and continuing profitability. What this all suggests, however, is the critical importance of capturing as many prospective clients as possible and booking appointments with them as systematically as possible. The more prospective clients you can attract to make the initial call to your office and the more of these callers you can engage in thoughtful discussion on the telephone and book for appointments, the more quickly and profitably your business will grow.

There are a few additional factors to consider when looking at the estimated projection of $435 for the first week. This example presumes that you covered your phone between the hours of 9:00 A.M. and 5:00 P.M. Start-up entrepreneurs in the resume profession consistently describe the additional number of calls they are able to handle (and new clients with whom they are able to book appointments) by being available to answer their phones after hours and on weekends. For the urgent job searcher, Sunday is the day when all the want ads are furiously scanned—and for the newly unemployed, that first Sunday is the day when, typically, he or she will realize, "I need a resume—and I need some help getting my cover letters prepared." Those most desperate will look in their local Yellow Pages, anxiously seeking several important words in any advertisements they find under the "Resume Service" category: *weekend appointments*. I heartily urge you to include "Evening and weekend appointments available" in your advertising copy. Just stating this does not obligate you to meet with clients every evening or even every weekend. You may opt, as I now do, to schedule a Saturday for meeting with resume clients just once per month, and perhaps set aside a weeknight only once or twice a week for client meetings.

A complete discussion of start-up costs appears in chapter 6, but this brief scenario illustrates the immediate cash flow a resume service is likely to experience. This fact, coupled with ease of start-up and the inherent low cost of getting into this business, makes it a highly desirable field for the motivated entrepreneur.

CHAPTER TWO

DO YOU "HAVE WHAT IT TAKES"?

MANY DIFFERENT EXPERIENCES ADD UP TO "THE PERFECT FIT"

No one candidate is ever the only "perfect" fit for a given position, and no one specific set of experiences or background can be said to be the "absolute optimum" in terms of ensuring the success of the entrepreneurial resume-writing professional. A combination of many different factors contributes to the likelihood of success, however, and these will be further explored below. Listed here, divided into three categories, are the traits and characteristics underlying success in the field of resume writing most often cited by professional resume writers.

SKILLS, ABILITIES, KNOWLEDGE, AND EXPERIENCE

- Excellent skills in writing English (good vocabulary, grammar, spelling, punctuation, and construction/syntax abilities)
- Strong communication and speaking skills (highly articulate and confident in presentation, particularly in telephone delivery)
- Ability to compose original documents with ease
- Background and experience in resume writing
- Good word-processing abilities

- Excellent eye for design and layout of documents
- Creative ability (including a flair for using adjectives and descriptors to highlight the salient points of a client's background)
- Educational background in a wide range of areas: business management, English/journalism, psychology, education/teaching, and human resources, to name just a few
- Work experience as a recruiter, hiring manager, human resources/personnel professional, placement specialist, counselor, trainer, social worker, or holder of other relevant positions in literally hundreds of fields
- Knowledge of many professions and areas of expertise
- Previous marketing or sales experience

CLIENT RELATIONSHIP

- Able to develop rapport with clients
- Maintains reputation for thoroughness, perfection, clarity, and brevity
- Able to provide a comfortable environment for clients
- Takes a personal interest in the individual client's resume
- Truly empathizes with client's plight (such as sudden unemployment)
- Able to focus on a client's key strengths, qualities, and accomplishments
- Enjoys talking with people and learning about their interests
- Genuinely relishes the challenge of "making people look good"

SPECIFIC SERVICE OFFERINGS

- Provides outstanding quality
- Guarantees 100 percent satisfaction with content and appearance of resume
- Promises and delivers fast turnaround of resume, cover letter, and other documents
- Heavily markets and provides customized cover letter services
- Delivers a range of "packages" to meet specific client needs; these may be flexible and range in price on the basis of client's background (student, midlevel manager, executive), time devoted to the project, or other criteria established in pricing structure
- Offers exclusivity—from distinction as the "only resume service in town" to possessing credentials as the only Certified Professional Resume Writer (CPRW) in the area
- Provides top-quality paper choices, including executive-class papers and uniquely designed specialty resume papers
- Has laser-printing capability
- Provides interview training and refresher courses to assist with career searches
- Maintains a library of books, publications, and videotapes for loan or lease to clients
- Provides free storage of resume and cover letter materials on computer or disk

Here's how Carla Culp, CPRW, president of Best Impression of Edwardsville, Illinois, described her key attributes as a resume writer.

1. Certified Professional Resume Writer (only one other in a 100-mile radius).

2. Experienced in the art of resume writing (but by no means know it all).

3. Genuinely interested in helping clients achieve success in their lives, however *they* choose to define it.

4. Can easily establish rapport with my clients; I'm easy to work with—flexible.

5. I enjoy what I do—writing resumes for people is my *choice,* not just a job!

Dawn LaFontaine, president of The Business Wordsmith of Ashland, Massachusetts, notes: "I believe everybody has something to offer, and I'm good at extracting that from even the most reticent, modest clients. I'm a good listener and I put people at ease, but I also ask very pointed questions to get the information that I require to do a good job for my clients. Then I write the resume with a real marketing perspective in mind, and I believe I'm really good at selling my clients to their prospective employers."

QUOTABLE INSPIRATION

"I am a resume writer and job search consultant. My mission is to make a difference in people's lives, to create a sense of energy, personal power, and hope in their lives, and to use my talents to accomplish these things on their behalf" (Kathy's business slogan).—*Kathy McConnell, CPRW, The Oval Office Resume & Career Services (St. Clair, Michigan)*

Jacqueline Herter, president of Professional Word Processing of Kodiak, Alaska, described her key attributes succinctly: "[I have] experience in the business world . . . an eye for display . . . and a way with words!"

As you review this comprehensive listing, can you say that you already possess or can immediately offer every one of these attributes, skills, and services? If so, you are the unique, "one-in-a-million" individual! Most of us probably already have a number of these strengths, but the vast majority (certainly myself included!) will recognize spots where we might say, "Yes, I could use a little more practice in that area." No problem. Just keep in mind as you are evaluating your "acumen for success" in the field of resume writing that the more of the attributes you possess, the more likely you will achieve success quickly. I fully believe that all individuals have potential for success in nearly any field they desire—with the right (read: high!) level of motivation, inspiration, desire, fortitude, and perseverance.

Remember that for every skill you may lack today—or simply not feel as well prepared in—there is always a solution. For example, if you are entering the resume-writing profession as a strong writer with human resources experience but lack the ability to type (never mind word-processing efficiency), you can do one of at least three things: subcontract the actual typing of resumes to an independent contractor, engage the services of a professional secretarial service to handle the production element, or hire a part-time secretary. Nothing says you can't "learn as you go." With keyboarding and word processing, many professionals become proficient over time, gradually learning their computer system and software. There really are no roadblocks to success in this field if you are motivated!

THE RIGHT BUSINESS FOR YOU?
CONSIDER THE BENEFITS!

At this point, some would-be resume-writing entrepreneurs may be thinking, "Is this field really for me? What is it actually all about? Would I be happy in this business?" Let's consider a sampling of the facets folks already in this field describe as their "chief rewards." As will be presented in greater detail later, more than 250 home-based resume service owners were surveyed for this book, using a very detailed questionnaire, and significant information was gleaned from their thorough responses. These men and women, entrepreneurs with wide-ranging experience and background, have operated their businesses anywhere from two to twenty-four years. In addition to many firsthand experiences drawn from my own background in this business, I will be sharing insights from these experts, whose personal experiences will expand your base of knowledge. Remember that it's just as important to learn the many ways to do things the right way as it is to be exposed to some of the mistakes to avoid when starting a resume business. And don't forget that you can do so efficiently, effectively, and, ultimately, successfully! On, then, to those areas of primary satisfaction described by your soon-to-be peers (you'll find a directory of these contributors in the Appendix and will note their specific recommendations interspersed strategically throughout the text).

INDEPENDENCE AND FLEXIBILITY

- Being my own boss! *(Janette Campbell, CPRW)*

- Complete flexibility and control over a process I love, without the potential burnout of a full-time, high-overhead storefront. *(Alan Ferrell)*

- The independence and ability to be creative. *(Cathy Cousear)*

- Don't have to deal with clients in person. *(Wendy Enelow, CPRW; as mentioned earlier, you'll be "meeting" Wendy Enelow, CPRW, later. Her business is conducted exclusively by telephone with clients from around the world)*

- The ability to "do what I want!" *(Anne Kramer, CPRW)*

- Flexibility of establishing own hours, setting own fees, and choosing own way to dress. *(Kathy McConnell, CPRW)*

- The independence and freedom! *(noted by everyone)*

SATISFACTION WITH CAREER AND SELF

- Being treated as a fellow professional (rather than "just" a secretary). *(Janette Campbell, CPRW)*

- Fulfilling my purpose. Helping people achieve their dreams. Satisfaction with the whole "lifestyle" that a home-based business provides. *(Barbie Dallmann, CPRW)*

- Small *and* large successes . . . making good contacts . . . getting lots of business in a short time . . . plus, I really like to write resumes. *(Jo Hammonds)*

- Ability to be creative! *(Anne Kramer, CPRW)*

- Ability to help someone develop qualifications and experiences in a resume format and assist that person in obtaining employment. *(Jo Hammonds)*

- Opportunity to meet interesting people from all walks of life, without the burden of working with (or for!) them day in and day out. *(Kathy McConnell, CPRW)*

- Pride that I help others. *(Cindy Patton, CPRW)*
- Personal achievements now . . . that were stifled by previous employers. *(Carol Ribar)*
- Enjoy meeting new clients and the variety this business provides. *(Jo Hammonds)*
- Enjoyment and satisfaction . . . enjoy challenge of assisting in career/job search. I take pride in hearing about comments clients received on their resumes! *(Penni Schratz)*
- Satisfaction for clients' success. It's a different kind of stress: energetic! *(Connie Stevens)*
- Because my perspective includes working as an employee for major employers and owning/operating a business from both home- and (formerly) office-based locations, I can truly say that I feel rewarded most as a home-based business owner in my freedom and ability to incorporate my professional goals with my choice of lifestyle (raising a large family [four children, including twin sons, something Carla and I share in common], maintaining a nice home, traveling, etc.). *(Carla Culp, CPRW)*

AVAILABILITY TO ONE'S FAMILY (IDEAS ECHOED BY MANY)

- Can be home when children get home from school.
- Can be home when children are home from school ill or on days when school is not in session.
- Can be generally available to one's entire family.
- Can provide children with a quality upbringing.
- Have the flexibility of scheduling work around family.
- Enjoy a schedule that allows for community and school involvement during traditional business hours (attending a school play, volunteering in a classroom, and other pursuits conventional employers might not tolerate).
- Able to provide care for aging parents.

ENVIRONMENT

- No time-consuming, stressful commute. *(Georgia Adamson, CPRW)*
- Can work on the computer in my pajamas. *(Vivian Belen, CPRW)*
- The flexibility of dress—don't have to dress up! *(Wendy Enelow, CPRW; Kathy McConnell, CPRW)*
- "Home-ability"! *(Jo Hammonds)*
- Have the flexibility of scheduling work around family.

FINANCIAL

- Low overhead, less temptation to eat meals out. *(Georgia Adamson, CPRW)*
- Money saved on car, fuel, clothes, dry cleaning, and lunches—plus nothing beats the thirty-second commute! *(Jo Hammonds)*
- Instant gratification of receiving money for service rendered. *(Carrie Kuntz)*
- Tax breaks. *(Jo Hammonds)*
- Money! *(Louise Kursmark, CPRW)*

QUOTABLE INSPIRATION

"This is an extremely rewarding business—professionally, personally, and financially. Great to find a way to 'make a buck' while providing a necessary service and support." (Note: details about how Wendy successfully works with clients 'long-distance' appear in chapter 3)

—*Wendy S. Enelow, CPRW, The Advantage, Inc. (Lynchburg, Virginia)*

A final note concerning the perceived financial advantages of operating a home-based resume service: 84 percent of the survey respondents indicated that they were either "very satisfied" or "satisfied" with the level of compensation. While perhaps reflective of the stance that you can never be "too rich" (or too thin!), only one person indicated that she was exceptionally satisfied with her compensation. No one reported being "extremely dissatisfied" with his or her remuneration.

Of the few respondents who indicated that they were "moderately dissatisfied" with their compensation, virtually all have been in business five years or less. One respondent, Cheryl Stoycoff of Stockton, California, added: "I'm only just starting [began part-time in September 1994, converted to full-time in January 1995], hoping to be 'very satisfied' soon!" Based upon the steps she is taking, I'm confident she will soon reach that level. Cheryl summarized her survey comments as follows: "The rewards of building your own business—having clients come to you, pay you, to do what you love, on your own terms—are incredible. I've never been so happy and would not trade my home office for a 'real' office for anything!"

CHAPTER THREE

STRATEGIES FOR AN IN-HOME BUSINESS

MAINTAINING THE BALANCE, KEEPING YOUR SANITY

I was seriously tempted to "outsource" this portion of the book as if to acknowledge "there's no way *I've* got a handle on this!" All joking aside, as a start-up entrepreneur in the field of resume writing, you'll probably find that one of the biggest challenges you'll face over time is being available to all of your clients as much as they'd like. That's where the balance comes in. In the very beginning, most of us try to be "all things to all people" and attempt to be as available as possible. As you will read, I advocate answering the telephone during off-hours to build the business more quickly in the beginning. But as things start to take hold and you begin to realize that your business has reached a point where you have a fairly steady mix of new clientele, repeat clients, and referrals, you'll want to give thought to planning organizationally in order to maintain the balance and keep your sanity.

The very draws of operating a home-based business oftentimes present the greatest hurdles with regard to achieving an even keel: You like being home based for the many benefits it affords you (low risk at start-up, the convenience of meeting with clients or handling production work when it suits you, flexibility in scheduling appointments, and so forth); your clients enjoy working with you from a home base because, chances are, especially in the beginning, you are more than willing to meet with them after hours, early mornings, and perhaps on weekends. And you often are available by phone at times convenient for them. If a client from the West Coast is in New York for a week (and you are in California), you may agree to be available at 6:00 A.M. (scheduled in advance, of course!) for a telephone consultation to modify some important cover letters. Extending these situations further, though, gets tricky as your business grows. While you now may be working on a full-time basis between the traditional hours of, say, 8:30 A.M. and 5:00 P.M., many of your original clients and those they refer to you will still expect you to be willing to work early mornings, late evenings, and on weekends. You may be perfectly amenable to doing this. But for you to achieve the all-important balance you'll need to succeed over the long term in this field, you'll have to develop clear policies about when you are working and when you are not available to clients.

There are no pat answers to this issue. I have found over the years that using my answering machine more has helped me place some controls over my schedule. I'm probably missing a fair number of first-time Yellow Pages callers—who keep going down the directory listings until they get "a real voice." Nevertheless, it's been years since I ran dripping wet from the shower to grab a business call. But it's a fair bet that all my existing clients will happily leave messages for me, knowing I'll return the call just as quickly as I can. And callers who have been referred by a satisfied client have probably already been informed, "Just leave a message on Jan's voice mail and she'll get back to you." To be quite honest, a number of my clients never expect me to answer the phone. They know I rely on voice mail and are prepared to dictate whatever their message is, knowing "it's in good hands." When I do answer the phone, I'm often greeted with incredulous surprise: "Jan, is that really you?" Just think—all you have to look forward to as your business becomes established and successful!

Once your business growth warrants, be sure to consider establishing certain days, or portions of days, when you don't book client appointments for any reason—and reserve these times for writing. Obviously, pick the times of day when you write most effectively. Likewise, a good strategy for managing yourself might be to book client appointments all together on given days and reserve the "off" days for marketing your services, producing materials, and so on. When working on this book, I scheduled myself "out of the office" on Fridays—though I actually was *in* the office interviewing, writing, and editing. But my message alerted clients all week long, after the standard greeting, that "the offices are closed on Fridays." I also did this with my first book and, once the manuscript was complete, erased that portion of my message. Do you know, for two years after that, some of my regular clients automatically expected that I was still closed on Fridays? This time I think I will continue to keep the offices closed on Fridays: I'll follow my own advice and reserve that as my day for client writing!

Challenges . . . and Strategies for Success!

If it's any consolation to you as you become established, many of your peers in this industry continue to state that balancing a home life with a home-based business is an ongoing challenge. Before sharing some of their comments, I will note that I, personally, think it's just as difficult to maintain a full-time position outside the home as it is to operate a business from the home. In fact, in many, many ways, I think it's easier, with good organizational skills, to work more hours from home than to work for someone else outside your home. I also think you'll find some good suggestions here from your prospective colleagues regarding other challenges faced by resume writers (by the way, these could easily apply to resume writers who don't work from their homes).

Jacqueline Herter, president of Professional Word Processing in Kodiak, Alaska, reports that a major challenge is "how to keep up with the ups and downs without driving my family crazy or neglecting them. I'm still in the process of overcoming this. I find I have to give them [family members] attention, then work late at night or early in the morning to help make it go smoother." She adds, though, that the chief reward of operating a home-based resume service is "the satisfaction of knowing I'm there when the kids really need me, knowing my kids don't have to go to day care, and knowing my kids don't have to come home to an empty house."

Alan Ferrell, president of ADF Professional Resumes in Lafayette, Indiana, notes that one of his greatest challenges is "having to learn to balance marketing costs against realistic part-time income. Therefore, [I put] more reliance on referrals. The nature of my part-time business means having some very busy and some very slack periods." The chief reward to operating his home-based business? "The complete flexibility and control over a process I love, without the potential burnout of a full-time high-overhead storefront."

For Penni Schratz, president of Resume Composition and Design in Traverse City, Michigan, the biggest challenge is "the other activities that I do in addition to the resume service. These include working as a full-time human resources professional, mother of three small children [ages nine, six, and four], serving as a Brownie/Girl Scout leader, involvement in hobbies, and memberships in local community groups. To overcome these challenges, I am trying to limit the number of activities in which my kids and I participate."

Louise Kursmark, CPRW, president of Best Impression in Cincinnati, faces two key challenges: "Doing it all (that is, finding enough time to do the work, manage the business, balance family life, and so on)" and "charging enough for services (being fairly compensated for much hard work)." Her strategies for the latter? "Networking and attending conferences are both very effective."

Cheryl Stoycoff, president of C&C Publications in Stockton, California, noted that her greatest concern "was having strangers come to my home when I'm alone. I always trust my instincts and when I get bad 'vibes' on the phone, I don't make the appointment. I've basically overcome the problem, however; I decided I had to if I wanted to be successful." She adds that the freedom "and time to spend with my two children, pick them up from school, attend conferences, and so on, represent the chief rewards of operating a home-based resume service."

Cheryl also states: "One of the main reasons (besides my children) I wanted to start my own business is that I wanted to do something every day that I enjoyed and that I could 'build,' because I did not want to be doing the same insurance customer-service job I had been doing for sixteen years for the next twenty years! Happily, it seems I have found what I was looking for!"

Connie Stevens, president of A+ Secretarial Office Support Services in Radcliff, Kentucky, shares an interesting challenge and offers some good insight: "There's a woman in town who will type anything for one dollar a page (we call her the DAP lady). I've talked to her, and she considers what she's doing a hobby! She likes to meet people and she's 'stuck at home' (the DAP lady's words) with small children." Connie provided lots of specific examples of how this competitor does not present herself as a professional—as described to her by a number of the DAP lady's former clients, who've since come to Connie for the "professional difference." "[This competitor's] conduct and manner hurts home-based professionals," Connie adds, "because people who meet with her then assume that all of us are like her. I always strive to present a professional, businesslike image, and I provide a high level of customer service. I also try to educate my clients as to what is actually involved in running a successful home-based resume service" (which Connie has been doing since 1973).

Jo Hammonds, president of Words Plus Secretarial & Resume Service in Douglasville, Georgia, describes two major challenges. The first is "a stigma attached to home-based businesses (that is, the 'typewriter-on-the-kitchen-table image'). To overcome this, I have a completely separate office—my clients do not enter our living quarters at any time. I have the office arranged in a professional manner and am probably better equipped than 90 percent of the small businesses in this area."

Jo's second challenge is to face the competition creatively in an already crowded market. "A printer here said he prints flyers every week for women wanting to do typing—and Douglasville is a small town! Most of my competition doesn't last long. The majority of new start-ups are young women who have a computer and think that's all they need to run a secretarial or resume service. They don't realize they need a good-quality copier, a laser printer, two phone lines, a fax machine, *plus the ability to produce quality work*. The problem this type of competition causes is [my] being unable to charge what the work is worth."

Jo Hammond cites with enthusiasm, however, her home-based business's chief rewards: "First, being able to help people put their qualifications and experience down in resume form and assist them to obtain employment. I did one young woman's resume twice—the first time two years ago and then again last month. She got the first job she interviewed for both times. She is very qualified and personable, but she gave 'my' resume all the credit!

"Second, I worked in Atlanta for three years and wore out two cars, spent a mint on gas, clothes, cleaning, and lunches. I also had to endure polluted air that was either too hot or too cold. My thirty-second commute wipes out all of that!

"Third, I get tax breaks by being able to deduct my office and some car expense. And lastly, I love being at home—being my own boss and controlling my environment. I enjoy meeting new clients and the variety my business provides."

Barbie Dallmann, CPRW, president of Happy Fingers Word Processing & Resume Service in Charleston, West Virginia, cites as major challenges "the poor economy and getting the word out about my expertise. There are others doing resume writing [in my area] for a fraction of the cost I charge. There's a big difference in the project, but the public doesn't know what that is. Educating the masses is a tough one! That's why I'm counting a lot on word of mouth from my current clients and focusing on a strong follow-up campaign." Barbie regularly surveys her clients by telephone, collecting valuable marketing data.

Barbie Dallmann also notes, "The chief reward in this business is fulfilling my purpose: helping people achieve their dreams. The knowledge that I'm 'on purpose' is the best thing of all. In addition, I have no commuting time and can be here when my son gets home from school. I'm a big believer in vacations. I took off thirty-eight days last year (besides weekends!). Where else can you make this kind of money and get seven or eight weeks' vacation a year? I'm totally satisfied with the whole lifestyle that a home-based business provides."

Rhodney LaLand, president of LaLand Resume and Career Services in Saudi Arabia, retired from the U.S. Air Force after twenty-three years of service and now works full time (by day) as an instructor and technical writer for a major aircraft company. He operates his home-based resume service weeknights and offers flexible appointment scheduling on weekends. He works about thirty hours a week in his resume business. He describes a typical day: "I get in from my 'regular' job (6:30 A.M. to 3:00 P.M.) around 3:30 and spend time with my wife. I start my resume business at 6:00 P.M., conducting all business (interview, writing, and so on) between 6:00 and 9:00 P.M. but am known to go on up until midnight.

"I keep to 6:00 P.M. because I've found that if I start before 7:00, my juices will still be flowing from the workday and I can easily get back into writing or whatever I'm doing. If I wait until after 7:00 P.M. to 'get down to business,' I'm into Santa Barbara reruns and I have *no* desire to do any kind of work!

"On weekends I start between 9:00 and 10:00 A.M. and end in the afternoon. I try to keep regular hours but sometimes find myself on a roll and will just continue until I get tired or am 'made to stop' by my wife.

"I work this kind of schedule because my resume business is my second job and these are the only times available for me. I put all this time into my resume business because it will be my only job when I leave this overseas assignment, and I believe that the more I put into it and learn, the better my chances for it to succeed as a home business."

Rhodney adds that his long-range goal is to operate his resume service on a full-time basis from home.

Wendy Enelow, CPRW, president of The Advantage in Lynchburg, Virginia, states that her major challenge is "making money! But . . . I've finally found the formula. Long-distance is much more lucrative than a local resume service. You can charge more." She recommends "identifying the appropriate additional services (aftermarket) for clientele, then negotiating cooperative alliances with the appropriate service providers." By the way, Wendy serves as a "consultant to other resume services and assists them in expanding their operations and increasing their revenues."

Wendy has effectively structured her business in a highly unusual way that—for many home-based resume professionals—would "solve some of the 'problems' of being home-based." Clients *never* come to her office—all work is handled by fax, phone, and delivery services. By her description, the nature of her business ("working with long-distance, executive clientele—[a] high-end resume and job search center") tends to be somewhat out of the ordinary. Her business slogan is "Complete Executive Resume & Employment Center." This is how the "basic system" of her business works (in Wendy's words):

> Client calls for information. We go through our "sales pitch" and have them mail or fax a resume, outline, or whatever materials they have put together. Becky (my associate) generally handles these calls. Once their information is received, I call them back for a free consultation. We discuss their search, results to date, my recommendations, and pricing. If they're interested, I then do an interview (at that time or scheduled at mutual convenience), write and typeset the resume, and mail or fax a proof (generally two to three days after the interview, faster if necessary). After proof, we discuss changes. We then print and [ship via] two-day UPS (overnight available at additional charge). Somewhere in the process we discuss search strategies in detail, which allows us to introduce and market our related services. When this is discussed depends upon the client and his or her receptivity.

In describing the breakout of her clientele, Wendy notes that "90 percent are senior management and corporate executives, of which (interestingly) 80 to 85 percent are males, ages forty to fifty-five. Five percent are students, young professionals, and wives (generally those of the executives we've worked with), and 5 percent are professionals with seven to ten years' experience (not just starting out, but not what one would consider the top management or executive tier)."

In pricing her services, Wendy offers no package plans. Each service is billed individually (á la carte), which gives the client the opportunity to select what is most appropriate for his or her situation. She states, "Generally, we provide the entire service (writing, typesetting, and printing), but sometimes only writing if clients want to print themselves—or writing, typesetting of original, and copying to a disk so that clients can do their own printing."

Here's how Wendy, who works between seventy-five and eighty-five hours per week, describes her typical workday:

- 3:00 A.M. to 6:30 A.M. [Wendy and I have *opposite* body clocks]—quiet writing time. Sometimes start earlier [ugh!] if necessary.

- 6:30 A.M. to 7:45 A.M. "Mom" time.

- 7:45 A.M. to 5:00 P.M.— the phone! Selling, doing interviews, and running the business. I talk all day long and learned years ago that I was unable to write during the day due to the constant phone interruptions. When we are busy, we probably get an average of forty to fifty-plus calls a day, in addition to scheduled appointments. During the day, most of my appointments are scheduled, although I will always take an unscheduled client who wants to immediately do an interview if I'm not already "with" a client.

- We are always open on "weird" holidays—Good Friday, President's Day, and so forth—great days for us because everyone else is off.

- Evening client appointments [always by phone]—scheduled as necessary.

Wendy also conducts client interviews on weekends, by appointment (as needed), and generally spends Saturday mornings writing. She adds: "All production work during the week is taken care of by my employee. She does all the typesetting, proofreading, printing, shipping, paper ordering, answering of phones, preparing our direct mail campaigns, and about a thousand other 'support functions.' My job is selling, interviewing, writing, and business management."

To manage a long-distance business effectively from a cash flow and collections standpoint, Wendy generally processes the full amount of a project at the time an order is accepted. "If we're not sure about the total on the project (if the client has not decided about the number of copies, for example), then we process a deposit for approximately half of the estimated total. The balance is processed *prior* to shipping. If a project has not been paid for, *it is not shipped*. No exceptions!" Wendy notes that 95 percent of her business is by credit card (Visa, MasterCard, American Express, and Discover), with the balance in money orders (no personal checks).

Wendy lists the following as key attributes that distinguish her business:

- Quality—quality—quality.

- Counseling and psychology background [she holds a B.S. in psychology]; display of concern for each client.

- Broad range of services that "position us" as a single source of job search support and services.

- Outstanding presentation over the telephone.

- Knowledge of virtually all professions—"I can 'talk' MIS, as well as finance and sales/marketing, as well as manufacturing. Comes from years and years of experience. This immediately allows us to establish rapport with [clients] and enhances their confidence in our knowledge and ability to prepare their job materials expertly."

Wendy's sole technique for cultivating referral clients? "Reputation alone."

SIMULTANEOUSLY MANAGING A BUSINESS AND YOUNG CHILDREN

As you no doubt have noticed by now, a number of home-based resume writers successfully manage their businesses while raising young children. While finding the right balance is challenging, this, often, is the source of greatest reward for these professionals. Draw some great suggestions and be inspired by the advice that follows.

Emily Goss-Crona, CPRW, president of Boulder Valley Secretarial Solutions in Longmont, Colorado, started her business in 1992 with the express goal of "developing a home-based business to stay home with my kids when I had them." Her first baby was born in January 1994, and, while she says that developing a work schedule was a challenge, "it is one I have overcome quite well." These are some of her strategies:

- I have a sitter Mondays and Thursdays, so I use those days to their fullest extent. I like to get started early, so I am at my desk anywhere from 6:00 to 7:30 A.M., depending upon what's going on with my daughter. She naps for two hours each morning, so I always count on working during that time. She also naps in the afternoon, so I book clients during that time.

- I add sitter hours during the summer. Typically, I begin writing resumes early in the morning, then do other tasks and phone calls, taking a break from the resumes. Then I return to the resumes with a fresh perspective for review or continuation. I also try to make all out-of-state calls before 8:00 A.M. my time.

- I often work late at night—my creative juices flow sporadically and I like to take advantage of the quiet hours, when I can count on few to no interruptions.

- I have established set hours for my work and really stick to them. I rise early each morning and get dressed for the day as though I were going to a job outside my home. This is imperative! Otherwise, the day never gets rolling and before you know it, it's midafternoon and no work has been accomplished.

- I try very hard to separate my career and personal life. Working at home provides the opportunity to work nonstop, and I find it very important to be very focused and work when I should be working—then close the door on my office and focus on my personal life.

Shelley Newman, CPRW, president of Ability Plus in Winthrop, Massachusetts, manages her resume business around an active four-year-old daughter (who she says serves as both the major challenge and the chief reward from her home-based business!). Compare her "typical" day with Emily's:

- A typical day usually starts around 10:00 A.M. (or whenever the phone rings). It rarely starts before then because my daughter needs my attention until then. I try to make the first few hours of the day "our" playtime. At 10:00 I make callbacks, work on resumes, or answer calls. I try to work from 10:00 A.M. until 1:00 P.M. Then I feed "us" lunch.

- My personal productive hours are from 2:00 to 5:00 P.M. I am at my best during those hours. Hopefully, my little girl is napping then.

- Most of my appointments are in the evenings, usually at either 6:00, 7:00, or 8:00. I have been known to have a client here until 11:00 P.M., but that is unusual. My daughter is now up until midnight, so forget real productive night hours. I try to get her to sleep by 9:00, but the average hour is 10:30. I then work from 10:30 or 11:00 P.M. until 2:00 A.M. My hours are very unpredictable, but I do whatever I have to do to survive.

Penni Schratz's children are ages nine, six, and four. Her typical day is of interest to those with not only small children but a full-time "day" job as well.

- I work as a human resource professional during the day and do the resume service evenings and weekends. A typical weekday would consist of working from 4:45 P.M. until 7:00 or 8:00 P.M. (consulting), then again from 10:00 P.M. to 2:00 or 3:00 A.M. (composing). I schedule consultations at the client's convenience.

- On weekends, I'll work from 10:00 A.M. until 3:00 P.M. on consultations and then do my composing from 10:00 P.M. until 2:00 A.M. I work approximately three or four days during the week and one day on the weekend.

- The reason for this schedule is to meet the needs of my clients. Most clients are happy to have evening appointments. They don't have to take off work. My philosophy is, "If I don't make myself available when the client is, someone else's resume service will"!

Cheryl Stoycoff's schedule includes raising two children, ages nine and six.

- I start work at 8:30 A.M., after taking my children to school. I begin on my most pressing project. I work until lunch, then will usually do errands at this time (banking, post office, office supply shopping). Then I work on projects or marketing until 2:30 P.M., when I pick up my children at school.

- We come home around 3:00; I help my son with his homework and reading until around 4:00. I sometimes start dinner, and depending upon my schedule and if I have an evening appointment that day, I may get in another half-hour on the computer.

- I schedule clients for the "work time" stated above. The exceptions are when I have clients scheduled for the evening hours; I will "fit" dinner around their appointments.

- Afternoon appointments when my children are home are fine; they are old enough to go in the other room to play when I have a client meeting.

- In the evening hours (7:00 to 10:00), I sometimes work on the computer, but mostly marketing stuff (too much noise for work that needs more concentration). This is not the norm, though—probably around two or three nights a week, depending on how busy I am.

My own schedule has changed considerably over the years as my kids have grown older. My youngest (Stephen, now seven years old), started first grade this past fall (full day!) and my twins, Danny and Westy, are in third grade. For the first time *ever* (going back to my business start-up in 1983), I am available in my office to clients Monday through Friday, from 8:30 A.M. until 4:00 P.M. Wow! What a big difference. Before the twins arrived, I had worked full-time days for my daytime employer—and ran my business evenings and weekends, as many do in starting their own business.

Then, when young babies and toddlers were in the picture, I squeezed in work around baby feedings, changings, naps, and laundry—and met with clients pretty much exclusively in evening and weekend appointments, when my husband was at home to care for the babies. As the kids got into preschool and half-day kindergarten, I took advantage of the morning time to meet with clients and afternoons (when the kids would be napping) to do most of my writing. Those clients with whom I already had an established relationship (and frequently who also had young children as well) would meet with me in the afternoon. Our kids often played together. (As a direct result, I believe, my children are very comfortable playing with other children and outgoing by nature! I think it's because they've always been around lots of children and adults—in the comfort and safety of their home environment—all their years of growing up.)

So the luxury of having what resemble fairly normal business hours comes after many years of paying my dues. But the conveniences are still very much there: I attend every school field trip, play, or special event and, in fact, volunteer in each of my sons' classrooms one day per week (on a rotating schedule) to deliver lesson plans in creative writing, character development, story structure, and so on. I also have the ability to keep home with me any one of my sons (sometimes more than one) who might be feeling under the weather. And I manage to get plenty of "creative thinking" time in while working in my garden in the middle of the day (or sunning by the pool deck). It's a lifestyle I wouldn't trade for anything!

The key to managing a home business effectively with young children around is to draw upon the flexibility inherent in the business and make no apologies either for being home-based or for having kids at home. When you are speaking on the phone with a client and your baby screams or your kids begin World War III, use the classic line, "Please excuse the background noise, my child happens to be in the office this afternoon." It's unlikely you'll ever get a negative client reaction to "having children," but an effective reply to, "Oh, you have children—you're home-based?" (when speaking with a first-time caller by phone who hears background "kid" noises) is, "Yes I do—and the convenience my being home-based affords my clients is most appreciated by them, since I offer flexibility around scheduling appointments in addition to the high-quality, professional work I produce."

A proven tip from most home-based resume writers with children is to have a reliable portable telephone for your business use—one that will allow you, when circumstances warrant, to duck into a closet or other room to complete a conversation in quiet. A hold or mute button is also recommended. Enjoy the flexibility that being home-based affords you both as a parent of young children and as a professional resume writer!

CHAPTER FOUR

BEFORE YOU BEGIN YOUR RESUME SERVICE

ZONING CONSIDERATIONS

Before actually launching a resume service, there are some critical steps you should take to ensure that your business can legitimately be operated from your home. It almost goes without saying that before you invest in anything for your business (from stationery to installation of a home office telephone line), you need to verify that your local zoning laws permit a home-based business in your locale and that you have secured any permits that might be necessary. As home-based businesses have become increasingly more prevalent throughout the nineties, more and more cities and towns are acknowledging their presence and addressing local concerns through changes in existing zoning regulations.

For a number of communities, obtaining approval to operate a home-based business is as easy as a telephone call to the town clerk. A simple, one-page application form and inexpensive filing fee (often as low as $10) may be required. With the advent of home-based offices, you may find that your town or city has "tightened" its zoning regulations so that a more formal permit is required. Typically, this involves no more than completing a still fairly basic form that outlines your intent to do business from your home, the nature of the business, the kinds of clientele you expect to serve, the means for attracting these clients, and the projected impact on the neighborhood.

Of primary concern to regulatory authorities in most any community is whether or not your business might have negative effects on the community (such as would potentially be experienced with a paint manufacturing business, a chemical company, or other industry generating noxious fumes or noise). Traffic and safety hazards are always a concern to planning and zoning commissions. It is generally a good idea to attach to any application that might be required a site plan of your residence (hand-drawn is acceptable). You should depict in the drawing the area of your dwelling in which you plan to locate the business. Check to determine if your town limits a home-based business to a certain percentage of the overall footage in the home.

Show access to and from your office area. Describe parking arrangements that will be available for clients (off-street is preferred). As will be explained later, it is highly desirable to operate your business on an appointment-only basis for a number of reasons. With regard to planning and zoning implications, you should be able to demonstrate adequate parking for one vehicle at a time. Planning commissions assess traffic flows differently, but in a typical single-family subdivision, a limited number of vehicle trips per day is allotted based on numbers of bedrooms in dwellings. It is probably not feasible (or advisable) to suggest that your traffic flow would be anything in the vicinity of fifteen or twenty client trips per day. For zoning purposes, simply indicating that you anticipate seeing "a client or two per day" should suffice.

Frequently, home business applications require that adjacent landowners be notified of your intent. A simple, one-paragraph form can be generated that states, "I, [neighbor's name], am aware that my neighbor [your name] is planning to open a home-based resume service at [your address]. Signed [neighbor's name], [neighbor's address], [date]." Prepare enough forms and have all adjacent property owners sign them.

Depending upon where you live, you may find it desirable to have a small, professional business sign located outside your residence, usually along the street. This is most frequently helpful as a locator to assist clients in finding you, not for attracting drop-in clientele. A sign of this type generally would have only your business name (or acronym, as does mine: CSP, in gold lettering on a maroon background measuring 1.5'x1.5' in size; I've continued to keep CSP on my business sign even though my name has changed from Comprehensive Services Plus to Absolute Advantage) or logo. Particularly if your residence is on a back road or in a well-developed subdivision, a business sign can be very useful. Be certain to check the provisions of your zoning regulations regarding signage. If signs are permitted in your regulations, you would be advised to mention that a sign is planned when completing your paperwork (even if you are undecided at this point).

If you live in a condominium, apartment complex, or cluster housing, you should check with the bylaws governing your residence to determine if any additional approvals are required beyond what your community stipulates. Evidence of a business in such dwellings is usually not permitted (for instance, a business sign will typically not be allowed).

NAME REGISTRATION

You will find specific points to consider when selecting your business name in chapter 5. If you are a sole proprietor, it is important that you register your business name with the secretary of state's office in your state. If you elect to incorporate (additional details appear later in this chapter), you should reserve your business name with the secretary of state's office. The process can vary depending upon the state in which you live; your local city or town clerk can provide details with regard to the procedure necessary to secure your business name. Many sole proprietors use a business name that includes their own, such as "Robert Smith Associates." For those who don't, the enterprise is registered under what is called a fictitious business name—for instance, "Access Resume Services." Particularly with regard to dealings with your bank or other financial institution, this fictitious name will be accompanied by the phrase "doing business as" (DBA). In this case, the business would be "Robert Smith, doing business as Access Resume Services."

In conferring with your town or city clerk's office, you should investigate the other documents necessary for your business. If your state collects sales tax on purchases, you will need to determine if resume services and related products are considered taxable items and, if so, obtain a sales and use tax permit number from your state's department of revenue services. If your community assesses property taxes on such items as assets of a business, you may need to complete a form indicating the purchase price of the computer equipment and office furnishings in your home office (and then be billed annually as part of your real estate tax bill). Your community or town may also require you to have a special license for sale of goods (separate from a home-based business permit). Again, the clerk in your town can best direct you to the appropriate agencies or offices for additional information.

SOLE PROPRIETORSHIP—OR MORE COMPLEX ARRANGEMENTS

The vast majority of home-based resume service operators organize their businesses as sole proprietorships. This is the simplest form of business organization for which to maintain tax filing documents and the easiest to begin. When you are operating as a sole proprietor, the financial records you maintain for your business are organized in such a way as to allow you to complete a one-page report (Schedule C) and attach it to your federal income tax form. You do not need the services of an accountant or attorney in order to start a business as a sole proprietor (although some individuals find it useful to consult these professional services when beginning any form of business). I opted, instead, to consult excellent documents provided by the Internal Revenue Service (IRS) and the Small Business Administration (SBA) when beginning my business, which continues to be a sole proprietorship (mailing addresses for the IRS and SBA appear in the Appendix).

If you wish to organize your business as a partnership, a Subchapter S corporation, a limited liability corporation (LLC), or a full corporation, you will require professional counsel. There are numerous documents to be prepared, particularly for a corporation, and complex financial and tax records to maintain for quarterly filing of returns. There is probably limited liability (from the standpoint of being sued) associated with operating a resume service; a sole proprietorship continues to be the easiest and most practical way in which to begin a business, in my opinion. Incorporating provides some protection against a lawsuit (as a sole proprietor, if you were sued, a plaintiff could go after your personal assets). If you have questions about the form of business organization that is right for your circumstances, contact an accountant or attorney who specializes in small-business organization.

INSURANCE

Early in the exploratory phase of your business start-up, check with your home insurance provider regarding options for operating a business from your residence. While it is possible to obtain strict business insurance for a resume service operated from your dwelling, it is quite likely that this will be very expensive—perhaps $500 or more per year for the premium. In all likelihood, you will be able to insure the possessions of the business operated from your home against fire and theft through a home office policy rider that can be as inexpensive as $10 or $20 per year, added on to the premium you are already paying for homeowner's insurance. I highly recommend obtaining an umbrella policy that will provide liability protection should someone be injured while on your property. The most likely scenario would be a fall by a client on your steps or front walk. (To prevent falls, I keep the rock salt companies in business during the winter months by religiously clearing my front walk and step of even the slightest bit of ice or snow.) An umbrella policy can be priced anywhere between $100 and $200 typically; it's good insurance for any home-based entrepreneur.

COMPETITIVE MARKET ANALYSIS AND EVALUATION

The final area of investigation before you "hang your shingle" is to determine what competition exists in the marketplace. This will be key as you undertake the next steps in getting ready to go into business and will help you to define your niche areas later on. The best place to start in your competitive review is with the Sunday newspapers serving your area and the one or two major cities nearest you, as well as the telephone directories serving these same locales.

If your phone company publishes its Yellow Pages separately from the white pages (as is common in major metropolitan areas), the Yellow Pages are all you'll need. It is a good idea to begin to build a library of telephone directories. Directories that provide address information as well as telephone numbers are useful for clients who wish to conduct direct mail marketing of firms in your area. In all likelihood, your telephone company operates an outlet from which you can obtain free directories for as many towns and cities as you wish (and can carry!). Your public library is another source for consulting the Yellow Pages and other business listings.

First, review the employment classifieds section of each of the major Sunday papers. Clip all ads for professional resume services and organize them alphabetically by company. Cross-reference any firms that advertise in more than one paper. To be most useful, this exercise should be conducted every week for at least three months to determine the frequency with which your competition chooses to advertise in the newspaper. Obviously, if you note any midweek advertising by competitors, clip those ads as well. Don't overlook competitors' ads in the weekly throw-away periodicals published in most communities.

Next, methodically peruse each phone directory's Yellow Pages. Consult the "Resume Service" category initially. Other potential categories to check for competitors' advertising include "Career and Vocational Counseling," "Employment Agencies," "Employment Consultants," "Employment Contractors," "Human Resource Consultants," and "Personnel Consultants." Pay close attention to whether companies in your area opt to run in-column advertising versus display advertising.

In-column ads vary in size from just a simple listing of a company's name to up to three inches of copy, usually surrounded by a box. The companies are listed in strict alphabetical order—at least this is at present the case in most areas of the country. I understand that in some locales, in-column listings are determined by seniority. Those companies new to a listing category are published at the bottom of the list.

Display ads are exactly that—ads ranging in size from a full page down to about 1½" by 2" and sprinkled somewhat randomly throughout the category section. The largest display ads usually appear near the front of the section, with the smaller ones near the end. Seniority can also play a role here as well; display ads for the most established companies may be printed near the front of the section. Chapter 8 includes detailed information regarding your advertising strategy and plan. In the evaluation stage, however, you want to collect as much information as you can about the competition. These details will be handy, too, when creating your business name.

I highly recommend that you use the information gleaned in your review of Sunday newspaper advertising and your Yellow Pages study to structure a grid analyzing the competition (see the accompanying samples).

Using this grid (you can photocopy the blank example or design your own form), establish a page for each competing company. Make notations on a weekly basis, indicating the date of that company's presence in the Sunday newspapers; identify in your "key" the name of each of the Sunday papers (for example, A: *Hartford Courant*; B: *New Haven Register*). If a company's ad varies from week to week, note either the change in ad size or the change in copy (perhaps a different service is featured each week, or a different promotion or discount is offered on a weekly basis).

For the Yellow Pages entries, identify in the key the locale covered by each directory (for example, A: Greater Hartford; B: New Haven County). Then, under each column for the respective phone book, record the categories in that book under which the competitor has advertised (resume service only, for instance), the size of the ad (2-inch in-column or quarter-page display, for example), and special features of that firm's ad (for instance, full consulting services, government applications [SF-171s], individualized cover letters, package pricing, credit cards accepted, and weekend appointments).

These data collected at the onset of your business start-up investigation will become the core of the marketing section in your business plan. The data also serve as a focal point for annual review as you assess, modify, and review your own advertising program. I strongly recommend that you analyze your competitors at least once yearly in such a methodical fashion. Using the grid sheets established for each competing firm this first year, you can then assess, on a year-to-year basis, newcomers to the profession, companies that go out of business, and trends within the field as reflected by changes in your competitors' advertising copy. Of course, companies that appear to have gone out of business may simply have

Competitive Market Analysis Grid

Company Name:	Town:	Sunday Paper A	Sunday Paper B	Sunday Paper C	Yellow Pages A	B	Other
Date:							
Date:							
Date:							
Date:							
Date:							
Date							
Date:							
Date:							
Date:							
Date:							
Date:							
Date							
Date:							
Date:							
Date:							
Date:							
Date:							
Date							
Date							

Before You Begin Your Resume Service

Completed Competitive Market Analysis Grid

Company Name: Access Resumes	Town: West Hartford	Sunday Paper A	Sunday Paper B	Sunday Paper C	Yellow Pages A	Yellow Pages B	Other
Date: 3/1	—	2" display "Resumes While You Wait"	2" display "Resumes While You Wait"	n/a	1/4" page display—CPRW	2.5" in-column display—CPRW	—
Date: 3/8	—	identical	3-line . . . "Why Take Chances? Call the Best!	n/a	4" in-column display—credit cards	—Guarantee— "Resumes with a Difference"	—
Date: 3/15	—	identical	3-line . . . "Aren't You Worth It?"	Business Card Directory	wide selection of papers—satisfaction guaranteed (Resume service only) | hours by appointment—CPRW on staff—Our resumes open doors"	after-hours appointments—credit cards (Resume service only) | "We invite comparisons"	
Date: 3/17	—	—	—	—			small display ad in weekly Gazette
Date: 3/22	—	identical	3-line . . . "Quality Makes a Difference"	—			—
Date: 3/29	—	identical	3-line . . . "Your Career Deserves Nothing but the Best"	—			—
Date:							
Date:							
Date:							
Date:							
Date:							
Date:							
Date:							
Date:							
Date:							
Date:							
Date:							
Date:							
Date:							

PAPERS
A= Hartford Courant
B= New Haven Register
C= New London Day

YELLOW PAGES
A= Greater Hartford
B= New Haven County

opted not to advertise because of heavy referrals—a practice I *don't* recommend. You should always maintain a presence in the Yellow Pages, even when that glorious day comes—and it will—when you are no longer desperate for new clients.

QUOTABLE INSPIRATION

"To newcomers: Count the cost; weigh the pros and cons of starting a service. It's quite a commitment—remember, you have to get out and get the work; it doesn't come to you. Research as much as possible and make sure you are qualified. Join NASS and PARW. Both of these organizations have been a tremendous help to me. I wish I had known about them when I started seven years ago."—*Jo Hammonds, Words Plus Secretarial & Resume Service (Douglasville, Georgia)*

Other methods for learning about the competition include querying everyone you know: "If you needed a resume prepared, where would you go? Do you know anyone who writes resumes?" Contact local colleges and universities and ask to speak with the directors of placement; ask them how they advise their graduating and postgraduate students. Keep in mind, you might be uncovering potential areas where you could subsequently market your services!

CHAPTER FIVE

DEFINING YOUR NICHES

LINKING YOUR BACKGROUND TO MARKET NEEDS

Having reviewed some of the attributes successful resume writers state are key in this business and having compared your own strengths and weaknesses to this listing, you should be in a good position to determine those areas in which you might first develop confidence and experience success in resume writing.

If, for example, your background includes significant recruiting activities in a particular field (such as placing advertisements, prescreening prospective candidates by telephone, interviewing, and, ultimately, hiring), this is a natural area for you to pursue initially. If your experience has included cold-calling and selling, for instance, and you enjoyed these activities, it would be a fairly straightforward process for you to begin cold-calling prospective clients: contacting companies in your area that might be contemplating a major layoff, introducing yourself to the director of human resources, developing a package offering, facilitating workshops for employees on developing their own resume and cover letter materials (and offering favorable package pricing for those who choose not to do it themselves), and so on.

Background that includes writing in some form (as a technical writer, journalist, English teacher, or administrative secretary, for example) is easily transferable to the business of resume writing (chapter 11 delves into the actual details of conducting client consultations and writing resumes "from scratch"). Regardless of the areas in which you've previously worked, you undoubtedly have developed good communication skills, you probably like speaking with people and working with them, and you perhaps enjoy (or believe you would enjoy) knowing that you have helped someone in pursuit of something typically ranked as one of the top five concerns of most human beings: a career.

Analyzing your list of key attributes (adding any unique qualifications you bring to the field beyond those mentioned in chapter 2) and examining the results of your competitive research place you in an ideal situation to determine your service niches. Let's suppose that you have skill as a writer and hope to capitalize on your ability to couple good word-processing ability with writing strengths and develop creative cover letters to go with your clients' resumes (which you also plan to write). As you review the findings of your competitive research, notice how many businesses in your broad geographic area list, in their advertising, that they provide writing or editorial services. You may find that most or all businesses mention this service offering—or, perhaps, none.

Your next step, regardless of the number of competitors who itemize this service (and others you determine to be areas in which you plan to "subspecialize"), is to conduct follow-up telephone research of your competitors in an attempt to learn as much as you possibly can. The areas listed below should be touched on in your "sleuthing." (Keep in mind that the intelligent person seeking to have a resume professionally prepared will be asking many of these questions—and remember that, ultimately, as a professional resume writer, you should be in a position to respond confidently to—and, in fact, direct—conversation along these lines when telephoned by your own prospective clients.)

- Background of the business owner or the person (in a larger office) who conducts the actual client consultations and writes the resumes

  Questions to ask: What are the qualifications of the person I would be meeting with? How many years has he or she been working with clients and writing resumes? Is the person certified (and, if yes, what does this indicate?)?

- Services available, package offerings, and pricing

  Questions to ask: Do you offer a range of resume services? Does this include cover letter preparation? How is this handled? Is there package pricing? How much will it cost to have a resume done? [Pay particular attention to the questions that follow.] Is there a flat fee? Is the charge based on time (An hourly rate? What is the rate?)? On number of pages? Is there a guarantee? What if I don't like what is written? Is there an additional charge involved to rewrite the resume? What is included (A single original of the final resume? Any additional originals on stationery?)? What do you offer for stationery? Extra cost for certain types? How about envelopes? Do you retain the resume on the computer or on disk? For how long? Any fee involved? Can I obtain a disk (What type of software, and so on?)? How do you handle resume updates? How do you determine the fees?

- Turnaround/timeliness

  Questions to ask: Do you meet with clients by appointment? What are my options for meeting with you [really pursue ease and availability of after-hours appointments, early morning appointments, and weekend meetings, if these are areas in which you believe you can offer time to clients]? How quickly after the initial meeting will my resume be ready for approval? Same day if necessary? Next day? Longer? How long does the first appointment take? Is everything completed at the second appointment, including revisions—or will I need to return a third time? Can you fax me a proof to save time at the second appointment (and are there any "conditions," such as full payment up front)?

- Payment options

  Questions to ask: How are the financial arrangements handled? Is a deposit required? How much? At what point must the balance be paid? Can payment be made with cash? By check? By credit card?

- Specials/discounts

  Questions to ask: Do you offer any special promotions or discounts? Seasonally? What about credit for referrals? What if both my spouse and I are interested in having a resume done?

It has long been recognized in this industry that the longer a resume service provider can engage a prospective client on the telephone discussing his or her requirements, the more likely it is that an appointment will be booked and a sale will ensue. Of course, as with the above scenario, you can expect that once you are in business, you, too, will be the recipient of calls from comparison shoppers and people who are thinking about entering this field.

By analyzing the information you obtain through the above "Q and A" with your competitors, you will get a very clear sense of what services are typically offered by resume companies in your area, how prospective clients perceive people engaged in the profession when calling for quotes, and how you can strategically place (and price) your business as you prepare to open shop. It almost goes without saying that being "user-friendly," professional, and helpful to prospective clients on the telephone can greatly increase your likelihood for success in booking appointments. Consider the times you have telephoned various companies, restaurants, or retailers for information. How customer-service-oriented are most of these people? Do you feel that your business is genuinely important to the person on the other end of the telephone? I can almost predict that as you call your competitors, many will surprise you by the way they don't appear to take your call or prospective business seriously. Once your business has started, you can immediately distinguish yourself from them on the telephone by always taking sufficient time to respond to queries, reassuring every caller, and anticipating and asking questions beyond what the client presents.

When studying what services your competition offers, you may begin to see areas where no one is claiming to specialize. For example, no one may be advertising or promoting the availability of individualized cover letter services whereby the client can telephone Sunday night or early Monday morning for immediate service in answering the employment classifieds. Shelley Newman, CPRW, president of Ability Plus in Winthrop, Massachusetts, began to offer this service in her first months in the resume business. She now offers up to ten clients (five to seven clients are ideal) a specific time for calling in their "job ads" from a current newspaper. While on the telephone with the client, she locates the desired ads in her copy of the newspaper. She then prepares individualized cover letters, which are faxed or mailed to the prospective employer along with the client's resume. "All my clients are impressed with this service," says Shelley. "They are glad to know it is available."

If you have an electric or electronic typewriter (in addition to word-processing equipment) and can type accurately, you may wish to consider offering application services to your clients. In this case, you could advertise, as a subspecialty, preparation of graduate school, college, employment, and SF-171 application forms. Combined with consulting, whereby you meet with the client to conduct an interview for developing the content of these application documents, application preparation can be very lucrative.

YOUR BUSINESS NAME AND SLOGAN

While many of the activities involved in starting a resume service are conducted in tandem, with lots of overlapping areas for research and analysis, this is probably the appropriate time to finalize selection of your business name. Given that you have done all the earlier research, you undoubtedly have been considering almost from day one the name you'd like for your resume business. You, of course, must select the business name before you can file it with the proper agencies (as recommended in chapter 4). Obviously, you cannot select a name already in use by a competitor in your area. Your research will have unearthed all the names currently in use by businesses in your part of the state. How should you position your service?

Selection of a business name takes into account many variables:

- The way you'd like your business to be perceived by prospective clients
- The ease with which your name might be remembered (and referred)
- The overall "feel" the business name imparts
- The ability to create a slogan or, perhaps, logo tied into the theme of your business name
- The ease with which you can "say" your business name in answering the telephone
- The placement of your business name alphabetically among its competition, particularly in the Yellow Pages listings in which you choose to advertise

That last point, though perhaps not as "ego-satisfying" as the other elements, is probably the most important to your initial business success. You will most likely not be the only game in town when it comes to competitors advertising in the "Resume Service" category of your local telephone directory's Yellow Pages. Therefore, if, as discussed earlier, those advertisements are placed alphabetically (particularly the in-column ads), it becomes apparent that your odds for getting a first-time caller will increase based upon your proximity to the top of the alphabetical listing.

QUOTABLE INSPIRATION

"Making you look good is what we do best!" *(Cheryl's slogan)* "I present myself to resume clients as having the expertise to write, design, and typeset their resume—rather than just 'type' it as Kinko's does. One of my goals is to double my prices, do half as much work!"—*Cheryl Stoycoff, C&C Publications (Stockton, California)*

What does this mean? That your business name must begin with the letter *A?* Not at all. But in looking at the competitors in your area, if 50 percent or more of them are located in the alphabetical spread between *A* and *C,* you'd be doing yourself a disservice in the beginning years of business to use a name such as Professional Resume Services. There are always exceptions: If there are only two or three businesses in your area and you prefer to select a business name that will fall at the bottom of the heap alphabetically, then it's probably all right for you to go with Superior Resume Service. Most prospective clients who call you upon seeing your listing in the Yellow Pages (as opposed to those referred by an already satisfied client) will probably call three services shopping for quotes. In this example, you'd make the cut and probably be called. But if there are fifteen or more professional resume services listed in your phone directory already and seven of them have names beginning with *A, B,* or *C,* you really should give thought to positioning yourself in this pack. And remember, as new services start up, they'll probably seek to be at the beginning of the group alphabetically.

Look at it this way: Few people have time to waste (even, or perhaps especially, the unemployed). If a prospective client calls two or three services, gets a reasonable and comparable price and service-delivery range from all three, and one of these providers "goes above and beyond" in terms of spending time on the telephone discussing specific requirements and how the potential client's key accomplishments can best be framed in an outstanding resume, isn't that person quite likely to book an appointment with the most helpful of these three? Most people will not go through an exhaustive list of competitors to interview every single service. With a large number of possible firms from which to select, they'll probably call the top three or so (and, if satisfied, book with one of them) or call on the basis of geography (that is, by looking for convenient locales or telephone prefixes that signify proximity to their home or office). People who call strictly on the basis of geography are beyond your ability to control.

As you will see in chapter 8, there are lots of strategies to employ in developing your advertising. For the home-based resume service professional, I recommend against encouraging drop-in clientele and, therefore, advise you not to publish your street address (while the telephone company will require a physical address when opening your telephone service account, they will agree, by request, not to publish your street in your Yellow Pages advertising). I recommend not placing an address on your business card, either. Beyond discouraging drop-ins, I believe it makes good sense for a professional working alone from home to take reasonable safety precautions. By revealing your physical location only after a discussion with a prospective client, once the appointment has been booked, you afford yourself a greater sense of security.

Getting back to selection of your business name, you may decide that your own name (if located at the top of the alphabet) lends itself nicely to something such as Browne Resume Associates or Alexander Career Services. There are possibly some advantages to using your own name as part of your business name, but there are equal benefits to developing an all-encompassing company name that reflects a breadth of services to prospective clients. Paging through the dictionary and thesaurus are time-honored ways of getting initial ideas for a company name.

If you travel out of your state, check the Yellow Pages of directories you find in your hotel rooms—something I do, to this day, every time I travel! Not only do I look at possible business names, but I also check to see trends in advertising across the country, the listing of new service offerings I may not have considered, and creative use of slogans in the advertising copy. You can also consider using the resources of a large public library, many of which have the telephone directories for large metropolitan areas around the country. Checks can be made—by you or an attorney, if you wish—to verify whether or not a potential name is already in use in your area. Have some fun in selecting your name. Play with fonts on the computer in stylizing how your name will look—on business cards, in advertising, and on letterheads. Repeat your business name over and over—and if you are getting close to a selection, try taping a message on an answering machine or a regular cassette recorder to hear how the name sounds when clients begin to call. Bounce your chosen name off colleagues, family, and friends.

Look at the acronym your name creates—does it lend itself to creative possibilities (or to an embarrassing letter formation)? I continue to use my former acronym (CSP) back from when my business name was Comprehensive Services Plus because of the obviously inappropriate acronym created by my newer business name, Absolute Advantage. All of my long-standing clients over the past twelve years or so know me as CSP and recognize not only my business sign with the gold letters CSP but also the registration plate on my vehicle, JAN•CSP. My "legal" business name is Absolute Advantage/division, Comprehensive Services Plus, though I frequently drop the reference to Comprehensive Services Plus and/or CSP in my voice mail messages and the like. How might a slogan be created that ties in to the chosen business name? Are you thinking of having a logo? Are any service possibilities hinted at in your prospective name? Is the name short and snappy? Professional sounding? Too long? Too many *ses*? Easy to articulate or garbled when said quickly (as you will undoubtedly do once it becomes very familiar and you've been saying it over and over—for a number of profitable years!)? All these points should be considered before you make your final selection. Always remember that your business name is important and should not be changed, especially in the formative years of your enterprise.

QUOTABLE INSPIRATION

Cindy's slogan is, "Quality resumes at affordable prices. I distinguish myself through strong knowledge of the local job market, a good design eye, and excellent writing skills."—*Cindy K. Patton, CPRW, Choice Business Service (Gulfport, Mississippi)*

A colleague and dear friend of mine, Louise Kursmark, CPRW, underwent an extensive process of changing her business name after successfully operating for ten years as Secretarial Services Unlimited in Reading, Massachusetts. In 1992 Louise decided to rename her business so that it was more reflective of the services she was specializing in and put her closer to the top of the alphabet. After much research and test-marketing, she settled on Best Impression, which perfectly conveys her image to prospective clients, both in the resume-writing and desktop publishing areas.

In 1995 Louise and her family relocated to Cincinnati, Ohio, and she is using two versions of her business name in her community: Best Impression Resumes and Best Impression Designs. The transition period back in Massachusetts was nearly a year long as she alerted existing clients of the impending change, then answered her telephone using both "Secretarial Services Unlimited and Best Impression" until the change was in place and her Yellow Pages advertising later that year reflected it. This change was undertaken after ten very successful years under her original business name and allowed Louise the opportunity to exploit the novelty and impact of her new name. A brand-new company would not be as well served by a name change during its first or second year in business. I strongly encourage you to give very careful consideration to this important part of your business planning.

In crafting a slogan to represent a business, I always recommend that people consider how they intend to identify themselves and their company in public. For example, if you are joining the chamber of commerce and being introduced in a networking meeting, how do you plan to talk about what you do? Networking-marketing specialists will advise you to confine your "minispeech" to twenty-five words or less (depending upon how quickly you speak, you perhaps can add a few to that). The following are some real-life examples from colleagues in our profession; these should help give you a good idea of the wide variety of possibilities for specialty in the resume-writing profession.

- Georgia Adamson, CPRW, president of Adept Business Services in Campbell, California, states, "When you 'look good,' so do we," adding that "my aim is to 'help businesses and individuals to communicate ideas effectively and organize information in a useful manner.' For resumes, this means creating a strong 'marketing' tool tailored to the client."

- Vivian Belen, CPRW, president of The Job Search Specialist in Fair Lawn, New Jersey, states: "The Job Search Specialist provides a rational approach to career assessment and job search in the fast-changing workplace of the nineties. Our clients gain new insights and confidence about marketing their credentials effectively."

- Cathy Cousear, president of the Institute on Human Service Resources in Fresh Meadows, New York, describes her business as "providing career development resources for individuals who work in the human service field, along with products for professionals."

- Barbie Dallmann, CPRW, president of Happy Fingers Word Processing and Resume Service of Charleston, West Virginia, emphasizes customer service and high quality in her slogan: "Friendly Service—Professional Results." "We position ourselves as 'the best,'" she adds, "and, consequently, most expensive service in the area." Among other services offered are professional resume development, including job search strategies and interview skills training.

- Wendy Enelow, CPRW, president of The Advantage, Inc., in Lynchburg, Virginia, categorizes her business as "a high-end resume and job search center working exclusively with top-level corporate executives nation- and worldwide." Her business card description reads, "Complete Executive Resume and Employment Center."

- Alan Ferrell, president of ADF Professional Resumes in Lafayette, Indiana, states: "The thrust of ADF Professional Resumes is to produce highly readable resumes whose content and readability appeal to industry recruiters. 'We do the hard part . . . we *write* your resume.'"

- Emily Goss-Crona, CPRW, president of Boulder Valley Secretarial Solutions, Inc., in Longmont, Colorado, has recently begun specializing in resume and cover-letter writing and interview-preparation training. She describes herself to prospective clients as "the only resume *writer* in town."

- Pat Kendall, CPRW, president of Advanced Resume Concepts of Aloha, Oregon, promotes her credentials as a "Certified Professional Resume Writer with thirteen years of experience with resumes for clients in all professions—blue collar to executives." She is also a published resume designer, with examples of her work appearing in JIST-WORKS *Gallery of Best Resumes.*

- Anne Kramer, CPRW, president of Alpha Bits of Virginia Beach, Virginia, characterized her business as "a freelance office center with expertise in resume preparation. We perform a complete range of services to fit the specific requirements needed to get the job done."

- Carrie Kuntz, president of Professional Typing and Resume Service of Ontario, California, always introduces herself as a "resume writer. The two slogans I use are: 'The Professional's Choice' and 'Professional Typing and Resume Service—An Authority in Resume Writing.'"

- Louise Kursmark, CPRW, president of Best Impression Resumes of Cincinnati, Ohio, states: "Professional desktop publishing and resume services for businesses and individuals. . . . We help you make your best impression!"

- Dawn LaFontaine, president of The Business Wordsmith of Ashland, Massachusetts, states: "I provide business writing and desktop publishing services to businesses and resume-writing and job search support services to individuals."

- Rhodney LaLand, president of LaLand Resume and Career Services of Saudi Arabia, uses "Your Success Is My Success" as his business slogan, adding, "I want my clients to feel that I take their success personally and, to that end, will do the best job possible."

- Shelley Newman, CPRW, president of Ability Plus in Winthrop, Massachusetts, "accents the multitude of resume services" she provides. She stresses that "my resumes are 100 percent guaranteed."

- Penni Schratz, president of Resume Composition and Design of Traverse City, Michigan, reflects her approach to offering a "multitude of services from à la carte resumes and cover letters to cost-saving packages, resume retypes, and employment campaign education" with the following slogan: "Invest in yourself . . . Invest in your future!"

- Connie Stevens, president of A+ Secretarial Office Support Services in Radcliff, Kentucky, uses "THE Resume Professionals" as her business slogan, noting that "we don't succeed unless you do." She stresses: "We care about the success of our clients. We provide career search materials and job enhancement training."

That's inspirational . . . if you look closely at how your competitors are defining their businesses and also consider how some of your colleagues from around the country are describing their niches and expertise, you should then be in a good position to draw from your own experience the attributes that will best allow you to define your business niche in your own geographic area.

CREATING A SERVICE MENU

What services should a resume business provide? In my opinion, the more of a generalist you can be, particularly at the outset with your business, the more quickly you will begin to establish yourself and acquire paying business. Then, as time goes on, you can opt to specialize in those areas that you find either most profitable or most interesting (or, ideally, both!). Thus, I recommend that you attempt to be a full-service resume business with offerings available to meet the needs of nearly every potential client. This includes the following services:

- Basic retype of a client's already existing resume (it might be completely handwritten, or professionally typeset with handwritten updates or revisions). The client requires no editorial services—or at least that's what he or she thinks—and merely wants you to provide a professionally "typed" resume from the material provided to you. No consultation is booked; this is the most "vanilla" of service offerings.

- Basic retype of a client's resume plus a miniconsultation to discuss the content of material that the client wishes to add as an update to the resume. This usually involves an additional charge for the editorial services, based on the time that it takes you to write the copy and conduct the short meeting. The time spent might be as little as fifteen minutes, but it can extend to an hour or more when clients see the benefit of the consultation. (They then ask you to review what they have already written.)

- Complete development of a client's resume "from scratch," accomplished through a client consultation. The discussion can be held face-to-face in your office, at a mutually agreed-upon location, or completely by telephone (in the case of a long-distance client, for instance). A minimum of one hour is generally spent in full consultation; this can be shorter for an individual with limited work experience and a fairly well articulated objective.

I often find that while students, for example, may expect "favorable pricing," such as a discounted resume package offering, they frequently are the clients with whom I spend as much time as I do counseling a high-level executive with thirty years of experience. This leads me to suggest, as I do later in this chapter, that if you find it advantageous to offer tiered package pricing—which I recommend—you will definitely want to build in parameters such as caps on the amount of time spent and a schedule of additional charges for any extensions.

In addition to the three basic resume services outlined above, you will undoubtedly wish to provide varying levels of cover letter service. You may opt to include a cover letter with the highest-level package (the complete development of a client's resume) or you may decide that offering this service as a separate component is desirable. Here, then, are suggested ancillary resume service offerings you'll at least want to consider:

- *Cover letter services.* These range from typing letters already drafted by your clients to creating them from scratch after you've written a client's resume. Different levels in this category include generic letters (addressed "To Whom It May Concern" with possible variations in the opening paragraph) and highly individualized letters, each tailored to a precise company or advertisement. Costs vary significantly, as indicated in the sample price sheet at the end of this chapter. Add to this offering "call-in" services (such as those provided by Shelley Newman, CPRW, of Ability Plus in Winthrop, Massachusetts, which were described earlier), and you can create a highly specialized service for clients in your area.

- *Providing supplemental career documents.* From preparing a list of professional references and a salary history to creating leave-behind materials that a client presents after an interview and follow-up thank-you letters, the category is wide open for add-on materials that you can market to your clients (chapter 12 has more on each of these items). Extending this profit center even further, you may decide to employ your "coaching" expertise and create careful scripts for your clients to use in cultivating interviews and, later, negotiating job offers and salary. You might also wish to draw on your editorial expertise and develop business plans for clients in senior-level sales, marketing, and executive management positions. This activity is creatively challenging and can be especially lucrative when carefully marketed.

- *Mailing services.* These can range from simply preparing envelopes (or labels for envelopes) to accompany each cover letter you provide, to printing a full resume/cover letter/envelope package for each advertisement, inserting a signature, collating the pieces, applying postage, and actually delivering the materials to the post office on your client's behalf. Pricing is based on the level of service desired.

- *Application preparation services.* From typing of college and graduate school applications to standard employment applications (as with teacher candidates) and SF-171s, this can be a lucrative market for those who don't object to sitting at a typewriter and doing somewhat laborious work. By offering this ancillary service—for which you might choose to charge a premium, especially if you are the only such specialist in your community—you can make a reasonable profit.

- *Job coaching services.* These can range from training in effective interviewing techniques to advising clients how to structure a job search. For those with the necessary qualifications, administration of professional testing (such as performing Myers-Briggs analyzes) can be a lucrative sideline to the resume profession. Many resume writers engage in training their clients for successful interviewing. Using materials such as those noted in the Appendix, they market videotapes, audiotapes, and publications for their clients' use (by purchase or lease) and work one-on-one in further developing these skills. This type of service usually commands the highest hourly rate a service charges.

- *Additional career and placement services.* These include listing client profiles with national databases, posting client resumes on the Internet (see chapter 12), providing subscriptions (for a fee, of course) to such publications as the Executive Search Bulletin, and providing access to services that offer individualized searches of massive databases containing job information.

- *Rush service.* Although I recommend that you include an extra charge in your price structure for express resume service, I can predict you will probably opt to waive the rush service fee (while always advising your client of this courtesy) in your desire to book as much business as possible when you start out. This is where the start-up business owner has an advantage: In the beginning, you won't be so busy that you can't offer rush service. Someone in my situation today can rarely offer a two- or four-day turnaround, let alone same-day service; I'm booked too far in advance with my regular clientele. But a new service without full bookings can easily accommodate these types of requests and make a decision whether or not to impose the rush service surcharge. Typical to the industry is a premium of between 25 and 50 percent for service delivered in under four hours (for example, a resume brought in at 9:00 A.M. for a miniconsultation and update, which you must typeset completely and have ready for the client by noon) and around 25 percent for same-day service. Some services deliver these types of turnarounds as "standard."

Always keep in mind that the desired goal is to build your business for the long term. If you can deliver in shorter turnaround windows than your competitors, that's great and will certainly please your clients. Just be sure to reflect these professional courtesies on your invoice (noting the standard fee for such service, with "fee waived as a courtesy," so that clients will know the *value* of what they are getting). You also want to be careful to set expectations with regard to what clients can anticipate receiving as far as service. If you always have personalized cover letters ready for clients the same day that they've faxed want-ad information to you but never mention that this is "special" service (even if you are not charging for it), these clients will come to expect this level of service always. Furthermore, as they refer others to you—which, of course, is what you want to happen (in fact, you will be cultivating this!)—these referred individuals will have the same service expectations. As you get busier and busier, these turnaround times may become impossible for you to achieve consistently.

DEVELOPING YOUR PRICE LIST

Pricing is, at best, an imprecise science—and to a large extent, an art. Before you can set prices, you must know and decide certain things. What image are you seeking for your service? The absolute tops in quality? With the perception that one "pays for quality"? Or a service that delivers quality work *at a reasonable price?* Do you deliberately want to price yourself at the very top in your area compared with your competition, or to price yourself slightly—or significantly—under what the market will bear? I strongly advise against pricing yourself as the lowest in your area. There is simply no advantage to trying to drive prices down, which is what will happen if you are good. Your business may grow more quickly in the beginning, but if the competition is smart, they'll be checking to see what *your* rates are. If you are doing well and "stealing the business that's out there," pricing around you will, by virtue of supply and demand, decline. No one benefits—because there's no point in being in business if you can't make a fair and reasonable profit. And there's no benefit to clients if you can't be in business, year after year, to serve their ever-increasing needs for service.

A resume is not a onetime proposition. Experts report that the average person changes positions nearly ten times in a typical career. While not every person will need a resume reflecting every change, you can be certain of the potential for literally millions of opportunities to write, or update, a resume. If a client has "invested" with you initially in developing a resume from scratch, in all likelihood he or she will want to return to your service for updating in the future. There are cost savings to working off an updated resume for a client, and there's significant profit to be made, over the long term, from working with clients throughout their careers. A number of my clients from more than ten years ago not only have continued to work with me over the past decade but have sent their neighbors, their spouses, their colleagues, and, now, their children to me for professional career assistance. Pricing your services right, to start, assures you of reasonable profitability over the long term and an ability to stay in business for as many years as you wish, thus affording your clients peace of mind and stability.

Keep in mind that the differing economic conditions in various areas of the country will significantly influence the rates charged and the fees that a given marketplace can bear. In a capitalist economy, you are free to charge whatever you wish, but you will have to secure and maintain paying work that is profitable. In other words, carried to an extreme, you might say that you won't do anything for under $100—even a simple resume retype. I can assure you that if you find a client who'll pay $100 for a one-page resume retype, you can consider yourself extremely lucky! I don't think there's an area of the country where an individual possesses such keen expertise as to demand $100 for a basic one-page retype with no value added.

Likewise, I believe it would be ridiculous to offer simple retypes for as little as $10, regardless of geographic area. An exception might be a carefully controlled special offer. For example: "The first five callers who book a retype of their resume receive one original for just $10. This is a limited-time offer. Call before January 31 to take advantage of this onetime special." Those services priced at the very top of the spectrum are counting on the profitability of a relatively small volume of work to carry them. Those at the bottom of the pricing spectrum are relying on high volume to carry them. For the sole proprietor beginning in this field, your best bet is to fall, in my opinion, in the middle-to-high range—but probably not at the highest end unless your area is unique and everyone is grossly underpriced. If you are fortunate enough to be the only game in town (as I have been over the years in some service areas), you have considerably more leeway in setting prices.

Prices are not cast in stone, but you should be careful to quote consistently, particularly when referrals are concerned. You are free to raise—or lower—your rates when you choose (ahh, the advantages of being the boss). You should not be changing prices every month or two, however, and you should try to settle into some kind of schedule. You may wish to implement annual price increases, or perhaps make adjustments every nine months, particularly if you become concerned that you have set your prices too low in the beginning. On the other hand, you may find it easier (as I do) to raise your prices by fairly hefty amounts every eighteen to twenty-four months, rather than going up in smaller increments more frequently. That way, you can "hype" increases (when there is a need to tell your clients) with the introduction, "Our first price increase in nearly two years." Once you get started, you'll find that quality work nearly always speaks for itself. Once you begin to have established clientele, and referrals, price is almost never a factor. But it *always* is important to the first-time caller.

Look back upon the research data you collected in assessing the competition. Examine closely the rates for varying services and draw up a detailed listing of all the services you plan to offer. Then begin to develop a model for what must be covered as a cost of your being in business. Factor in projected costs, including time, for completing specific service offerings. The following breakdown represents a hybrid pricing model, drawn from my experience of more than fourteen years in the field as well as the experiences of respected colleagues throughout the country. First there is a "clean" price list (the kind that would be posted in your office or readily available for a client to peruse upon request). *Note:* This sample resume service price list may not be representative of pricing for your geographic area; however, service and pricing distinctions should be somewhat consistent. The information that begins on this page provides the rationale behind the service charges. This is just one model that you can "bounce your numbers against" as a reality check.

Rationale for the Resume Service Price List

The following narrative explains in detail the major entries to the Sample Resume Service Price List presented on the next page.

Resumes

This first entry is for the basic retyping of a resume, with no editorial or consultation services. This fee is derived on the basis of *total* time spent in typing a basic, one-page resume. This *includes* the time spent in the five-minute or so discussion with the client at the time the material is dropped off and the ten or so minutes the client spends approving the resume when picking it up. The time it takes to print the five originals on stationery the client selects at pickup *and* such overhead as time engaged in "selling" the service by phone when the client first calls, costs of retaining the material on disk, and the general cost of sustaining the business as a whole are also components of this fee. Forty-nine dollars is representative of an hourly fee designed to cover strictly word processing, in this sample price list (again, fees in your area may vary, perhaps significantly). Actual time an operator should spend in properly preparing, typesetting, laying out, designing, and proofreading an existing one-page resume should be no more than a half-hour.

- *one-page resume (includes 5 originals on stationery) $49*
- *two-page resume (includes 5 originals on stationery) $69*

SAMPLE RESUME PRICE LIST

Resumes (basic retyping, no editorial or consultation services)

- one-page resume (includes 5 originals on stationery) — $49
- two-page resume (includes 5 originals on stationery) — $69
- additional pages of CV (curriculum vitae) — $25 (each)
- revisions to existing resume or original printouts of revised or existing resume (in addition to copy charge); there is a minimum charge of $10 (the hourly rate is $85) — $10 (min.)
- consultation (actual time billed) — $85/hour

Complete Resume Package — $300

- 1- to 1.5-hour consultation (time spent in consultation exceeding 1.5 hours is billed at hourly rate of $85)
- preparation of draft resume for approval/revisions
- 20 originals of final resume, choice of stock
- pro forma cover letter (one included)
- Student Discount (40 percent off)—maximum .75-hour consultation — $180

Cover Letter Services

- create one unique cover letter template — $40
- prepare individualized cover letters (based upon time, usually about six per hour) with matching envelopes; charge includes time client spends in discussion—if more than five minutes, time is separately billed at hourly rate of $85) — $44/hour

Editorial/Consulting Services — $85/hour

- discussing career objective, career search materials, interview training and preparation, mock interviews, follow-up to actual interviews, etc.

Laser-Printed Originals

- on selected stationery; discounted for high volume
- executive class paper, $1.00 each (each page) — 75¢

Photocopies (each; discounted for high volume)

- standard white bond, letter size, 8 ½" x 11" — 25¢
- legal size, 8 ½" x 14" — 30¢
- blank resume stock (ten varieties, including executive class) 40¢–$1.00
- matching envelope 40¢–$1.50

Fax Service *Transmit/Receive:* $3.50 first page; $2.00 all subsequent pages

- additional line charge for overseas only
- no charge for material faxed by client to resume service

Rush Service Add 50% to hourly rate

Disk Copy of Resume/Cover Letter — $5
All resumes are retained on disk indefinitely at no additional charge

For a two-page resume, the same premise as above is followed . . . except that it generally should take only an additional fifteen minutes to prepare the second page of the client's already written resume. Review time and print time are a little longer on the return visit.

■ *additional pages of CV (curriculum vitae) $25 each*

The same premise described above is used for every page after the second: $25 is the overall fee per page, with no more than fifteen minutes spent per page.

■ *revisions to existing resume or original printouts*
of revised or existing resume (in addition to copy charge);
there is a minimum charge of $10 (the hourly rate is $85)

For a client who calls up to receive ten more originals of his or her resume with no changes, there is a flat minimum fee of $10 (plus the charge to print, usually .75¢ per page unless an executive-class paper is used). If changes are required to the resume (client-initiated, not correction of typographical errors), these are made at an hourly rate of $85, with $21.25 being the minimum, quarter-hour charge.

■ *consultation (actual time billed) $85/hour*

This is the basis on which any time spent by telephone or in person with a client is computed. Client services could include discussion of the objective, use of cover letters, miniconsultation for altering portions of resume or cover letter, and so on. Time charged is billed in tenth-of-an-hour increments, with a quarter-hour representing the minimum charge ($21.25).

Complete Resume Package

As stated, this package *includes* a consultation of up to one and one-half hours in length. The client is informed of this at the time the consultation is scheduled and is reminded about the time limit as the consultation begins. Should both parties deem additional time to be appropriate, consultation will continue at an hourly rate of $85.

While there is a great deal of deviation in the industry, you should anticipate that with practice and experience, you will ultimately spend about the same time writing, reviewing, and proofreading a client's resume (from scratch) as you do in collecting the data during the consultation. In other words, with experience, a one-and-one-half-hour-long consultation should yield material that you then spend, in total, about an hour and a half on to review, organize, write, and proofread the resume (one or two pages, does not matter).

That said, it is easily possible, particularly in the beginning *or* with unusual client situations, difficult employment histories, and so forth, to spend significantly more time writing—perhaps two or more hours. Some colleagues have said that with a really trying client situation, they have spent even four hours altogether in writing, rewriting, and preparing the resume. With all of that deviation in mind, you should also take into account that when the client returns to your office to read the resume you have developed, he or she may spend only ten minutes at this task and completely love what you've prepared, with no corrections (the ultimate—but, alas, unlikely goal!). More realistically, the client will correct several facts (which he or she might have presented incorrectly in consultation), change several phrases or words, or perhaps modify a summary statement.

The average time that a client *should* spend in reviewing a full resume developed completely from scratch is about fifteen to twenty minutes; this includes time for noting any minor revisions or corrections. Then, as part of a full consultation in which a specified number of originals are provided, time is required to select the paper and print the finals. This can take another ten or fifteen minutes. If you have included development of one pro forma cover letter with the package, the review and revision will add even more time to the total.

Hence, once you tally all the components, primarily time, you can see why a package might carry such a "high" price tag (as the $300 I quote). Use this as a *selling* point when marketing your packages to clients. An effective strategy is establishing different levels of complete resume packages:

- Using the above example of $300 for a complete resume package, this might be labeled your *Platinum* service offering.
- A *Gold* package could be priced at $250 and include up to a one-hour

consultation and twenty originals of the final resume (the pro forma cover letter is extra).

- A *Silver* package could be priced at $210 and include up to a forty-five-minute consultation and ten originals of the final resume (pro forma cover letter extra).

A discounted offering for students is designed for those "with focus"—that is, those with very clear job objectives, a degree supporting their interest, and a fairly well-organized employment/volunteer/academic history. A student resume should be one page in length (probably one of the few absolutes that I can think of). Therefore, if the consultation comes in under the forty-five-minute mark, the pricing, as in my price list example for $180, is good. Students availing themselves of this service offering should be reminded at the onset of the consultation that the hourly rate is $85 (or whatever you have determined) should the consultation period require more than forty-five minutes.

Cover Letter Services

The example in my sample price list of $40 for a cover letter presents a flat rate to a client for developing a unique cover letter on the basis of (a) having completed a consultation or (b) having conducted a miniconsultation and retype of a resume so that you are comfortable with your knowledge of your client's background and objectives.

The $40 charge listed to create one unique cover letter is based upon roughly a half-hour at the top hourly rate, $85. The fee of $44 per hour quoted for preparing individualized cover letters is based upon the traditionally lower hourly rate established for word-processing services. This time is spent personalizing the information in each cover letter. I typically quote that I can prepare about eight individualized cover letters per hour (using the previously developed template letter with minor modifications to slant each letter to each respective ad; also included is preparation of the matching envelope). Note, however, that if a consultation is required to "discuss the merits of various want ads" or approaches in responding to advertisements, the client should be billed for that portion of the project at the top hourly rate.

Editorial/Consulting Services

Basically, any time spent in consultation by phone or in person with a client to discuss career objective, career search materials, interview training and preparation, mock interviews, follow-up to actual interviews, and the like, represents billable time at the top hourly rate. There are some exceptions: If a client with whom you've been working regularly calls in briefly (no more than five or, at most, ten minutes) to report results of a given interview, you may decide (as I do) *not* to charge for this time . . . unless it becomes an extended discussion wherein advice is being sought.

Rush Service

As mentioned earlier in the text, particularly if you are a new service, you should feel free to waive this fee, but always note it on the invoice (as in "Typical 50 percent surcharge for rush service has been waived as a courtesy"). In this way, clients will know—and appreciate—the professional courtesies you have extended.

Disk Copy of Resume/Cover Letter

In today's highly computer-literate society, more and more resume clients will want to have a copy of their resume (and cover letter, if one has been developed) on disk. Depending upon your equipment and compatibility with your individual client's system type, you will want to make this service readily available. However, it is important to clarify several key points at the initial consultation as well as to develop policies that will work for you down the road.

I recommend including on your work order a query that asks about the need for a disk copy, the type of platform (IBM or Mac), and the preferred software (see chapter 7). I also recommend that if you know in advance that the client will want access to his or her resume on disk (say, for preparing cover letters independently or perhaps using a fax modem to send his or her own resume), you determine the preferred font that matches something on the client's system. I further suggest that you advise clients (if this, as with me, is the case) that you are *not* a computer/software specialist but, rather, a professional resume writer; as such, you cannot guarantee their success in being able to access the resume from a disk copy that you will provide (software versions could be different; clients might not be familiar with their own hardware or software, or they might have a poor-quality inkjet printer that spreads to two pages the one-page format you have created on your system and so on).

Over the past few years, I've noted a marked increase in the number of clients wanting a disk copy of their resume. I've also seen a commensurate rise in the number of calls I receive "after the fact" of clients experiencing problems with their software (or being totally lacking in knowledge of "how to use Word") once they try to work with the resume/disk copy. I have learned the hard way (by spending significant amounts of time in telephone diagnosis to an IBM user who is clueless as to how to use the system and doesn't know how to use WordPerfect—I'm a pure Mac lover and use Microsoft Word to write nearly all the resumes I prepare) and have perfected ways of stating up front that I will retain all resumes and indefinitely at no charge to my clients for future access and updating (the latter, updating, for a fee, of course). I charge a flat $5.00 to provide clients with their resume on disk. And in addition to preferred software format, I always provide an extra copy of the resume as a text file on the disk.

I also have a firm policy of never accepting disks back—in other words, the client will call to say, "I've updated the content of my resume on that disk you gave me . . . but when I go to print it, it doesn't look good or fit on one page. Can I bring you the disk and have you print it?" In my opinion, this is a lose-lose proposition. The client may or may not understand the need for additional formatting once you open the disk (if you decide to even take the risk, run virus protection, and accept a disk onto your system—I've had two hard-drive failures from this practice, thus the reason for establishing my policy!). The client may or may not be willing to pay for the time you will inevitably spend in formatting and fine-tuning the document. And clients may or may not be willing to pay for the time you will undoubtedly *want* to spend in making revisions, corrections, or enhancements of those areas they "think" they've written perfectly. While perhaps not intentionally so, it's frequently a case of "something for nothing." This is almost always true when the client has, in all actuality, spent hours and hours trying to do what you are an expert at—and the client is probably at a high frustration level when his or her software or printer doesn't cooperate.

When I present a disk copy to clients, I remind them that while it's "theirs to do with as they wish," I don't accept disks back onto my system and that I retain their materials indefinitely at no charge. I also indicate that if they do wish to undertake their own updates but would then like my services at a future point, I'm happy to work with them—from their printed copies. I also remind clients (this happens frequently) that if/when they do bring in printed updates of their resume, unless they've carefully marked up changes made on the original document *I provided,* I may have to spend a significant amount of extra time simply reviewing what they present against the original (that's in my system) on a line-by-line basis to discern *where they've made changes.* I've had this happen a number of times: A computer-savvy client will update and make reasonably good changes to his or her resume over several years, possibly reflecting two career changes. Then the client loses access to the computer he or she made these changes on (spouse "gets" computer in a divorce settlement, child takes computer away to school, client no longer works for employer where computer was used, and so on). Such clients will need "only an address change," but when they bring the printout of the resume to me, it's clear that it's *not* the resume I originally prepared! I then have to spend that time in line-by-line review to see what else has changed. When I'm charging by the hour (using the $85 per hour fee), I don't mind expending the time at all, providing the client understands the necessity for this review.

It truly becomes ineffective, from a cost and quality standpoint, for most clients to undertake their own updates unless they are very proficient on their own systems and have excellent-quality laser printers. By basing all fees off a time schedule (and hourly rate), I protect myself from spending inordinate hours in what would seem, to many clients, to be "unpaid work." I urge you to develop similar policies.

CHAPTER SIX

WRITING A BUSINESS PLAN— THE "ROADMAP" TO SUCCESS

WHY A BUSINESS PLAN?

As Laurence J. Peter said in his infamous management tome of the late 1960s (*The Peter Principle,* source of the popular quote, "In a hierarchy, every employee tends to rise to his level of incompetence"), "if you don't know where you're going, you will probably end up somewhere else." Especially with a business, if you don't at least commit your wonderful ideas and plans to paper, you may never know when you've reached your goal. Even if you are not seeking outside financing, your business plan will force you to consider all aspects of starting a resume business (including the risks, which are relatively few, in my opinion). And a business plan will allow you a great measure of pride when you review your accomplishments twelve months after setting your goals.

THE SECTIONS OF A BUSINESS PLAN

The key areas of a business plan are listed below. While you should certainly touch on all of these facets in your business planning document, feel free to combine sections where it makes sense in order to maintain the fluidity of the document as a working tool for your business. In each of the worksheet sections below, I've provided examples that illustrate my background and how I would reflect it in a business plan. You should note your unique attributes, experience, distinguishing market features, and so on, creating a business plan that symbolizes *your* approach to your market.

Mission Statement and Executive Summary

Using the information presented in chapter 5 about defining your market niche and creating a business slogan, you can easily add the narrative necessary to create a strong objective statement for your resume service. This information is typically included in the "Executive Summary" portion of a business plan; this section of the plan is usually a page or two in length at most (oftentimes it is just a paragraph or two), and it should be written last. Here is where you should outline your plans for the business, provide concise information about your qualifications and background in the field (review the attributes you developed earlier), and describe the types of clients you intend to serve.

Company Background and Industry

This category of your business plan should provide more detailed information about you, your background, and the company you are planning to operate. You should also touch on the industry and include information about the field of resume writing in general.

General Description of the Business

In this section of the plan, you should describe such things as the condition of the current marketplace, your competition, what specific services you expect to offer, the equipment you will use to operate your business, the suppliers and vendors from whom you will procure specialty resume papers and office supplies, and how your schedule will operate to allow you to meet with clients and handle production. You should also mention areas that you may eventually develop in your business (that is, potential profit centers beyond your resume service, such as interview training, and videotaping).

Marketing and Sales Planning

In the marketing section of this category, you should detail your competition, including price and service differentials, as well as define your distinctions in the marketplace and your pricing strategies. Include an actual price list. (By the way, I also advise keeping a copy of every version of your

COMPANY BACKGROUND AND INDUSTRY WORKSHEET IDEAS

For instance, as president of Absolute Advantage, I have been in the professional employment/job search field for more than ten years. I hold the credential of Certified Professional Resume Writer and am an active member/contributor to two of my industry's professional associations, the Professional Association of Resume Writers and the National Resume Writers Association. I have written more than 7,000 resumes and helped nearly 10,000 clients conduct successful job search campaigns. The resume-writing industry is a rapidly growing field reflective of the economic trends in our global society: The typical twenty-five-year-old today can expect to hold positions with at least ten different employers in his or her lifetime. That necessitates, in all likelihood, a revised resume about that number of times. In addition, more and more employers in fields that traditionally did not require a resume are now seeking one. Because of the gross undersaving of the baby-boomer generation, the elimination of secure, long-term employment with one company that guarantees a hefty retirement pension, the lack of security in the social security system, and the desire for maintaining costly lifestyles, today's biggest generation, the baby boomers, will work well past their early sixties . . . and require dynamic career search materials to help them accomplish successful searches in highly competitive times. Lastly, with the Internet explosion, more and more clients require not only well-written resumes on paper but the ability to have their career profiles posted (sometimes confidentially) on the Internet.

price list in your permanent files. You will find it very interesting ten years from now to look back upon the services you initially offered and the rates that you affixed to them. When I review my price list from my first year in business, 1983, I laugh to think that I charged just $10 an hour for consulting and editorial services and that a one-page resume was $25—complete, including the consultation and writing services!)

In this category you should also describe your plans for advertising your business, list projected costs for your advertising, and provide details about how you will attract clientele. Also discuss the "sales cycle" (primarily by telephone) that you plan to use.

Contingency Planning

This is a brief section! What are the risks to this type of business? Well, not attracting clients quickly enough to ensure profitability could be one. What is the contingency plan for such an outcome? One solution (and, in fact, a recommended step for your start-up months—at least until yellow pages advertising "hits") is advertising "two-fer" specials in your local weekly newspaper and then offering a different discount or attractive special every week for at least two to three months. A 2" x 2" ad each week (perhaps printed in reverse—that is, a black background surrounding letters that appear set in "white") can bring name recognition and serve as a reminder to potential clients of where to find you before they can locate you in the book. That in itself can be a good strategy; in your newspaper advertising and any flyers you generate, always include the statement "Make a note of our telephone number! You won't find us in the Yellow Pages till spring [or whenever the next Yellow Pages edition is released]!"

Another example of contingency planning might be that you have opted to start your resume business on a part-time basis while continuing either full- or part-time employment during traditional business hours. You might plan to do this until the business begins to demonstrate the strength to operate full-time.

To digress slightly, I effectively started my own company in this fashion (on a part-time basis). I worked in a traditional office environment as a manager at Digital Equipment Corporation from 8:00 A.M. until 5:30 or 6:00 P.M.; I scheduled my own client appointments from 7:30 P.M. until 9:00 or 9:30 P.M., though sometimes business needs warranted that I meet with clients even later. I also booked consultations on Saturdays and Sundays. During my lunch hour I managed to return telephone messages left on my answering machine, and I did so again upon return to my home office after a regular day at work. I didn't explain to my clients that I had a job away from the home office during the day; most simply presumed that I was with other clients. And because I marketed my evening and weekend availability as an advantage to my clients, they perceived it as such.

A difficulty has been weaning these clients, and their referrals, to a more traditional schedule. My business has been running full-time since 1988, concurrent with the birth of my first children (twin sons), and while I generally prefer to see clients for consultation during the morning hours, I still offer one evening a week and one Saturday out of three for those clients unable to schedule appointments during regular office hours.

Financial Data

Financial information in a formal business plan (one that you'd bring to a bank for financing purposes) should include a financial summary, a profit-and-loss statement, a cash flow analysis, and a projected balance sheet. The Small Business Administration (address in the Appendix) publishes excellent booklets on developing these documents. Should you decide to seek financing but not feel comfortable compiling the financial data for your business, set up a visit with an accountant or finance professional. The most important financial document for a start-up business, however, is the expense sheet (see example). This is the document off of which your planning with regard to hourly rates and overall profitability will be determined.

For instance, examples of advertising planned for the Yellow Pages, supplementary advertising/direct mail marketing campaigns, special offers planned (seasonal, targeted two-fer specials, and so on), any promotional purchase offers (credit for referrals), and regular marketing efforts (postcard mailings, newsletter mailings, and the like) would all be included.

Projected Costs for Business Start-Up

In this part of your business plan, you calculate how much you'll need to spend to launch your home-based resume service. The cost breakdowns here supplement the lists presented in chapter 1.

Essential equipment and other start-up expenses. First list the items you'll need at bare minimum.

- Word Processor ($500, for a used computer system, to $2,000, for a new one)
  - Seek adequate storage capability on hard drive, plus disk backups.
  - You'll need a reasonable selection of fonts. The seven or eight fonts embedded on your system will be adequate to start; later, consider adding five to ten highly readable yet distinctive type-faces to enhance your ability to provide distinctive resumes.
- Laser Printer ($500 to $2,000)
  - Absolutely necessary to produce the high-quality documents that clients will expect.
  - A resolution of 300 dots per inch (dpi) is certainly adequate. If you can afford a laser printer featuring 600 dpi, "go for it." (Costs have really dropped on these.)
- Telephone Service ($20 to $400, including Yellow Pages advertising costs)
  - For your base service, an in-home office line fee can run as low as $15 or $20 per month.

For instance, in reviewing the ideas mentioned on the previous few pages, select and tailor to your own situation those points that reflect most closely the strategies you would employ to ensure the start-up of your business (including return to part-time or temporary work in order to cover resume service expenses while building the business).

— Yellow Pages advertising costs vary greatly nationally. In part, determinations are based on the population of the circulation area, the number of categories you choose to list under, and the number of directories in which you want to appear.

■ Telephone Answering Machine or Voice Mail System ($75 flat fee for a machine versus a one-time installation fee of about $20, then a monthly bill of about $10 for voice mail service)

— Automated answering is absolutely critical so that clients can leave messages for you when you are not available. This is particularly true for "sunlighting" individuals who are away from their home offices during traditional 9-to-5 hours.

■ Business Cards and Stationery ($40 and up—way up, if you wish, but I advise against this)

— Have your business cards professionally printed but use a camera-ready mechanical you have prepared yourself. (This ensures that you are able to replicate the font chosen for your card on your computer system and are able to create matching stationery, brochure copy, and similar items yourself). The professional printing results you will get may cost no more than if you print the cards yourself on the specialty papers commonly available today from such vendors as PaperDirect and Quill. Plus, the quality of good business cards speaks volumes about you and your business (and remember, you really want to get those business cards "out there," attracting clients for your business, cultivating referrals, and so on).

EXPENSE SHEET

(Project expenses on a monthly basis for the first year;
not all expenses occur monthly)

For the month of_____

- Business Telephone Service
(monthly base/toll charges) $_____
- Yellow Pages Advertising $_____
- Other Advertising Expenses $_____
- Fax Telephone Service (if dedicated) $_____
- Utilities/"Rent"/Security/Monitoring $_____
  (proportion of household expenses based on
  the percentage of space your office occupies
  relative to your house—typically anywhere from
  5 to 25 percent) $_____
- Business Insurance $_____
- Medical Insurance $_____
- Taxes and Licenses $_____
- Bank Service Charges/Fees $_____
- Office Supplies $_____
- Postage $_____
- Delivery Services $_____
- Printer's Charges $_____
- Office Equipment $_____
- Leased Equipment Expenses $_____
- Software $_____
- Service Agreements on Hardware/Copier $_____
- Repair/Maintenance Expenses $_____
- Periodicals/Subscriptions $_____
- Professional Dues/Memberships $_____
- Business Auto Expense $_____
- Parking/Tolls $_____
- Travel Expense $_____
- Entertainment $_____
- Freelancer/Subcontractor Pay $_____
- Salary/Draw $_____
- Miscellaneous $_____
TOTAL $_____

— In the beginning, there's really no need to invest in expensive stationery for your business. Off the top of my head, I can think of no instance when I've ever needed 8 ½" x 11" stationery to communicate with clients. When I'm writing a note, say, acknowledging a successful job search following a full consultation and development of materials, I use professionally printed note cards on which I handwrite my personalized message. I do use brochures with my clients and have found that the preprinted thirty-eight-pound papers of companies such as PaperDirect are appropriate and ideal for this purpose. But I made the mistake of ordering stationery and envelopes from a printer in my early years and ended up giving most of it to my kids for scrap paper because of several changes I later made on my letterhead. I invested in a dedicated fax line, so the number I had printed on the letterhead (originally sharing the fax with my residence line) was no longer correct . . . and I changed my business slogan as time went along so that the first no longer reflected my business focus.

— As soon as you can afford it, have half-sheet padded stationery printed (5 ½" x 8 ½" sheets, glued at the top to cardboard to create pads of fifty or seventy-five sheets each). Beyond giving these pads to certain clients as promotional items, I use them all the time to jot the quick cover notes I send out with newspaper clippings, press releases, and other materials I pass along to clients.

■ Paper for Clients' Career Materials (costs detailed below)

— Offer at least four basic paper colors. Pure white, an ivory or cream, a very light stone gray, and a very light blue are sufficient. All should be quality papers—parchment or at least some cotton content. The choice of finish will be up to you, though I personally hate what is called a "laid" finish. Depending upon the supplier (many are listed in the Appendix), you can anticipate paying anywhere from $3 to $10 per box of 100 sheets, with the cost decreasing slightly when you purchase a ream (a package of 500 sheets). I have always liked having boxes of 100; as the boxes empty, I keep them in storage for use as shipping containers. I carry ten different types of paper and keep about 500 sheets of each on hand, but you don't have to maintain this type of inventory until you start to have "turn." For start-up you should have at least 200 sheets of paper available in each of the colors you offer.

— Offer envelopes in colors matching the resumes. As a minimum, you should have number 10, traditional business-size envelopes, and I highly recommend carrying 9" x 12" envelopes in matching or coordinating colors. If you use papers provided by a company such as PM Resource or PaperDirect (my favorites), for example, 9" x 12" envelopes to match the resume papers are available, but are quite costly. Beyond these, I carry 9" x 12" envelopes in a traditional buff color, as well as white ones that I obtain from economical bulk office supply stores. For those clients unable, or unwilling, to purchase the more costly matching envelopes, these provide an effective alternative: as you will read later, prospective employers *vastly prefer* receiving resume materials mailed flat, as opposed to folded into a number 10 envelope. The cost of envelopes is higher per piece than stationery, varying anywhere from fifteen cents per number 10 envelope to more than a dollar for the custom, oversize envelopes. You'll want to have on hand at least fifty in each of the colors you provide.

- Business Checking Account (usually $25 or $35 to open)
  - Expect a monthly fee of between $7 and $15.
- Licenses and Permits
  - Fees vary (from $10 to nearly $100) depending upon your town and state.
- Furniture and Furnishings
  - These investment costs can be nothing—if you already have a furnished section of your home that can be considered your office, and an area in which you can meet with clients—or they can be substantial. I started in my basement, then moved to a spare bedroom, and finally ended up constructing a lovely 22' x 24' office adjacent to my home on my business's seventh anniversary. The first seven years, I spent virtually nothing on "space," and I was able to get all of my office furniture used for under $100 through a corporate tag sale.

- If you need to purchase a desk, a file cabinet, a table, a chair for yourself, and two for client purposes (for couples or a parent and a grown child), definitely investigate used office-furniture outlets. Costs can range from a few hundred dollars to $1,000.

■ Lighting (cost varies)

- Don't skimp on lighting, particularly if you will be working in a basement office or during evening hours.

- Task and ambient lighting may already be available in your work space or you may need to spend upwards of several hundred dollars to purchase and install adequate lighting.

Optional equipment and other expenses. Now that you've covered the essentials, list the cost of any special items—the add-ons you plan to use to enhance your service.

■ Fax Machine ($300 and up)

- I consider this nearly a requirement in up-front expense for a resume service. Clients who pay in advance may want you to fax copies for their approval or fax already approved copies to prospective employers.

■ Merchant Account Status (about $400)

- This may appear to be a luxury, but your ability to accept major credit cards will quickly enhance your overall profitability. Being able to accept credit cards will enable you to work with clients on a long-distance basis. For instance, former clients who have moved out of your area may need updates and want you to mail materials on their behalf immediately. You don't have to wait for receipt—and clearing—of checks in order to send out their work. Plus, credit card companies report that customers consistently spend more money when they are able to charge their purchases. A price-resistant client who is short of ready cash may wind up buying an expensive resume package if you can offer the option of charging the purchase and financing the cost over a few months.

■ Electronic or Electric Typewriter ($200 and up)

- If you plan to prepare application forms for your clients, you will need a good typewriter in addition to your word processor.

- For cover letter services, you will need to prepare oversize

Writing a Business Plan—The "Roadmap" to Success

envelopes on a typewriter to facilitate client mailings.

- Photocopier ($500 to $2,000)
  - Consider a fax machine with photocopy capability.
  - A copy machine will allow you to market photocopies of client resume materials at a cost lower to you and your client than laser-printed originals.
  - You will be able to sell extra copies of client letters of recommendation, transcripts, and so on.
  - You will be able to make file copies of client work orders and completed applications efficiently.
- Professional Brochure ($100 and up)
  - If you opt not to produce a brochure for yourself using desktop publishing skills and your own laser printer, you will ultimately wish to have one printed by a professional.
- Advertising (varies widely)
  - In addition to traditional (and recommended!) Yellow Pages advertising, you may wish to consider various forms of direct mail and other print advertising.
  - It is possible to spend as little as $10 or $15 per week on a small, in-column classified ad in your weekly newspaper. Or you can spend upward of $1,500 a month, as does Wendy Enelow, CPRW, of The Advantage, Inc. (the amount she allocates for her advertising in the *National Business Employment Weekly*, a highly recommended periodical for your own reference and library).
  - Direct mail advertising costs could involve something such as a quarterly client newsletter that you prepare "in-house." I highly recommend this approach (chapter 10 has details); the costs can vary between $100 and $300 per quarter.
- Professional Library ($100 to $500 or more)
  - Costs vary widely to stock a well-designed professional library with materials for your own use in preparing professional resumes and cover letters plus resources your clients may consult, borrow, or lease when conducting their own job searches. (This book's Appendix contains recommended materials to consider.)

Appendix and Resources

In this final section of a business plan, you will want to include your own resume (if not included as part of the Executive Summary) as well as mention materials you will use in preparing professional career search materials (list the items you plan to include in your professional library).

QUOTABLE INSPIRATION

"I've made a policy of paying my way and letting my clients' needs dictate the equipment and supplies that I have obtained. For instance, a few years ago I made a cold call on a tattoo parlor (OK, so I'm creative!). He wanted to know if I could laminate his pictures. I said, 'No problem' and proceeded to find out how much a laminator would cost, the supplies, and then gave him a quote based on the information I had gotten. His job paid for my 'new toy,' and every job thereafter was profit."—*Janette M. Campbell, CPRW, Business Assistants (Washougal, Washington)*

CHAPTER SEVEN

OFFICE DESIGN AND ADMINISTRATION

ESTABLISHING YOUR ENVIRONMENT

Many home-based professionals situate their offices in spare rooms in their homes, often an unused bedroom or finished basement room. If you are lucky, you will have an office area with separate access from the rest of your house. But if this is not the case, don't worry—many successful resume writers meet with clients at their dining room table or in the living room (whichever is closest to the front door, so that there is minimal traipsing through the house or apartment). I began my business from a tiny, dark room in my basement that had access off my laundry room, down an open set of wooden stairs and past the furnace. I dragged unsuspecting clients into this office for three years before moving out of state and into a home that did not have suitable client access to the basement (although that was, again, where my office was located). In that house, I met with clients at my dining room table.

Two years later my family was again relocated, not so incidentally back to house number one in Connecticut. This time, I set up shop in an unused bedroom (it was after the twins were born but before my littlest one had arrived). With the exception of just a handful of "close" clients, however, I was reluctant to drag clients into the bedroom end of my house. I therefore again met with my clients at a dining room table. One year later I designed an "official" office, broke ground in the fall, and, six months later, moved into a dedicated 22' x 24' office adjacent to my home with its own entrance and lavatory. *Heaven!* But as I've pointed out, I paid my dues. Not only that, I achieved success and a high degree of profitability right in my initial basement location. So I would encourage anyone just thinking of starting out as a professional resume writer that it is very feasible to operate your business with minimal enhancements to your dwelling.

Safety and Security

As the operator of a home-based business, you must consider the aspect of safety and security, particularly if you intend to meet with clients at times when you are the only occupant of the dwelling. There are a number of effective strategies for bolstering your confidence and safety while conducting business from your home. I believe it is generally reasonable to assume that a prank caller is not going to engage you in relevant-sounding discussion by telephone for ten minutes or more in an effort to obtain your physical address and then cause you harm (presuming, as I recommend, that you do *not* publish your street address in any of your advertising materials, including your ads in the Yellow Pages). Because I further suggest that specific directions be the last thing you communicate to prospective clients, you should be in a good position to assess the "legitimacy" of every caller.

Trust your gut-level instincts: If you sense something is amiss or are uncomfortable in any way when speaking with an unknown caller, there are several things you can do. Pretend that a client has just arrived for an appointment and ask for the caller's telephone number, indicating that you must meet with the client now but will contact the caller later to complete the discussion and finalize an appointment. A prank caller is certainly not going to provide you with an actual telephone number. You may also opt to schedule an appointment with the caller, then ask for a telephone number, advising that it is your practice to call to confirm each appointment the day before it is to occur and to provide specific directions at that time. Some of my colleagues schedule appointments only for times when someone else will be home. Here are a few creative suggestions shared by a colleague and friend, Kathy Keshemberg, president of Computron of Appleton, Wisconsin, during her presentation at a recent professional conference.

- Place an enormous bowl of dog food near your office door or in the office area to give the illusion of the presence of a large, protective guard dog.

- Place a pair of worn men's work boots near the door of your office (to create a similar illusion).

- Hang a man's overcoat or hat on a coat tree in your office.

- When opening the door for an appointment with a client you feel uneasy about, call out something such as, "John, I'm about to meet with a client—we can finish our discussion shortly."

- Leave a radio playing in an adjacent room on a talk station, low volume, to give the impression of the conversation of others.

- Park your vehicle outside the garage (if you have a garage and normally use it), with the garage door closed, to give the impression that perhaps someone else besides you is also at home.

- Arrange for a friend or colleague to telephone you midway during the time you anticipate meeting with a questionable client to determine that "everything is fine." Establish some kind of code in advance to indicate to the caller if there is a problem or if you'd like the person to call you again in ten or fifteen minutes.

- If you have a close friend who lives near you and will be at home, explain that you are meeting with a client about whom you have some reservations at a certain time of day and ask the friend simply to be alert. Or, as I've heard some folks indicate they have done, call this neighbor and leave the telephone lines "connected" so that you can call for help and be heard by the neighbor in the event of a problem.

All of these ideas might give the impression that there is cause to be paranoid about operating a home-based business. In my years of operating exclusively from my home, I have never experienced a threatening situation (and I see on the order of eight to ten clients per day). I've had calls from a few individuals about whom I suspected there was something odd, but I followed the suggestion of obtaining a phone number to "confirm appointments before giving directions" and either found that there was nothing suspicious to worry about or that the number was, in fact, fictitious. I've conducted consultations with a handful of people over the years whom I found to be a little peculiar, perhaps, or unusual—but, again, never threatening. I believe if you follow basic, commonsense precautions and approach the business professionally (without worrying excessively), you will find that these types of risks are minimal.

If you live alone in a somewhat isolated location where there could be particular risks associated with meeting with "strangers" in your home, condominium, or apartment, you might opt to begin your business by holding consultations at a local fast-food restaurant, coffee shop, or diner. I am aware of successful colleagues in this field who prefer to meet all their clients off-site in such locations—so you do have options to only meeting clientele in your home. Just keep in mind that if you do choose to conduct off-site consultations, you may end up with a third appointment for each client (typically, it is a two-appointment process, as explained in chapter 10: the initial consultation and the return visit to approve, correct, and finalize everything). Meeting off-site would mean that any revisions agreed upon during the second meeting would have to be made at home and possibly represented in a third meeting (or, if you obtain full payment of the balance at the second meeting, you could arrange to ship or mail the final materials to the client instead of holding a third meeting).

QUOTABLE INSPIRATION

"Owning your own business requires much dedication and long hours with minimal pay *at times;* however, generally the satisfaction of personal independence and recognition received by accomplishments is rewarding. Determination of success is a must at all times."— *Carol Ribar, Professional Office Services, Inc. (Island Lake, Illinois)*

LOGISTICS AND OFFICE LAYOUT

This section assumes that you plan to meet with clients in your home. You will want to create an office area that can allow for meeting with two people at a time. (Occasionally, you will find a client bringing a spouse or friend to the consultation; also, a number of your clients will probably refer their children upon graduation from college, and they may choose to accompany them to the initial consultation). Having experimented over the years in my various home offices, I find my clients to be most comfortable when meeting at a table where I can position myself at a right angle to the primary client (with a "guest," when present, situated directly across from me). A table makes it easy for the resume writer to take notes and provides a surface for the client to lay out and present materials (performance evaluations, old resumes, past cover letters, and so on).

In the waiting area of my office, I have a large, wraparound sofa. I have tried conducting consultations with clients seated at a right angle to me on the sofa and simply found that I wasn't as comfortable maintaining the Q-and-A process in this setting. You, however, may prefer such a setting and I encourage you to experiment. Role-play with family, friends, or neighbors before you actually "open for business" to see what works best for you. In my "dining room years," the table in that room served very satisfactorily. When I moved into my "real" office, a conference table proved ideal, with plenty of room for three people to sit comfortably around it and still leave space for work materials.

At the suggestion of some colleagues, I also experimented with conducting consultations with my laptop computer and, even before that, my main computer at hand, directly keying in client responses as we talked. In my case, I found this practice severely limiting and constricting—for both me and my clients. It's a funny thing: Clients would assume that if I didn't type in a comment they were obviously taking their time with to explain to me, "it must not be important" and they would "shut down." On the other hand, some clients would attempt to look over my shoulder as I typed and "correct" me as I went along, not realizing that I was deliberately editing out some of what they were saying to keep the points focused. I also found that by introducing a computer—even my low-profile laptop—into the consultation, I was creating a barrier between the client and myself. This prevented the smooth and open exchange of information and, even more important, thwarted good eye contact—an element essential to a successful interview and consultation.

Keep in mind—and this is a point I emphasize with my clients—that a resume consultation between a professional resume writer and a client is not unlike what the client will experience in an actual interview with a prospective employer. Now, I don't tell my clients this until the *conclusion* of the consultation interview—at which point, many remark, "Why, you are absolutely right . . . and I wasn't even *nervous* with you, Jan." I respond, "Precisely! And that's what you should strive for through role-play once you get home with your completed resume, so that you will interview comfortably and naturally!" True to the time-tested proverb, practice *does* make perfect: The more a client can test-interview, the better prepared he or she will be when presenting for an actual interview (more information to provide to your clients on this topic is included in chapter 12).

Two or three chairs and a table are really the only requirements, logistically, that you must have in order to meet with your clients. Beyond this, however, consider ways in which you will outfit your office (or the area where you will be meeting with clients) to give the best impression of you and your business. Particularly if you are meeting in "shared space" (such as your home's living or dining room), you'll want to develop a quick way to transform the meeting space into a professional-looking room almost designed for that purpose—and just as quickly to restore it to its original look once you are done with business for the day. One of the plastic "milk crates" available at many office superstores is ideal for assembling the materials you'll want immediately at hand for a consultation that is in a nondedicated room of your house. As you will find in chapter 11, you'll want to have the following available:

Materials for Client Consultations

- A supply of client consultation/intake forms
- Pads of paper on which to take your notes (experiment to determine if you prefer loose-leaf paper, a loose-leaf composition notebook, a steno pad, or letter- or legal-size paper padded at the top)
- A supply of pens (pencils, if you prefer)
- Business cards
- Brochures
- Professional articles copied for distribution to clients (generic articles might be appropriate for every resume client and pieces

specific to a particular industry for only certain clientele)

- Your professional certificates and credentials
- Paper samples
- Receipts for deposits (including credit card slips, if you are established as a merchant, as detailed later in this chapter)
- A bulletin board or loose-leaf binder of testimonials and thank-you letters from satisfied clients
- A resume sample book, if you decide to have one. I no longer make one available to my clients, because I found a number of them getting overly hung up on the *content* of the fictitious samples. No matter how many samples I created, I couldn't possibly have one for every unique client need. Instead, I rather quickly learned that it is in the best interest of both my clientele and myself to assure clients that I will develop the most effective format, select the most appropriate font, and design a resume to best portray them; no one has ever taken issue with this. Of course, if a client presents a sample resume that he or she prefers (whether it be in terms of design, typeface, layout, or what have you), I will review the document with the individual. If I believe a feature the client likes is not as appropriate as something else, I will offer my professional opinion, then defer in the final decision making to the client. (You know the old adage: "The customer is *always* right.")

For those resume service operators with an established home office location for meeting with clients, the above items will simply become a part of the office space.

Provisions should be made for clients to have access to a lavatory. When you consider that most full consultations can extend easily to an hour and a half, it is not unreasonable to presume that some clients will need to use the facilities, just as you would expect to be able to do while visiting with your attorney or accountant. Obviously, the bathroom located in nearest proximity to your office is preferable. From a logistical standpoint, if the closest bathroom is in a different section of your home, it's certainly appropriate to escort the client to the bathroom, then discreetly "post guard" in an adjacent area so that you can escort the client back to the office (so as not to leave the client at the opposite end of your home for a long time).

I believe it is also common courtesy to offer a beverage to a client upon arrival. While I'm a constant coffee drinker and nearly always have a pot brewing, I also offer iced water or tea to my clients. Most folks get pretty thirsty while talking for an hour and a half. If I happen to have a batch of cookies just out of the oven (ahh, the joys of being home-based—even when one works the number of hours I do, I *still* have the flexibility of squeezing in the "extras" when I want!), I always offer samples to my clients. The Christmas season is very popular in my office; regular clients know they can count on nibbling from a full candy dish and sampling whatever I happen to be baking that day. These recommendations may sound like trivialities, but, really, combined with excellent service and an outstanding product, these are the finer points that will put perceptions of you and your business "over the top" for many of your clients and lead to many referrals.

BOOKKEEPING AND ACCOUNTING SYSTEMS

For many creative individuals, including some resume writers, the book-keeping aspect of running a business is not the most appealing, at least initially. To run a business efficiently and profitably, however, a business owner must be on top of the financial details of the operation—including how much money is in receivables and how much money is owed to others at any given time. The financial forms presented in the business planning section of chapter 6 provide the documents accounting professionals will generate (or ask you to provide) if you decide to use the services of an accountant or finance professional. Determine to maintain your financial records in a way that allows for the smooth flow of data into standard accounting forms.

Complex accounting practices aside, though, what should you do about the day-to-day records for your resume service? You need an efficient way of tracking client billing, first and foremost. All clients must be invoiced in a consistent manner—and one that allows you to build records on a monthly basis at minimum (weekly may ultimately be desired). If you go with a monthly time frame, your system should let you see, at a glance, how much revenue was generated in a given month and in what categories (or profit centers). In other words, for a service billing $1,000 a month in one of its early months, $400 might be in consultation charges, $300 might be in typesetting and other production charges, and $300 might be in cover letter generation and supplies. Your recording system should allow for you to "trap" other expenses that are billed to your clients such as charges for overnight delivery, long-distance telephone calls, postage, extra sheets of paper, fax services, and photocopies. There are many good software programs available for PCs today; Quicken, Quickbooks,

QUOTABLE INSPIRATION

"I have to fight the temptation to cut prices, so I encourage all of us to understand our markets and maintain fair prices, even at the risk of slower growth."—*Alan D. Ferrell, ADF Professional Resumes (Lafayette, Indiana)*

Peachtree Accounting, and Dollars & Sense are just a sampling of the excellent programs that will easily automate your record-keeping process.

As you establish the books for your business, pay close attention to creating the proper mechanisms for funding and filing quarterly estimated taxes (Form 1040-ES on the federal level; individual state requirements vary). If you are uncertain about how to proceed, request documents from the Internal Revenue Service and then, if something is still unclear, consult an accounting professional. If your state requires you to collect sales tax on resume services (many do), be sure that you follow the proper filing procedure and timing (usually quarterly) for this as well.

To use your accounting information to best advantage, you'll soon want to assess your true costs of doing business, calculate a break-even point for your resume service, and count up your profits. If you base your fee schedule on an hourly rate as I advocate, it is easy to use a simple formula to check that the rate you have settled on is, in fact, one that not only covers the costs of doing business but yields a reasonable profit. To start with, you must determine the number of billable hours you will have in a week. Being conservative, start with the assumption that you will be able to bill clients for roughly 50 percent of the time you are working. Time that you aren't able to bill clients for directly includes the hours devoted to handling all administrative work related to operating your resume service, developing marketing and advertising materials, completing bank deposits, ordering supplies, visiting printers, and so forth. In round numbers, if you work 40 hours a week and 20 of these hours are billable, your gross for the week, based on a hypothetical hourly rate of $50, is $1,000.

Now, in calculating an annual gross, you'll want to take into account the amount of time you anticipate taking off for vacation, attending professional conferences, and so on. Let's suppose you plan to have five weeks of unbillable time per year; that leaves 47 weeks, at 20 hours per week (940 hours) and $50 per hour, or a gross of $47,000 for purposes of this exercise. *That's not your profit.* We haven't looked at expenses yet!

In reviewing the numbers you developed for your expense sheet in chapter 6, take the total and use it in the equation below (I'll supply a figure of $36,000 for purposes of the exercise). Before running the calculations, you'll want to project an amount to plug into the "profit" line—a figure separate from your salary (although they end up being reported the same, with the same tax implications, on Schedule C of your federal tax return); this is the amount that you would like to see the business generate for a profit. In the first year it's unlikely for most businesses to roll much to a profit line; to pull out a salary is doing well. In any event, I'll plug a hypothetical $4,000 into the equation.

Total Annual Expenses ($36,000) + **Projected Profit** ($4,000) = **Total Expenses and Profit** ($40,000) ÷ **Billable Hours** (940) = **Effective Hourly Rate** ($42.55)

When considered with all other factors—market conditions in your area, what competitors are charging, the number of hours you *really* expect to be working, and so forth—you can use this equation to play out a number of useful "what if" scenarios that will help to shape the financial picture of your business.

Client Record/Invoice

Unless you opt to use an automated invoice-generating program (not necessary), a document developed in your word-processing program that becomes part of the computer file for each client works well. The accompanying examples show the client record and invoice form I maintain on my computer for each of my clients. By maintaining up-to-date information in the client record, which is the first "page" of the invoice file, I am easily able to recall all business transacted with a given client each time we speak or meet (even if it has been two years since he or she required my services). There are other benefits to this record. Many of my clients will contact me for income tax purposes in the first quarter of the new calendar year to request a summary statement of all charges incurred during the previous calendar year. By maintaining this record, I can easily generate such a document, without having to review my paper invoice files or go into my accounting program.

As a backup to my bookkeeping system, I maintain a copy of each client's invoice in this same computer record. When new charges are incurred and it is time to generate a new invoice, I simply take a copy of the most recent invoice (retaining that original "intact" on the system) and then overwrite with the correct information. Hence, I can scroll through one document to review the complete history of financial transactions with a given client.

ESTABLISHING PAYMENT POLICIES, BILLING, AND CREDIT

Your success in operating a profitable, thriving resume service is closely related to your consistency and ability to establish sound procedures from the beginning. Most entrepreneurs have heard time and again that cash flow problems can bring a small business to a halt very quickly. Especially in the beginning, it is difficult to imagine the likelihood of such a problem for a resume service—but unless you are careful to determine how you want to work *financially* with your clients, problems may ensue.

SAMPLE CLIENT RECORD

Client Profile:

ED JONES
123 Main Street
Anytown, USA 66666
Office: (222) 222-2222
Residence: (666) 333-3333
Beeper (333) 666-6666
Fax: (666) 333-1111

Stationery: Stone Gray Exec.
Envelope: 9 x 12 matching
Source: MGC Yellow Pages
  "Resume Services"
Costs: $85/hour
  $1.00 per sheet
  $1.25 per env.
Format: two-page res., one vers.
  only + prof'l refs. and salary
  history

Personal Data:
- wife Jane (psychotherapist)
- two high school/near
college-age sons
- avid golfer

Payment History: Visa
Account #666 666 666 666
Expir. 2/98

Client Referrals:

Sue Smith (3/1/96, full resume package)	$300.00
Jane Jones (5/1/96, mini resume package)	130.00
Dave Edwards (11/1/96, full resume package)	300.00
Total Referrals to Date:	$730.00

Activity	Date	Revenue
• Full Resume Consultation (package)	1/20/96	$300.00
• Interview Training Techniques	2/1/96	185.50
• Cover Letters	2/15/96	53.00
• Cover Letters	2/22/96	53.00
• Cover Letters plus orig. resume printing	3/1/96	106.00
• Cover Letters/Follow-Up Letters	3/8/96	79.50
• Cover Letters/Follow-Up Letters	3/15/96	79.50
• Resume Update	3/17/97	219.95
Total Client Revenues to Date:		$1,076.45
TOTAL CLIENT/REFERRAL REVENUES:		$1,806.45

*[Note: The computer file record is followed by the individual invoices
for this client in chronological order.]*

ABSOLUTE ADVANTAGE
P.O. Box 718
Durham, CT 06422
(860) 349–0256
(860) 349–1343

Invoice for Services Rendered   **Date:** March 17, 1997

Ed Jones
123 Main Street
Anytown, USA 66666
(222) 222–2222
Visa Acct. #666 666 666 666, expir. 2/98

Date of Service	Project Description	Hours/Rate	Subtotal
Mar. 17, 1997	Miniconsultation to update resume	.8 hr. @ $75	$60.00
	•editorial services	.5 hr. @ $75	37.50
	•modifications to - professional references and salary history	.3 hr. @ $75	22.50
	•ten originals sets of four–page package (stone grey pebble granite, Executive Class)	40 sheets @ $1	40.00
	•ten matching envelopes	10 @ $1.25	12.50
	•overnight FedEx delivery to Marriott/Atlanta		5.00
Payment is due upon completion of project.		**Subtotal**	$177.50
		Sales Tax	12.45
Thank you!		**TOTAL**	$189.95

Professional Resume, Personal Marketing, and Career Services
Our Business Is Making <u>You</u> Look Good!

Operational Recommendations

- Develop a concise, one-page work order form for consultations (see the accompanying sample). This document should be used with every first-time client as well as with all repeat clients (such as for resume updates or ongoing cover letter services); for those clients with whom you are providing weekly cover letter services, a signature on the initial sheet is probably sufficient, as you will undoubtedly be handling much of this work via the telephone and fax machine.

- Be certain to obtain client signatures at the onset of any major project (including complete resume consultations, miniconsultations, and resume typesetting projects); always date the document and provide clients with a copy.

- Provide estimated costs (or flat package pricing, if relevant) in the appropriate area of the work order form.

- *Always collect a deposit from new clients.* Once you have established a relationship with a client and are dealing locally (in other words, the client picks up all work from your office and pays you at the time of the pickup), you may opt not to charge a deposit with repeat work.

- As the sample work order form shown here reflects, I collect a deposit of $150 (cash, credit card, or personal check) with full resume consultation projects; for other work (miniconsultations, straight typesetting, or cover letter projects), I ask for roughly 50 percent of the anticipated total charge as the deposit amount.

- For long-distance clients (resume consultations conducted by telephone, for example, or updates to materials of clients who have moved out of your area), I recommend receiving payment in full before you ship the final materials. Here's where having "merchant account status"—the ability to accept credit cards—can aid you significantly (see last bullet of this section). If you do not plan to offer credit card charging privileges, obtain full payment by check before mailing the completed work.

- Unless you are working with a long-standing client, I also recom-

ABSOLUTE ADVANTAGE
Celebrating 14 Years! · 1983-1997
P.O. Box 718
Durham, CT 06422
(333) 555–3333 ● Fax: (333) 555–1111

Date/Time Initial Appointment_____

Client Name _____

Address _____

Office Telephone _____ Home Telephone_____

Fax _____ E-mail Address _____

Project _____

Source (which YPgs? referral? repeat?) _____

Font Selection_____ Stock Selection _____

copies _____ # originals _____ Envelope Selection_____

Special Instructions_____

Disk Copy? _____ yes _____ no   IBM____ MAC____

Software _____

Return Appointment Date/Time _____

M/C · Visa · Discover · American Express   Estimated Cost: $ _____

Acct. # _____   Tax $ _____

Expir. Date _____   Less Deposit   – _____

                                             Total $ _____

The above estimate is provided to the best of our ability following initial review/consultation. Final invoice is based on actual project requirements. Significant differences between estimated total and actual requirements will be discussed with the client prior to completion of the work.

A nonrefundable deposit of $150 is required for all complete resume consultations; other project deposits as mutually agreed. All written materials and consultation services must be paid for in full upon receipt of completed product; completed work will not be released until full payment is made, unless alternative billing arrangements have been made in advance. **Please note: Final proofreading is the responsibility of the client** (please be certain to verify all dates, spelling of proper names, etc.).

The client hereby agrees that any inaccurate, incorrect, or misleading information in the resume or other materials provided to the client by **Absolute Advantage** is not our responsibility and that the client had an opportunity to review the materials and approve the entire content prior to delivery and/or reproduction. The client's signature below certifies understanding of and agreement with all the statements in this document.

Signature _____   Date _____

Professional Resume, Personal Marketing, and Career Services
Our Business Is Making <u>You</u> Look Good!

mend against releasing work "in person" without payment of any balance in full; over time, you will begin to develop an understanding of which clients you can work with "on credit" and which you cannot. To start, though, I recommend caution.

■ If you collect "as you go," you won't have any client billing to worry about, never mind billing problems! And your cash flow picture should be seamless.

■ In the area of credit, as your business begins to become established, do explore merchant account status (see the Appendix for contact information). Typically, for under $400 you can be set up to offer electronic acceptance of MasterCard, Visa, and Discover credit cards (as well as others, if desired). The processing fee (called a "discount") is generally around 2 percent—so a $200 resume package, for instance, processed with a Visa card would have a $4 charge for the privilege of allowing the client to use his or her credit card. In other words, you would have $196 automatically deposited into your business checking account *without* worrying about a bouncing check. By the way, you cannot charge your client extra for the ability to use a credit card, but you may want to offer a cash discount. Primarily for the client convenience they afford, and the ability they give you to market higher-end services, accepting credit cards is an excellent idea. Particularly if you intend to engage in the high-end business of long-distance resumes, credit card services are essential.

Other policies that you'll need to consider include your hours of operation (most likely, "by appointment"), your standard turnaround for materials (as well as a policy covering rush service—and an appropriate surcharge), and any guarantee of satisfaction you may wish to provide. Some resume services provide guarantees in writing ("100% Satisfaction Guaranteed!"); many services also develop a statement of policies for their business incorporating the points just articulated.

SCHEDULING

Refer to chapter 11 for the sample scheduling of a resume package for one client. Then consider the following hypothetical week in terms of coordinating and scheduling. Three new clients are scheduled for full consultations between Monday and Friday; six clients are booked for miniconsultations (some existing clients for updates to existing resumes or for tailored cover letters and some new clients for resume typesetting with miniconsultations). These are anticipated to last anywhere from twenty minutes at a minimum to an hour. In addition, you expect that by Friday you will probably receive one "rush" full resume consultation booking as well as two miniconsultation bookings for immediate turnaround (updates to existing resumes). Lastly, in a given week you generally work with five existing clients on generating minor updates to resumes you've already written (change of address, telephone number, association membership, and so on). Let's look at the scheduling calendar tracking how this is likely to come together in terms of your schedule for the week. Keep in mind that while all of this activity is being scheduled—and occurring—you are providing phone coverage, handling marketing and administrative tasks, actually doing production work (which is reflected on this calendar), and scheduling appointments into the next two weeks.

As mentioned earlier, I believe it is critical that the home-based professional resume writer meet with clients *by appointment only*. Unless you plan to expand your business to the point of having a receptionist, if you were to allow drop-in clients, you would have no way of professionally greeting those who happened to drop in or to protect the confidentiality and privacy of the client with whom you were already meeting. In addition, one of the benefits of working from a home office is the ability to structure your time so that you have one day or more per week when you do nothing but work on writing resumes, cover letters, and marketing materials. On those days, naturally, you won't want to dress formally in a business suit—yet if you were to welcome drop-in clients, casual dress, of course, wouldn't be appropriate.

As many of my colleagues know, I've had my share of humorous experiences running a home-based business over the years, a number of which relate to scheduling. There's the story—these are all true, by the way—of the client who mixed up his appointment day and arrived for his appointment at the same time his boss was in my office for a resume! Then there are the unannounced client drop-ins, such as the regular client who, feel-

WEEK OF MAY 1:

	7	8	9	10	11	12	1	2	3	4	5	6	7-?
Monday			Full cons. Jane Doe		Mini Cons. Don Adams	Write Adams, start doc. (↕)		Mini Cons. Steve Smith	3:30 Client A cons. -update while wait		Full cons. RUSH for Tues a.m. Bob Edwards		Write Edwards (↕)
Tuesday	Bob Edwards P.U.			Full Cons. Joe Davis		mini Cons. RUSH Kathy Thomas	Write Thomas, Doe (↕)		Mini Cons. Dan James		Kathy Thomas P.U. / 5:30 Adams P.U.	Write Thomas, Doe (↕)	
Wednesday		8:30 Jane Doe P.U.		Write Davis (↕)		Steve Smith P.U.	Client B Cons. -update while wait (↑)			Joe Davis P.U.		Dan Jones P.U.	
Thursday		Client C cons. update while wait	Full cons. Paul Jackson		Mini Cons. Kevin Spooner	Write Spooner (↕)		Mini Cons. Client D update while wait	Mini Cons. RUSH Donna Roberts		Kevin Spooner P.U.		Write Roberts (↕)
Friday	6:30 Roberts P.U.		Mini cons. Lisa Booth	Client E minicons. update while wait		Mini cons. Jerry Norris	(↓)			Write (←)			
Saturday			10:30 Jerry Norris P.U.						Jackson, Booth, Norris				

ing so comfortable with my office—and with me, evidently—walked right into my home office and proceeded to walk through the house until he found me—*in the bathroom!* I've also been walked-in-on while nursing my babies—and, as many folks know, caught at my desk attired in an even more embarrassing fashion than just my old pj's (which a few "regulars" have seen): One time I was eight months' pregnant and naked.

Personally, I like to choose when to make myself available to my clients—subject, of course, to *their* schedules. I'm fairly flexible with clients who run late if my schedule permits me to be adaptable. When a client is late, I point out that we have a certain amount of time still available but that another client is expected at a specific time. If a client is really late and the parameters are too tight, I'll offer to reschedule another day. I've been late myself (caught in traffic problems beyond my control or whatever), so I do try to be understanding and flexible when possible.

Another important factor you should take into account when scheduling appointments and planning production time is whether you are a "morning person" or a "night owl" and when you are most efficient at performing various tasks. Fortunately (given my somewhat chaotic schedule, heavy client load, and three small children), I am able to be creative and can easily write at any time—day or night. I am, by virtue of my genes, a proverbial night owl, but the demands of the real world force me to be available to family and clients from early in the morning. I seem to get by on less sleep than I could years ago—and more caffeine than I probably should! As you define your optimum production and meeting times and the needs of your clients, you'll create shortcuts and adapt to a flexible schedule that works smoothly for you.

CHAPTER EIGHT

BUILDING AN EFFECTIVE ADVERTISING PROGRAM

THE BEST WAYS TO ATTRACT NEW CLIENTS

Before sharing with you my specific advertising strategies, I'll present information gleaned in my survey of professional home-based resume writers around the country. Their number one method for attracting new clients is Yellow Pages advertising (more details later in this chapter). The next most effective techniques—other than cultivating referrals and repeat business—include weekly local newspaper advertising, flyers, direct mailers, and networking. A few other areas to explore include postings on student bulletin boards at university campuses and maintaining a presence at job fairs and workshops. Consider offering students special introductory rates and marketing such a resume program through on-campus support services or career service centers.

Penni Schratz, president of Resume Composition and Design in Traverse City, Michigan, suggests "offering companies special rates for their employees as part of a severance package or layoff. Advertise in brochures or booklets through local organizations (such as Newcomers' Group); donate full packages to be auctioned at local fund-raising events."

Connie Stevens, president of A+ Secretarial Office Support Services in Radcliff, Kentucky, recommends providing brochures to employment agencies and nearby state employment offices. As with many other resume writers, she, too, suggests posting flyers at libraries and post offices throughout the county. She sends her monthly newsletter not only to clients but to local and state employment agencies, college counselors, and personnel managers at all the major companies in her area.

If your community provides job search support groups, see how you can get involved—or at least supply promotional materials about your service along with tips for writing effective resumes. Some resume writers have "exploited" their talents through teaching workshops on resume and cover letter writing (as I have done—details about a workshop kit I market appear in the Appendix). Don't overlook, too, the cost-effectiveness of brightly colored flyers (neon is perfect) placed under windshield wipers of cars parked in busy shopping malls and office park complexes; high school students can often be employed very economically to do the legwork involved in this type of promotion.

QUOTABLE INSPIRATION

"I help my job-seeking clients outshine and 'outsell' the competition with a well-written and attractively designed resume and cover letter package" *(Carla's business slogan)*. "I help my clients make their 'best impression' on paper—in the form of a resume, curriculum vitae, or qualification brief—to market themselves to potential employers or clients in order to get a coveted position or assignment."—*Carla L. Culp, CPRW, Best Impression Resume Writing & Design (Edwardsville, Illinois)*

Newspaper advertising can range from a small "Resumes Typed" ad in the help-wanted section to a quarter-page display advertisement. Costs can run from as low as $10 a week to more than $300 a week. Some resume writers have success including their picture in their local display advertising. Cost-effective ads can also be placed in university newspapers directed to students. If your chamber of commerce publishes a monthly newsletter or tabloid magazine, investigate running a regular ad (your business card might be ideal) in this medium.

Chapter 9 provides recommended niche areas for marketing professional resume services (to audiences such as recruiters, human resource professionals, career counselors, printers, and secretarial and word-processing services). In addition, be sure to check the recommendations in chapter 9 for cultivating repeat and referral business.

GAINING PRESENCE IN YOUR COMMUNITY

Becoming visible in your own community is probably the easiest way to begin to build recognition for your business—even before your advertising efforts commence. What are some of the proven ways for capturing attention and becoming more visible? Volunteerism, always touted for heightening awareness, is an excellent way not only to secure more attention for you and your business but to make a personal contribution to your community as well. By volunteering to serve on a personnel policy committee, for example, with your local town government or board of education, you will become involved with professionals in your community and have something vital to share with your new colleagues.

Involvement with the chamber of commerce is highly recommended for any business entrepreneur, but it pays particular dividends to someone in the business of preparing professional resumes. Virtually every other member of the chamber is a potential client or employs potential clients for you and your business. In order for this networking to work, however, you must become active within the organization. In some communities, the chamber of commerce serves as a vital link between businesses and the public. There is a lot of power—and a lot of business being transacted—within many chambers. Typically, the chamber of commerce publishes a booklet in which members briefly describe their businesses. As you become known within this organization, referrals will flow freely. It's good business to do business with people you know and respect. By participating actively and contributing to the chamber's causes, you will quickly gain a reputation and recognition for the work you do. Many functions and activities of the chamber of commerce are scheduled as early breakfast meetings and after-hours "social" events. Participate to the full extent that your schedule will allow; the benefits will accrue to you and your business in no time at all.

There are probably other civic organizations in your community worth investigating. From the Exchange Club and Rotary to local women's clubs and fraternal organizations, nearly all towns have a variety of civic-minded organizations, some more powerful or visible than others. You won't have time to do everything while building your business into a highly successful enterprise, but try to select one or two groups to which you can contribute your efforts and benefit through participation.

Networking is always an effective way to build visibility in your community and "leads clubs" are springing up around the country in response to the myriad benefits of networking and building alliances. A typical rule of membership in a leads club is that there can be no more than one of a given business type represented in the group (in other words, you'll probably find just one CPA, one attorney, one florist, one banker, one resume writer, and so on). The group gathers (often as frequently as weekly) for short meetings at which members exchange marketing ideas, business cards, and leads for one another. Dues are usually quite inexpensive, and the "effectiveness" of such an organization is highly contingent upon the membership. Check out your town to see what is available—or consider starting your own networking group by inviting professionals from other fields to join you over coffee in your office on a given day. The group can build from there, if interest and motivation dictate.

Contributing your professional services to a local cause is another good way to build visibility and publicity. For instance, if a local civic group is raising money via an auction, you might wish to contribute professional resume-writing services (a package, for example) as a means of helping out the group—and gaining local visibility as well as a client. In exchange for donating an auction item, you will have the opportunity to work with someone who might not have found you otherwise. Upon completing that person's resume, you are in a good position to provide business cards and promotional coupons for that individual to give to friends and colleagues. Plus, you generally get the opportunity to write the copy about your donation that is read during the auction; use some pizzazz to spread the word about the professional services you provide.

PRESS RELEASES AND OTHER MEDIA PITCHES

As you prepare to open shop, carefully targeted press releases are an effective way to begin to gain publicity, particularly in newspapers. Nearly all dailies and weeklies published locally are hungry for editorial copy. If you enjoy writing about the human resources and resume field, why not propose authoring a regular column for the business or lifestyles section of your local newspaper? If this isn't already being done, chances are very good that the business editor will look favorably upon such a contribution. You may or may not be able to negotiate payment for your work, but that shouldn't be a concern. Even if you were to be paid for your articles, the nominal amount usually allocated to freelance writers by newspapers is laughable. You will, however, achieve visibility with your byline and with the identifying paragraph at the bottom of your column, which might say something such as "Contributed by John Edwards, President of Access Resume Services, a firm engaged in providing professional resume and career support services to clients of all backgrounds. For more information, contact Access Resume Services in Memphis, 555-5555."

Developing effective press releases requires several skills: an understanding of the slant of the publications for which you are writing, knowing how the information you possess is relevant to the readership, and an ability to find the hook on which to hang your story, the all-important "angle." As news editors will quickly tell you, just opening a business in and of itself is not particularly newsworthy—unless you are the very first resume service to operate in a town or you provide career services never before available in your area. For instance, if you intend to market aggressively and capitalize on the emerging use of electronic resumes (appropriate for scanning), you might make a pitch about this fact, coupling it with your company's being the first dedicated resume service to operate in Oshkosh. If you are changing careers to begin your resume service—particularly if you are an individual who has been affected by corporate reengineering and, especially, if you are in your late forties or older—you can create a story hook around these points. Try to find the human interest element in your situation as well as the business angle. This will help to create feature-story appeal in the mind of the editor, as opposed to generating a bland three- or four-line paragraph reporting the opening of a resume service.

Always attempt to include statistics and evidence of trends in your press releases. Depending upon your geographic area, you might wish to reflect upon the ever-increasing numbers of unemployed—and the unique strategies you intend to implement to help this situation (providing a free workshop each month through the public library, for instance, to help the newly unemployed with their resumes). Giving talks in the community is an excellent way to gain credibility as an expert in the field of resume writing. This is especially important for the entrepreneur new to this field. While your formal background may be in a related area, if you've just opened the doors to your business, you'll want to try to establish yourself as the "pro" throughout your community as quickly as possible (without waiting for five or more years to pass to gain that distinction automatically!).

YOUR YELLOW PAGES ADVERTISING

Yellow Pages advertising is absolutely critical to the resume professional, particularly in the start-up years. Down the road five or more years, you'll find that you could probably—almost—stop advertising altogether on the basis of the heavy referral and repeat business that will be well established for your enterprise. I don't, by the way, necessarily recommend against ceasing your advertising effort simply because you are successful and busy. You will always want to cultivate continued new business, for a variety of reasons. In the first few years, however, it's essential that you be where prospective clients will think of looking for you—and the Yellow Pages of local telephone directories are, undoubtedly, where a prospective client will go if he or she has not been directed to a service provider by an already satisfied client.

By the way, among the resume writers around the country who responded to my survey, Yellow Pages advertising was consistently named the number one generator of new clients. (The amount of money spent per month in Yellow Pages advertising varied widely, however, from a low of $20 to more than $300.) Georgia Adamson, CPRW, the president of Adept Business Services in Campbell, California, stated: "Yellow Pages and referrals from clients and colleagues [are my] primary means for attracting new clients. I didn't have a separate ad under 'Resumes' until

March of 1994. Prior to that, I just listed resumes in my 'Word Processing' and 'Secretarial Services' ads. The separate ad [under 'Resume Services']—just a 1-inch in-column ad—made an immediate impact when the new phone books came out!"

It's very obvious that upon opening up the telephone directory, most prospective clients will consult the "Resume Services" category. At a minimum, you definitely need to have a presence there—as large as you can afford, relative to what the competition in your area is doing. After you have assessed your competitors through a study of the Yellow Pages (as suggested in chapter 4), other categories you may wish to consider for placement of Yellow Pages advertising include:

- Career and Vocational Counseling
- Employment Agencies
- Employment Consultants
- Employment Contractors
- Human Resource Consultants
- Personnel Consultants

For the start-up entrepreneur, however, a well-written ad in the "Resume Services" category *will certainly* bring queries from prospective clients who refer to the Yellow Pages. In reviewing the notes from your study of the Yellow Pages in your area, determine whether in-column advertising alone is more popular than large display ads accompanied by a short listing in-column and a cross-reference such as "See our ad on page 333"—which directs consumers to your display ad.

By now, you have already selected your business name and reviewed my recommendations with regard to a choice that is as near the front of the alphabet as possible. For the most part, this will dictate where in the Yellow Pages listing your ad will appear. Near the "top of the heap" with regard to your competition is definitely preferred.

Listed below are various taglines and slogans you might include in your advertising copy (not only in the Yellow Pages but in flyers, brochures, and print advertising as well). Keep in mind that an attractively designed ad is important. Don't cram too much copy into a small ad; let good use of white space draw the reader's eye to your message. Remember, however, that individuals who consult the Yellow Pages are looking for specific information, so be sure to address their "need to know."

Possible Taglines to Highlight Benefits and Services

- Resumes and CVs
- Cover Letters/SF–171s/Applications
- Word Processing and Laser Printing
- Consultation and Writing/Editorial [or Composition] Services
- Quick Turnaround [or Prompt Service]
- Next-Day Service [or Same-Day Service, if you can deliver!]
- Professional Services
- Confidentiality Ensured
- Expertise in Numerous Occupations
- Resume Packages for Every Budget
- CPRW (Certified Professional Resume Writer)

- Member, PARW (Professional Association of Resume Writers)
- Member, NRWA (National Resume Writers Association)
- Free Disk Storage—Indefinitely
- Free Resume and Cover Letter Pointers
- Photocopies and Fax Service Available
- Mailing Service
- Customized, Individualized Cover Letters
- Personalized Secretarial Support Services
- Entry-Level Graduates to Executives
- Interview Training/Video- and Audiotaping
- Career and Job Counseling
- Job Search Strategies
- Interview Preparation Kit
- Nationwide Computer Job Network
- Flexible Hours and Prompt Service
- Entry Level through Executive
- Scannable/Key Word Resumes
- Specializing in Working with New Grads (or the Unemployed, Those Reentering the Workforce, Military-to-Civilian Conversions, or Career Changers)
- Specialty or Custom Papers Available
- Personal Marketing Materials
- Call for a Quote
- Areas of Specialty: Academic, Administrative, Banking, Creative, Executive, Financial, Health Care, Insurance, Managerial, Medical, Retail, Scientific, Technical
- Hours by Appointment
- Evening and Weekend Appointments Available
- Appointments Available Seven Days a Week
- Satisfaction Guaranteed
  Credit Cards Accepted
- Ten Years of Resume Writing Experience (or, after you have been in business for at least five years, "Since 1989")

Possible Business Slogans

- Presenting You at Your Best
- Resumes and Cover Letters That Open the Doors to Interviews
- We Know What Employers Want
- Building Better Careers Through Distinctive Resumes Since 1989
- Simply Put, There Is No One Better!
- When a Form Resume Won't Do
- You Deserve to Be Seen and Heard
- Be the One They Want to Interview and Hire
- Let Us Put Our Expertise to Work for You!
- Your Satisfaction Is Our Best Advertisement!
- You Have Just One Chance to Make the Right Impression!
- When You Look Good, So Do We!
- We'll Give You the Edge!
- Personalized Attention . . . A Customized Approach
- Resumes That Get Results
- We've Worked with More than 5,000 Satisfied Clients
- Put Our Experience to Work for You!

Sample Copy for Yellow Pages Advertising

Here is what my Yellow Pages advertisement looks like. It runs under "Resume Services" in two directories as a 3-inch, in-column ad.

INTERNET MARKETING POSSIBILITIES

With the vast explosion of information services and rapidly growing access to the Internet and the World Wide Web, to say nothing of the potential of these services to job seekers, no book about resume services would be complete without a discussion of the use of these high-tech tools. This text will address two key areas: In this chapter the marketing potential via the Internet and World Wide Web will be presented for the resume service provider (that's you!). Later, in chapter 12, you can read more about how some of the on-line services and the Internet can be used to good advantage by your clients in their job search campaigns.

Although I was one of the first people (never mind businesses!) in my town to go "on-line" with an account through America Online nearly four years ago, I pretty much isolate my on-line activity to active E-mail use and regular participation in certain on-line forums. If you have an account on AOL, as America Online is called (and this *is* highly recommended for the new and seasoned entrepreneurs in our industry), a good area in which to "hang out" is under the key word *Strategies*. From that section of AOL, you can access the "DTP, WP & Office Services" folder. In that folder there are about thirty-five subfolders—all filled with excellent business operational "posts" from other users of AOL (including a number of experts in our field). One subfolder, in particular—Resume Development/Writing—is especially recommended.

While I occasionally go on the Internet to check what other businesses are doing, I confess to being so overwhelmed by client work and writing projects on a continuing basis that I have not *yet* created my own page on the Web. Nor am I an expert by any stretch of the imagination in this genre. Therefore, I did what any self-respecting professional does: I consulted with professionals in the development of this section of my book. I conducted extensive interviews with two well-recognized leaders in this field, both of whom gave freely of their time and expertise in "educating" me. Lisa Freeman, president of Advanced Office and Résumé Services in Florence, South Carolina, and René Hart, CPRW, president of First Impressions Resume and Career Development Services in Lakeland, Florida, collaborated with me to provide an introductory primer on the use of the Internet and the World Wide Web in marketing your resume service (consult the Appendix for additional information about their services, including offers of several outstanding packages; in addition, both women provide consultation services regarding Web page design to other resume writers—call to inquire about their fees and to schedule telephone appointments).

If you haven't yet considered expanding your marketing efforts to the on-line community, or if you're not sure where to begin, this is the place for you. There's little doubt that computers have become a mainstay of our existence, and more and more people are turning to the Internet for research and information about products and services that they have a need for or an interest in. Expanding your business on-line can be a fun and profitable venture—and it's easy to do even if you've never been on the Internet before!

The Internet and World Wide Web Defined

What exactly is the Internet? In the simplest of terms, it is a global network of computers connected to one another via telephone lines, satellites, and so forth. If you were to connect several computers in your office, then you would have a local area network (LAN). If you were then to connect those computers to your branch office across town, you would be working with a wide area network (WAN). The Internet is a worldwide collection of multiple networks, in addition to the individual computers that may connect with it along the way. More importantly, the Internet is people—a market to which you can sell your services. No one really knows how big the Internet is, but it has been estimated that more than fifty million people are using it (and it is literally growing by the tens of thousands every day).

The World Wide Web, sometimes referred to as the Web or the WWW, is the Internet's graphical interface. Using the Web is as simple as pointing your mouse at an object and clicking on it. If you've ever used a Windows help file, you can use the Web (and if you haven't used a Windows help file, don't worry—it's really easy!). The Web enables the user to enjoy multimedia and interactive capabilities, handling not only text and pictures but also audio and full-motion video. The variety of information contained on the Web is as diverse as its users. Site topics range from computer technical support (software and hardware vendors) to hobbyist information (stamp collecting, gardening, and so on) to virtual storefronts (anything anyone could possibly think of to sell, including resumes!).

How Can Marketing on the Internet Benefit Me?

If you're still not convinced that Internet marketing is for you, just think how many more prospective clients you could reach if you advertised on the Web! Having a storefront on the Web makes your services available to fifty-million+ potential customers across the globe. Your virtual store is open for business twenty-four hours a day, seven days a week—without the extra staffing expenses. It enhances your public image by showing your clients that you are enlightened regarding the latest and greatest technological advances, and it promotes customer service by answering your clients' common questions and directing them to related resources on the Internet. Furthermore, unlike Yellow Pages advertising, your Internet marketing can change its focus as often as you choose. In fact, many Internet visitors say that the key to maintaining a popular site is to update it often—keep it fresh!

René Hart, CPRW, recognized the opportunity a Web site could pro-

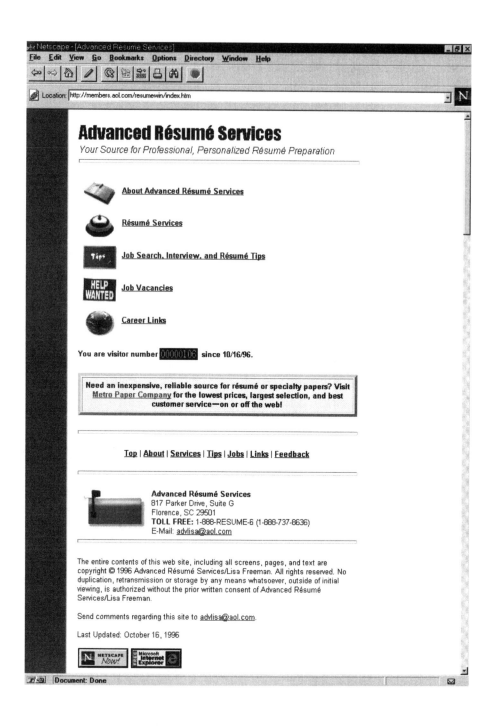

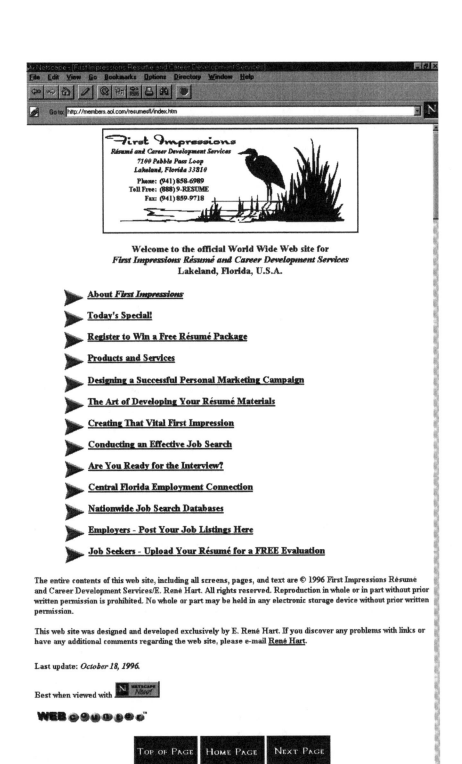

The entire contents of this web site, including all screens, pages, and text are © 1996 First Impressions Résumé and Career Development Services/E. René Hart. All rights reserved. Reproduction in whole or in part without prior written permission is prohibited. No whole or part may be held in any electronic storage device without prior written permission.

This web site was designed and developed exclusively by E. René Hart. If you discover any problems with links or have any additional comments regarding the web site, please e-mail René Hart.

Last update: *October 18, 1996.*

Best when viewed with

vide. "My goal in creating the Web site was to enhance my business's credibility and increase visibility within my own community," she says. "Beyond that, I really didn't expect to get a lot of inquiries from people outside central Florida." René admits that she has been pleasantly surprised at the number of people interested in her business. "It amazes me how people will hop onto the Internet to investigate a particular service or product sold thousands of miles away without first investigating the services available to them in their own city," she remarks.

Lisa Freeman concurs: "About a month after my Web site was listed in a few of the Internet search engines, I started getting inquiries about my services. In the first three months, my total resume bookings increased by about 15 percent. In fact, some weeks would have been very meager were it not for the bookings I received from the Internet." Lisa goes on to say that many of the clients who contact her as a result of her Internet advertising are already sold on her services. "They act more like referral clients than first-time customers," she says. "With Yellow Pages customers, I have to really turn on the charm and 'sell, sell, sell' to get the booking. However, Internet clients have usually made the decision to buy when they make contact with me, and my close rate with them is nearly 100 percent. It's very refreshing!"

Perhaps the best part about building a Web site for your business is that it costs little or nothing but your time and creativity. Many Internet Service Providers (ISPs) lease cyberspace for a minimal monthly charge; others include it as part of their regular service. America Online, for instance, includes space for a Web site as a part each account.

Do you feel that spark of excitement building yet? Are you eager to get started? By the end of this section, you'll have the tools you need to create your very own Web site and begin doing business on the World Wide Web.

Getting Started—Accessing the Internet

First, the essentials. In order to access the Internet, you need a computer with a fast modem, an Internet Service Provider, and the appropriate software. The easiest, though not the least expensive, way to get on the Internet is through an on-line service such as America Online. On-line services have staff and other resources available to answer your questions and help you get started—this can be a lifesaver in the beginning. Additionally, on-line services provide their own built-in programs for accessing the various parts of the Internet, so you don't have to worry about confusing software configurations. Costs for using on-line services vary according to how much time you spend on-line, but they generally start at around $10 per month. In most cases, the base fee includes a small number of free hours, with additional hours costing anywhere from $3 to $7 per hour.

The less expensive route for gaining access to the Internet is via a private Internet Service Provider. A private ISP will provide you with Internet software applications and a local telephone number for establishing your dial-up Internet connection. However, the user is generally required to handle most of the software setup and many other issues on his or her own. If you're new to the Internet, make sure the company you choose has excellent technical support, available twenty-four hours a day if at all possible. "It is extremely frustrating when your ISP proves to be unreliable," René commented. "Sometimes you have to go through several services to find the right one." Costs for private ISPs vary, but more people can find a company that allows unlimited access for around $20 to $30 per month.

Using the World Wide Web

If you're new to the on-line scene, you'll probably want to familiarize yourself with the service before jumping onto the Internet feet-first. As noted earlier, America Online offers a number of popular areas frequented by many of the same professionals you'll read about in this book (the DTP, WP & Office Services folder of "Strategies"). The ongoing discussions and posts have proven to be an invaluable resource to many just starting out.

Once you become familiar with making your way around America Online, you can quickly and easily jump out to the Internet. Each Web site has its own identity, called a URL (Uniform Resource Locator). If you have a particular site you'd like to visit, hit Ctrl-K (for Keyword) and fill in the URL. For step-by-step access, select "Internet Connection" from the main screen of America Online; then click on "World Wide Web." From there, type the URL (address) on the bar labeled "Current URL." For example, if you wanted to find out about tomorrow's weather, you could visit The

Weather Channel's Web site by inputting its URL, http://www.weather.com, and you would be instantly transported to its site.

If you're not sure which Web site you'd like to visit, or if you're feeling adventurous and want to explore, you'll want to visit one of the Internet's search engines, such as Yahoo! or WebCrawler. These search engines are easy to use—you just plug in a few words and it brings up a list of Web sites all pertaining to the subject of your search. From this list you can click on the site of your choice and be directly connected to it.

As you visit more and more sites, you'll begin to acquire a sense of what you want to do with your own site. You'll see different ways authors have chosen to present their information and start to develop ideas to use in your own site. One word of caution here: You should strive to be original and make a distinct effort not to duplicate what another Web site author has developed for himself or herself. As with any printed material, authorship is taken very seriously on the Internet.

Where Do I Start?

Now that you have a basic understanding of the Internet, it's time to give consideration to what you should include as part of your own Web site. If you're still not sure whether this is a project you're ready to tackle, you may want to consider paying someone else to create your site for you. If, however, you're feeling up to the challenge and want to create the site on your own, read on!

Planning and active involvement in content development are key to creating a profitable Web site. Think of your Web site as an electronic brochure for your business. It should contain much of the same information as your printed brochure but in more detail. Your site must be able to answer a greater number of your customers' questions because you can't be there to provide additional information—at least, not right away. The materials need to be organized in a logical fashion, so that visitors can quickly and easily find what they're looking for. If your site is difficult to navigate, visitors will lose interest and move on to the next site.

"I started out by getting on the Web and visiting as many resume- and career-related sites as I could find," Lisa notes. "Using the search engines—several of them—I found hundreds of sites. After I got a feel for what was 'typically' included in resume service sites, I sat down and decided what was important to my business. From these notes I developed a loose outline of my own Web site's current organization."

What Information Should Be Included in My Web Site?

Any electronic storefront should answer, at a minimum, four key questions:

- Who are you?
- Why should I do business with you?
- What are you selling?
- How do I make my purchase or get more information?

Who Are You and Why Should I Do Business With You?

Responses to the first two questions are fairly straightforward. On each page of your site, have your business name and/or logo prominently displayed. You will also want to set aside a place for people to go to find out more detailed information about you and your business. "I chose to devote a separate page, called 'About Advanced Résumé Services,' which gives a brief bio of myself and my business," Lisa said. If you have special credentials, such as CPRW status, you should highlight those here as well as any professional organizations to which you belong. Mention the number of years you've been in business (if it's been more than two or three years). Your bio page would also be well served with your company's mission statement, which also may be sprinkled throughout your Web site.

What Are You Selling?

Taglines that you commonly use in your promotional materials should figure prominently throughout your Web site. For example, just below her business name at the top of every page on her site, Lisa uses the phrase "Your Source for Professional, Personalized Résumé Preparation." Additionally, both Lisa and René have separate pages devoted to resume packages and the other products and services their businesses offer. When developing your services page, be mindful that benefits sell better than product descriptions. A certain amount of product description will obviously necessary, but remember to always point out the benefit of that particular package or product.

How Do I Make My Purchase or Get More Information?

Some customers will be perfectly happy to send you an E-mail message to request more information, or even to conduct their entire consultation. At some point, however, most people will want to talk to a real person. Your telephone number and E-mail address should be included in at least one prominent location at your Web site. You can also include your fax number and physical address, if you like. Both René and Lisa felt it would increase their bookings to provide a toll-free number for customers to make direct contact with them. René comments, "I was a little apprehensive at first about paying for a toll-free line, but after researching several long-distance companies, I found a package that not only was affordable on the toll-free end but also saved me money on my outbound long-distance calls."

Ideally, payment options should be made as easy as possible for your customers, while also protecting your interests. While this is best achieved through credit card acceptance, it is not an absolute necessity. Lisa wasn't ready to bear the expense of purchasing or leasing a credit card terminal, so she accepts out-of-state checks. "I will conduct the client's telephone consultation before having payment in hand; however, I will not proceed with writing the resume until I've deposited the funds. Surprisingly, all of my clients have been satisfied to do business this way. Some even prefer it to giving out their credit card number to a stranger," she says. René goes on to say that, when dealing with clients outside central Florida, she prefers to receive a cashier's check or money order as payment: "They are virtually the same as cash, and I don't have to delay in getting the client's materials completed while waiting for their check to clear."

While talking to first-time clients, the more helpful you are with solving their problems, the better they feel about you and the more likely they are to make a purchase from you. Therefore, in addition to answering their basic questions, you can enhance your image in your clients' eyes by including other information that would be of interest to them—and keep them coming back for other services or future updates.

Lisa notes, "I knew my site needed to be more extensive than just an electronic product catalog, so I decided to include some job search articles. I am also developing a page where local employers can list their job openings with me." René also realized that providing more than the basics would boost her credibility, stating, "My specials page is where I can showcase my creativity while promoting a particular service." Both Lisa and René saw the benefit in providing hyperlinks for their sites' visitors to use in locating career opportunities worldwide. Each of them has a dedicated page that provides extensive links to other career-related resources on the Internet.

<u>Hyperlinks</u>

Hyperlinks are text items or graphics that, when you click on them, will take you to another place on the Internet. The hyperlink's destination can be another page at the same Web site or another Web site altogether, or it could bring up an E-mail program or Internet newsgroup.

HTML Basics

Out on the Web, it doesn't matter whether you're using a Mac or PC to access the Internet; nor does it matter what brand of software you use. Why? Because the programming language that makes the Web's existence possible—called Hypertext Markup Language, or HTML—is based on plain old ASCII text. For this reason, the appearance of Web pages stays mostly consistent, regardless of what variety of equipment and software the millions of Netizens (Internet Citizens) are using. HTML commands, called "tags," are easy to remember once you've used them a few times. René noted, "I have absolutely no programming experience whatsoever. I took the obligatory Intro to Computers course in high school and can remember beaming at my first successful GO TO statement. While I was apprehensive about my ability to learn HTML, I actually found it very easy to use."

Anyone who can use a simple word processor can design his or her own Web site. There are also programs, called Web editors, that help automate the process of programming your Web site. Lisa notes, "When I was first starting out, I used a text editor to write the HTML code manually but shortly discovered an editor that lets you see what your page is going to look like as you're creating it. This, for me, made things much easier."

Lisa enjoys the ease with which Web pages can be created using the HTML editor but says that learning the HTML codes was still a necessity to create some of her site's more advanced features.

RESOURCES FOR LEARNING HTML

There are many excellent resources available to guide you through the process of learning HTML. Some that are well worth a trip to the bookstore include:

- *HTML for Dummies,* by Ed Tittel and Stephen N. James; IDG Books Worldwide, 1996.

- *Teach Yourself Web Publishing with HTML in a Week,* by Laura Lemay; Sams Publishing, 1995.

- *Visual Quickstart Guide HTML for the World Wide Web,* by Elizabeth Castro; Peachpit Press, 1996.

- If you have an account on America Online, use the key word *Web Diner* to access Web Diner HTML Tutorials.

- From the Internet, access the following: http://www.yahoo.com/ Computers_and_Internet/Internet/World_Wide_Web/Page_ Design_and_Layout/ *(this is a list of URLs to excellent resources on the Web).*

Web Page Layout and Design

The overall look of your Web site should be graphically balanced and pleasing to the eye and should entice your Internet customers to explore your site further. Most importantly, you should maintain consistency throughout your Web site. Give consideration to what image you want your site to project, and maintain that style in both your layout and graphics choices. In all likelihood, the style you settle on will reflect your own personality.

René and Lisa suggested the following points to keep in mind when working on your site's layout and appearance:

- The colors of your text and background should contrast well enough with one another to ensure readability. You wouldn't want to put light green text on a yellow background. On the other hand, you wouldn't place yellow text against a red background because it's very painful on the eyes.

- Avoid the temptation to overuse graphics, or use ones that are too large. If a page takes too long to load (more than thirty seconds), potential customers may become frustrated and go elsewhere. René says: "The very first graphic I fell in love with was this beautiful blue marbled box with built-in buttons. Nobody told me that once the graphic was uploaded to the Internet, it would take about two minutes for it to fully load!"

- Using blinking text sparingly. It may seem like fun at first but can quickly become an annoyance. There are better ways to emphasize text, such as bold or italics.

- Rather than having one continuous page constitute your whole Web site, it's better to split your site into separate pages by topic. The exception to this rule is when you're presenting articles or other information that your visitors will want to sit and read.

- Make sure your site is well organized and the information your prospective clients are looking for is easy to find. Organize your documents using headlines and lists, so visitors can see what's included on that page with a quick scan. Include a location on each page of your site where users can link back to the main page or any subsequent pages.

Getting the Word Out—Advertising Your Site

Simply creating and placing a site on the World Wide Web does not guarantee automatic business. As with anything, you must get the word out.

As mentioned earlier, having an electronic storefront is great for generating good PR locally. Add your site address (your site's URL) to all of your printed materials—business cards, brochures, letterhead, and any other promotional materials you give to prospective clients. If you have a client newsletter, include an article about your site. Write a press release and send it to the local newspapers and business journals.

Gaining business directly from customers on the Internet is dependent on their being able to find you. Fortunately, there are Web sites, called search engines, that are devoted solely to sifting through and organizing topics on the Web. You can submit your site for inclusion in these search engines' databases, so that when a job seeker goes to that search engine looking for resume services on the Internet, your site will appear on that list. Lisa comments, "I originally submitted my URL to about ten different search engines using a free submission site called SubmitIt! [http://www.submitit.com] so that I wouldn't have to go to each search engine and request submission individually. My listing with Yahoo! [http://www.yahoo.com] appeared within a couple of weeks, and the rest trickled in within two months after that."

Monitoring Your Site's Activity

The true test of any marketing strategy is its ability to draw paying clients to your business. To that end, you want to track how many people are responding to your Internet advertising. Adding a counter to the site is an excellent way of monitoring the amount of traffic that visits your site daily.

There are other ways to observe how many people visit your site: You can ask visitors to E-mail you with their feedback or comments regarding the site, or you can set up a minisurvey for them to complete and send to you. The counter can tell you only how many people visit your Web site; ideally, you want to find out who visited your site. The perfect way to do this is to incorporate some kind of response form into your Web site. René says, "I have a 'Register to Win!' form in my site that promises visitors a discount coupon and the chance to win a free resume package just for taking a few minutes to fill out the form and electronically transmit it to me. The form is actually an oversize E-mail and, when completely filled out, gives me quite a bit of information about the person."

Checklist for Creating a Successful Web Site

You've just learned the basics of creating your business's virtual storefront. Once you've had a chance to delve into your Web design project, you should consider the following points:

- Have you answered the four basic questions: Who Are You, Why Should I Do Business with You, What Are You Selling, and How Can I Make My Purchase or Get More Information?
- Have you given your prospective clients a reason to continue viewing your site after the first few seconds? Have you given them a reason to come back?
- Is your site logically organized and the materials easy to find? Are the most important materials near the top of the page?
- Have you double-checked your typing to make sure there are no errors?
- Is the visual appearance of your site pleasing and reflective of your business's image?
- Have you avoided the use of large graphics or the overuse of graphics in general?
- Can visitors easily move from one part of your site to another?
- Have you promoted your site in your printed materials as well as on the Internet?

Next, take into consideration the following:

- Work on your site when your mind is fresh—not at 3:00 A.M., after six servings of the caffeinated beverage of your choice. At that hour of the morning, HTML might as well be a foreign language because it makes just about as much sense!
- Carefully plan the content of your site. Visit other sites; determine what approach seems to flow best for you. You don't want to get in the middle of this project and then decide to scrap it and start over!

- Choose graphics, colors, and typefaces carefully. Make sure that the page is easy to read you don't want the visitor to squint while trying to read light green text against a yellow background. Be cognizant of the time it takes for your graphics to load onto the visitor's screen. Remember, the average Internet attention span is minimal!

Of course, the most important consideration when creating your Web site is that you are satisfied with the end result. The site represents your business and, as such, must convey your image professionally as if you were standing there to greet those fifty million potential clients yourself. The Internet is quickly becoming too important for any resume service entrepreneur to ignore when developing his or her marketing plan.

MARKETING TO SPECIALTY NICHES—EXPERT ADVICE

EXPAND YOUR MARKETING OUTREACH

There are several distinct groups to whom you may wish to market your services specifically. Some of these people comprise audiences about whom you will want to be well informed so as to provide the optimum level of service to your clients (from the standpoint of possessing the most up-to-date information and perspective about hiring managers in your area).

Using direct mail in the resume service industry can be effective. In theory, while every adult is conceivably a potential client for your business, any form of direct mail to this audience-at-large would be outlandishly expensive and impractical. So let's look at the best methods of marketing (including direct mail) to specific groups with the most likelihood for potential business.

In gathering information for this book, I interviewed many professionals in the fields of human resources and counseling as well as representatives from numerous professions and industries who are on the "other side of the table" in the hiring process. These are the people your clients are attempting to market themselves to, the people whose attention they want to attract. These individuals are the all-important decision makers who, through subjective process or objective strategy, review the paperwork presented and determine which candidates they'd like to interview. While the steps of the entire employment process can be termed subjective, I found it incredibly interesting and validating to learn of the many common denominators existing across most professions at nearly all levels of the career ladder.

The individuals quoted throughout this text—including those on the recruiting and hiring sides as well as those in the profession of writing resumes—shared valuable insight from which professional resume writers and candidates alike can learn. In addition to reviewing the information shared in this chapter by specialists in human resources, career counseling, and recruiting and placement, be sure to consult the specific advice in chapter 12, which has been culled from interviews with dozens of professional resume writers and hiring managers in a number of professions.

Now let's delve into three key areas and "talk" with professionals in the fields of recruiting and placement, human resources, and career counseling.

RECRUITING AND PLACEMENT

Before exploring the human resources and career counseling fields, consider making professional recruiters your marketing focus. Why recruiters? Professionals in the field of recruiting and placement are in a position to work with literally hundreds of clients. Besides having up-to-date knowledge regarding hiring practices in your area, they are in a unique position to observe trends in resume writing. Beyond this, recruiters equipped with knowledge about your expertise, specialties, and the overall quality of your work may be in a position to refer candidates to your service.

QUOTABLE INSPIRATION

"New clients are important, but you need to build your business primarily on referrals and repeat customers. This involves marketing, developing update programs, using fax machines and 800 numbers, sending out reminder postcards, newsletters to clients, and so on."
—*Pat Kendall, CPRW, Advanced Resume Concepts (Aloha, Oregon)*

Professional Recruiting Expertise

With more than twenty years in the fields of human resources and counseling services, Walter S. Truscinski, CPC, is president of Professional Staffing Services of Shelton, Connecticut. Walt specializes in positions in marketing and sales, distributed processing client/server computing technologies, and placement of senior technical and mid- and executive-level management candidates. Drawing upon his experience working with large numbers of candidates and the in-depth information he has accumulated about what companies are looking for, Walt offered very specific advice on what employers want to see in resumes and cover letters.

- With regard to length of resume, Walt believes that candidates should not sell themselves short, but if a second page is going to be used, applicants should be certain that the information justifies the increase in length. Reflecting upon feedback from hiring managers, Walt says: "If you get through one interesting page, you won't have a problem reading the second page of a resume. If, on the other hand, you have just looked at one page of 'fluff,' you certainly won't bother reading the second page." "Brevity is always the watchword," Walt added. "The resume should be a simple roadmap that identifies chronological history, technical or specialty skill areas, key accomplishments, statement of educational background, and community involvement. I like to have some sense of how involved this person is within the community and within their profession."

- In terms of information provided in the resume, Walt notes that employers today prefer a chronological history that includes quantifiable accomplishments. (By the way, this observation was mirrored by virtually every person I interviewed who is in a position to consider the credentials of a prospective employee.) "Also demonstrate, particularly if you are a highly technical candidate, that you have remained current in your field," Walt suggests. "Show the continuing education process."

- Many employers appreciate the use of an overview statement (referred to as "Summary of Qualifications," "Career Perspective" or "Career Overview," or, simply, "Summary") on the resume, located immediately after the identifying information and before the category outlining professional experience.

- Timeliness of information is critically important today, particularly for clients who work with professional recruiters. In the interest of time, recruiters usually request a faxed copy of a resume (on plain white paper). With that in mind, Walt recommends that prospects consider developing two versions of their resume. The first format can use a sophisticated but understated font (such as Garamond or Century Schoolbook), feature appropriate use of italics and boldfaced text, and be printed on a textured, lightly speckled gray paper, for example. The alternate version should always be printed on plain white paper (for maximum in faxing/scanning quality), feature plenty of leading (the space between lines), use a Geneva or Helvetica (sans serif) font, and have minimal features with regard to italics and boldfaced text. The content can be virtually the same.

- Walt Truscinski recommends that candidates always follow up a faxed copy of their resume with an original in the mail (or hand-delivered, if possible). This holds true with resumes sent to recruiters as well as with those sent to companies directly. He notes that recruiters maintain paper files on all prospective candidates; even if a particular position advertisement to which a client may be responding does not lead to a job interview, that client can become a candidate for a subsequent opportunity. Walt indicates that recruiters will always check their files first for appropriate candidates before running an advertisement.

- Follow-up activities by prospective candidates are a bit of a dilemma when working with recruiters. Walt points out that unless a job hunter is paying for a recruiter's help ("less than a quarter of the industry"), the recruiter's first allegiance is to the *employer,* that is, the client that they represent. Therefore, if your clients are attempting to open opportunities for employment through recruiters, they should keep the recruiter's allegiance in mind; too much follow-up can easily be perceived as a nuisance. Walt observes that "the smart candidate . . . recognizes that employers are the recruiter's focus . . . [but] still goes the extra yard and maintains professional contact." He suggests that reasonable contact is a short letter updating the recruiter perhaps once a month, ideally pointing out changes in situation, completion of a project or program, additional training, and so on. "What I don't appreciate," he adds, "is when a candidate calls back once a week for ten weeks running when it is obvious that I don't have anything appropriate."

- Compensation and relocation are two factors that can be "deal killers," according to Walt. "Addressing these issues up front with a recruiter is recommended. Salary history is fair game . . . and if a candidate is uncomfortable with being 'boxed in,' then a simple statement of fact—without inflation—is the way to go: 'My current salary is $_____K.'" With regard to relocation, he recommends that candidates indicate which geographic areas they would consider or, alternatively, that they are unwilling to relocate.

- Walt Truscinski's final, and key, watchword in working with clients preparing resume paperwork? Honesty. "To the extent possible, ensure that the paperwork you are preparing for your clients reflects the truth. Encourage your clients to be 100 percent honest. In no way should information, including educational credentials, be deliberately falsified."

Susan E. Rietano is the director of Flexible Resources, Inc., an eight-year-old company with offices in Greenwich and Simsbury, Connecticut, as well as Chicago and San Francisco. Her business specializes in two key areas: placing part-time, typically executive-level resources and consulting with corporations wanting to develop flexible work plans for their organizations.

Her corporate client list reads like a *Who's Who*/Fortune 50 club, particularly for the Northeast. In describing the employment trends that have fueled the need for such hybrid placement services, Susan points to those corporations in need of highly specialized, "great talent . . . that they can't afford with a fully loaded compensation package." By using part-time executive resources and offering a flexible schedule, these corporate clients are able to get the expertise they need at a price they can afford. Consistent with this trend, the individual clients Susan places achieve their goals of maintaining a challenging professional position without being tied to a typical work schedule. "Flexible scheduling and part-time placement of resources offer a real departure from the traditional nine-to-five, five-day-a-week work schedule." Susan points out, "With telecommuting and a flexible work week factored in, many options are created."

The types of individual clients Susan works with typically possess dual degrees as well as significant management experience in their given field. Many of her clients—CPAs, engineers, attorneys, CFOs, and so on—have been employed at very high levels for ten to fifteen years with one corporation. Sixty percent of Flexible Resources' clients are women fitting the above profile, many now with young children. They are seeking an alternative to the traditional workweek, yet are very committed to remaining in their profession. Susan described, as an example, an attorney she recently placed. This woman was interested in a flexible work schedule and desired a three-day-per-week position. The company with whom the "match" was made wanted top legal talent but could not afford the $100,000-plus such a professional would command. Through negotiation, a deal was struck whereby the attorney is now working with the company earning $400 per day, three days per week. The company is pleased to be getting this level of expertise—but for $62,400 per year instead of $104,000.

The remaining 40 percent of Susan's individual clients are professionals seeking project work on an interim or contractual basis, generally for a finite period. These individuals have often been affected by corporate outplacement, downsizing, or reengineering.

The database of individual clients Flexible Resources works with numbers more than 3,000. "Nearly all clients come to us by referral, often from another client with whom we have successfully worked," Susan noted. Her company gains good visibility through print media, including the *Journal of Recruiting Firms*.

As someone who sees literally thousands of resumes (and in her former corporate role as district sales manager for Xerox Corporation in Connecticut, she hired all that firm's sales, marketing, and support personnel), Susan offered concrete resume and cover letter marketing suggestions for candidates.

- "Don't make me work too hard [to find the details I need], don't conceal age, and certainly don't omit important experience. It's key that I understand how you 'got to where you are'. . . . Show me the progression in your career path."

- Susan is of the group of professionals who prefer a summary on a resume and says that "one which also conveys an objective and gives me an idea of this person's purpose is a plus." She comfortably rattled off the following by way of illustration: "Senior-level marketing professional with fifteen years in product development and specific strengths in financial products."

- How long can a resume be? "It is not inappropriate at all to use a two-page format for a high-level individual," according to Susan. "In fact, I don't care if it's four pages long—provided that it is well written, engaging, presents me with four pages of accomplishments, and doesn't include fluff."

- Susan Rietano's pet peeve: "A resume that is not accomplishment-oriented. I want to see a chronological summary of professional experience, with dates. I like short sentences and the use of bullet statements. I *don't* want to know what you [the candidate] are 'responsible for'; I want to know *what you did.* Include numbers to substantiate your claims, list awards and recognition, anything that is measurable."

- In describing the salient points she looks for in the content of a resume, Susan said to "present transferable skills, give me a clear understanding of what you do." She suggests candidates show their resume to people who "know absolutely nothing about your business and see if they can understand it." She cautions: "Don't use jargon or acronyms; don't assume anything. Be sure not to define yourself and your accomplishments in terms that people outside your industry won't understand."

- A last point from Susan on writing resumes (and there is considerable variation in opinion on this issue among hiring managers): "I like to see interests on a resume. In fact, the three key things I used to look at while at Xerox were summary, objective, and interests. The latter allow you to get a good feel for people. I would look for athletics, an interest in diverse areas, volunteerism, involvement that suggested high energy, and a person giving something back to his or her community."

- Cover letters should "mention the connection. I like when a candidate shows they know something about my business and the cover letter doesn't scream 'form letter.'" Susan also likes the use of bulleted points in a cover letter: "They're short, to the point, easier on the eye, and provide a visual break from running narrative."

- With regard to presentation, Susan prefers that resumes be mailed flat, in a large envelope, feature an attractive layout that's "not too busy," and be distinctive "but not loud." She doesn't want to see unusual papers or catchy graphics "unless the person is in advertising."

Patricia Frechtman, CPC, of Indianapolis, Indiana, has more than twenty-five years' experience in the human resources and training fields. She notes, with great pride, that she gained her initial training and experience with the firm of Snelling & Snelling when she was "a single mother with four young children, had not [at that point] completed my college degree, and hadn't worked for pay for fifteen years." At that time employment candidates paid most or all of a recruiter's fee. After completing her training, Patricia started her own private employment agency (as firms in the field were known a number of years ago) and earned credentials as both a Certified Personnel Consultant and a Certified Temporary Consultant. Calling upon her years in the business, she reflected on a number of key points employment candidates should consider in packaging themselves so that "they sizzle."

- Patricia recommends that candidates "remember that whether they are speaking with a recruiter, a human resources person, or the actual hiring authority, people always hire in their own image." Therefore, from the moment you first present yourself, you should be attempting to demonstrate the "fit" to the prospective employer.

- Patricia underscored a well-established axiom in this area: "You never get a second chance to make a first impression. If that resume doesn't have sizzle, you are never going to get to the second step."

- In contrast to some of the other professionals offering advice (which demonstrates the notion that there are few "rules" in this industry), Patricia is adamant about confining a resume to one page, regardless of years of experience. "The employer is *not* interested in your life history, in what your hobbies are, or whether you played on the swim team. You've got thirty seconds to capture a person's interest. Your resume needs to say 'notice me.'" Patricia encourages omitting anything that's irrelevant, including, for those in senior positions, their first few jobs. And "always list in chronological order, most recent experience first."

- For the candidate without professional paid experience, "pull out the stops in presenting every community experience in which this candidate has had responsibility, supervision experience, financial/accounting expertise, and so on" (as in running a rummage sale for a nonprofit organization, serving on various boards or commissions, and so forth).

- Patricia favors use of bulleted statements on a resume and likes to see "duties, responsibilities, and accomplishments." She adds: "Use the cover letter as the tool for making the connection between the resume and the job being applied for. Definitely link it to the employer with demonstrated knowledge of the industry or field and that company's efforts."

- For presentation, Patricia prefers ivory stock, high quality, and either black or brown ink. She doesn't like "cutesy papers" and believes candidates who don't look completely professional on paper will not be treated professionally.

- Patricia advocates developing several different resumes based upon a candidate's background. For instance: "One resume which focuses on the candidate's supervisory experience, another emphasizing hands-on background, and perhaps a third which details innovations and creativity, new ideas, and resultant increases in profitability or sales." She finds that "too many people try to generalize and cram everything onto a one-size-fits-all resume."

Theresa M. Bachhuber, B.S.N., R.N., C, serves as director of clinical services for Home Care, Inc., of Wallingford, Connecticut, and its division Nurse Registry Home Care of Bloomfield, Connecticut. Her background includes five years of clinical experience and more than seven years in health care management. She handles recruiting and hiring for the health care agencies she represents, attracting paraprofessionals in the field through job fairs, newspaper advertising, word of mouth, and contacts with nursing departments at hospitals and schools. Theresa shares her impressions about resume and cover letter presentation below.

- Contrary to what many professionals in the resume-writing field counsel concerning paper, Theresa indicates that, particularly for health care candidates, ivory, a very pale blue, or a light dusty gray are advisable colors because they "allow the resume to stand out in a file of white papers." Of course, she prefers a quality-grade stock.

- While one page is "preferable," Theresa says that for candidates with many years of experience, two pages are acceptable. She likes a chronological format, with dates at the left-hand margin and text to the right. "Use of a summary with an embedded objective is positive," she notes, but "be sure that the objective isn't too general." A slightly different style that Theresa says she likes is a "two-page resume printed on the front and back of the same sheet of paper."

- As with every recruiter, hiring manager, and human resources professional I interviewed, Theresa expects perfection (with regard to spelling, grammar, formatting) and completeness in a resume and cover letter.

- In terms of content, personal information is not of interest, she says, but mention of civic or professional involvement, articles written for publication, and certification should be included in the resume.

- Cover letters, according to Theresa, should be prepared to match the font and paper selected for the resume. "Make sure you know the spelling of an individual's name," she cautioned. She also suggested that the cover letter is an appropriate location for highlighting a professional summary, particularly if space on the resume itself is very tight (or if including the professional summary would cause the resume to spill over to the second page). Always mail items flat in an oversize envelope.

- Regarding cover letter content, Theresa also recommends that if at all possible, candidates provide a daytime phone number for contact purposes, supplemented by an evening number. She suggests that if this is not feasible, candidates should establish a voice mail box and state that messages can be left at any time at that number, which will be checked frequently.

- Theresa nearly always requests a salary requirement in her recruitment efforts. "I want to see a range," she says. "There is always room for negotiating." She adds, "If information that we have requested [in our ad] is not provided, it can be annoying and does not appear as professional."

- Follow-up telephone calls are appropriate, according to Theresa. If a candidate has responded to a Sunday advertisement with a mailing on Tuesday, a call placed on Friday would represent good timing; but, she cautions, "one follow-up call is sufficient. Anything more than that is pestering." Theresa also appreciates follow-up correspondence after the interview ("either handwritten, neatly, or professionally typed would be fine; this can be a definite plus").

- Her suggestions for positioning a client as the "ideal candidate": "Make sure the resume and cover letter are very professionally prepared and concise, outline the high points of his or her employment, and accurately reflect his or her achievements."

HUMAN RESOURCES

In targeting some of the most likely prospective clients, consider the hiring practices of large companies in your area. If there are layoffs occurring (or rumors of downsizing, "rightsizing," or reengineering), contact the human resources (HR) department and schedule an appointment. Your objective? To offer a package of services that can be coordinated through the HR office. As a minimum, your brochures and business cards can be provided to exiting employees. Optimally, you might arrange for a workshop session (company-paid, directly to you) with employees to discuss

1. Keep the resume concise (*you* decide which camp you're in: "always a one-page format" or "two pages when warranted").

2. Present a mix of abbreviated narrative with concrete, action-oriented language and bulleted points to illustrate accomplishments; support this with quantifiable data wherever possible.

3. Tailor the cover letter to relate specifically to the opportunity being pursued; reflect industry knowledge and information.

4. Use a straightforward chronological approach complemented by a summary of qualifications and background at the top of the resume (immediately below address information, before professional experience).

5. Use high-quality, professional papers of at least a twenty-four-pound weight; select subtle, professional colors (nothing clever or "cute," particularly for management positions).

6. Ensure that grammar, spelling, and syntax are perfect: Proofread, proofread, proofread!

7. Address cover letters to a particular individual and spell that person's name correctly.

career search strategies as well as provide resume and cover letter services on a contracted basis through the company. Or, you might negotiate a hybrid arrangement, with the company engaging you as a consultant for training programs with resume services provided on an individual, employee-paid basis. Your opening into such opportunities is via direct mail: a well-written letter of introduction accompanied by your company brochure and business card. The accompanying letter illustrates the type of effective direct mail piece you could target to specific companies in your area. As with the cover letters you generate for clients, it is always preferable to personalize such letters and ensure the correct spelling of individual and corporate names.

SAMPLE DIRECT MAIL LETTER TO CORPORATIONS UNDERGOING DOWNSIZING

Dear Human Resources Professional:

Having read of the ongoing strategy of the XYZ Company to align its workforce to meet fiscal objectives and the projected demand for services, I am aware that you have implemented a reengineering program throughout the organization. I am writing to introduce myself and some of the services that ABC Career Consultants provides to companies and employees throughout the Greater Boston area.

As a professional resume writer [be sure to state Certified Professional Resume Writer if you have earned this credential], I have worked with hundreds [or, thousands, if true] of clients in nearly all professions, teaching relevant skills in personal marketing, job search strategies, and effective interview techniques. I have developed many workshops [or, if you haven't yet done this, "The programs I deliver to my clients can be effectively packaged for delivery in a workshop setting"] that could be delivered as lunch-hour or after-work sessions at your worksite and complement the programs you already have in place. In addition, the range of specific resume package services I provide could be tailored to the needs of your company and its employees. The details can be quickly arranged to meet your requirements.

I am confident that the background and expertise I possess could prove to position me a beneficial partner to the efforts of the Human Resources Department at XYZ Company in effecting a positive reengineering of its number one asset: its people. I look forward to discussing additional ideas I have as well as understanding your challenges and critical needs. I will contact your office to arrange a convenient appointment in the next week. In the meantime, please feel free to contact me if you would like any additional information.

Sincerely,

Susan J. Smith, CPRW
Enclosures

Professional Human Resources Expertise

Cynthia B. Cannon is a human resource consultant in Durham, Connecticut, who has expertise in the areas of organizational development and employee relations. She has concentrated in health care during a nineteen-year career that has combined extensive hospital experience with key pharmaceutical industry background. Before starting her own practice, she most recently served as the employee relations manager for Bristol-Myers Squibb, a major pharmaceutical company. There she supported a client base of 400 employees and focused on human resources issues, including staffing and recruiting, internal placement, employee relations, training, organizational development and design, compensation, performance appraisal systems, conflict resolution, and benefits counseling.

Having recruited thousands of people for positions ranging from the nonprofessional to the Ph.D. level, Cindy has seen it all and speaks succinctly about what attributes, in the way of initial presentation, separate a candidate who will be contacted for an interview from the many hundreds of individuals whose paperwork will not get a second glance after the initial twenty seconds. "Number one, I'm looking for something that's polished, error-free, grammatically correct, and with perfect structure. Number two, I don't want to see candidates who blatantly try to force themselves down my throat. This oftentimes is evident in the cover letter, where a candidate will strongly state what an asset he or she will be to the company. That has no bearing on whether or not this individual is even a right fit for the job."

Professionalism of presentation is an overriding factor when initial cuts are being made. Obvious shortcomings will rule out a candidate. Crumpled, stained paper, handwritten documents, resumes produced on poor-quality copiers, mistakes in spelling or grammar, and typographical errors serve to cast a big negative over a prospective candidate. Cindy's specific comments and recommendations about candidate presentation appear on the next page.

Wendy Pease is a human resources officer with Fleet Bank, formerly Shawmut Bank, one of the oldest financial institutions in the country (its dual headquarters are in Boston, Massachusetts, and Hartford, Connecticut). Her career includes more than fifteen years of human resources expe-

- Concerning resume length, Cindy Cannon suggests that a "two-page maximum is the most you would ever need for the majority of candidates. An exception would be a candidate for an academic position, in which a CV can easily run three or four pages. I've seen them as long as ten pages for scientists with an extensive number of patents, significant research background, and numerous publications to their credit."

- In Cindy's opinion, a cover letter should not be a "sales" piece; it should be a "brief summarization of the candidate's attributes."

- The resume should be sequentially driven in chronological format. Cindy does not want to see a listing of hobbies ("inappropriate for the culture of an organization such as Bristol-Myers Squibb"). Such personal details, however, would not be "a major faux pas for the recruiting I do for nonprofessional positions, such as those within hospitals."

- Cindy strongly endorses a "traditional presentation of resumes and cover letters, with regard to paper. Convey creativity with language, not use of gimmickry in paper." She recommends a shade of gray or ivory.

- Cindy emphasizes how important spelling accuracy is. Spelling of the contact name should be perfect, as should that of the company (when working with Bristol-Myers Squibb, Cindy was in a position to see many misspellings).

- Cindy indicates that in fields with high-volume hiring, professional follow-up, preferably in writing, is appropriate. ("A short, two-paragraph letter a few weeks after mailing the resume and cover letter is about right.") While a barrage of phone calls is "the last thing busy recruiters want," Cindy says that if a candidate is inclined to call, after 5:00 or 5:30 P.M. is the recommended window (and not first thing in the morning).

- The bottom line for Cindy Cannon: "For the overall presentation—from the first paper in the door [the resume and cover letter] to the in-person interview—what counts is organization and the ability of candidates to truly look like and demonstrate that they know what they are doing."

rience in the insurance and banking industries. She has recruited professionally for nearly all levels of an organization, from clerical and word-processing positions to customer service and data processing jobs to middle- and upper-management positions. She has expertise recruiting undergraduates for entry-level management positions and also recruits graduate students with MBAs.

Working for an institution with a labor pool in excess of 3,000 employees, Wendy needs to recruit frequently. "Newspaper advertising is primarily used to attract a candidate pool," she explains. "We typically place display advertisements on Sunday in the major papers with proximity to the office where the hiring will occur. Beyond the major dailies in the Greater Boston and Hartford areas, we will also use the *New York Times* and the *Wall Street Journal*."

In response to queries regarding the key elements comprising effective candidate presentation, Wendy Pease made the points that follow.

- "I look for professional presentation, fairly conservative—nothing flamboyant. I don't want to see a photograph, nor do I care for flimsy paper." In terms of paper color, Wendy indicates, "I have no problem with pure white; ivory, gray, or a light blue are acceptable, too."

- Wendy looks at the resume to provide concrete statements of "what you [the candidate] have done . . . and *how well* you have done. I generally look for a strong work record, which would mean no large breaks in employment. I like to see employment with respected corporations as well as growth in a job. Show me that you have taken on increased responsibility in your positions and that this is a logical progression."

- A summary of attributes with "buzzwords appropriate to the industry being approached" is a positive touch. Length of a resume? "Two-page maximum—and, yes, there are circumstances where experience really warrants use of a second page." A chronological format is preferred. Wendy cited the most common objection to the functional style of presentation: "It's used to hide things."

- In Wendy's opinion, there is no place on a resume for personal information or details about hobbies. Depending upon the position sought, however, civic and community information may be important (for a bank branch manager's position, for instance, involvement in the community will be key).

- Wendy notes that for a candidate with a lengthy gap in employment (such as a woman who stopped working while raising a family), it is very important to convey involvement in the community, any volunteer experience, background demonstrating leadership abilities, and administrative and organizational expertise. New college graduates should show their on-campus involvement, again, highlighting leadership positions and breadth of experience.

- Cover letters, which Wendy "definitely likes to see," should clearly convey why a candidate is applying and reflect knowledge of the organization to which an applicant is writing. (An interesting side note: Wendy reports that she frequently sees the line "I will contact you within the next two weeks" in cover letters from applicants and then never receives a telephone call.) A cover letter personally geared to the recipient is vastly preferred over a generic one, but a generic letter is better than no letter at all.

- Wendy notes that a salary requirement is requested in nearly all her ads (and, occasionally, a salary history). "I find it's generally more realistic to ask for a requirement, as a very strong salary history might exclude a candidate from consideration when a career change is being considered." Such a request is often effectively skirted with the following type of disclaimer in a cover letter: "My salary requirement is open; I am more interested in the challenge that presents itself here. My experience would appear to be very beneficial to your organization, and I would like to pursue this opportunity with you."

- A last thought on the mailing of the resume and cover letter: "Respond quickly and with enthusiasm. If I run an ad on Sunday, the managers for whom I'm recruiting are looking for responses on Wednesday." And if a candidate has an opportunity to fax a resume to a number listed in an ad, "always follow that up with a hard copy," adds Wendy.

- Follow-up correspondence is very important, in Wendy's opinion. In fact, on one of the days we spoke, she shared with me that she had just received three "thank-you notes" following on-campus recruiting activities of the week before. She assessed this correspondence as follows: "One note was handwritten on a note card preprinted with the words 'Thank You' surrounded by flowers on the cover; this, by the way, was from the number three student in the entire class, a candidate who might have expected to be invited back for another interview. The whole presentation was entirely unfocused and unprofessional looking. The second note was typed, at least, but on a thin piece of paper; it lacked content and felt generally less professional than it should have all the way around. The third note was actually a letter, very professionally written and word-processed on a heavy bond paper. This candidate already had presented herself well and this was the final positive touch." Wendy emphasizes: "In business, particularly, it is important to be professional and formal. A handwritten note is much too informal and personal."

Just as there are numerous ways for candidates to present themselves professionally in an interview (or on paper), human resources professionals have equally diverse opinions about "what works and what doesn't."

June N. Walker is the employment manager at Data Switch Corporation. Located in Shelton, Connecticut, the company designs, manufactures, markets, and services products for large-scale, high-speed data networks. June handles mid- and upper-level management recruiting for both executive staff positions and highly technical slots. Her human resources background includes nearly fifteen years in such fields as retail photofinishing and commodities trading. An employment generalist, she has significant background in Equal Employment Opportunity/ Affirmative Action Plan (EEO/AAP) and employment law.

Data Switch has undergone impressive growth in recent years, and this has resulted in lots of recruiting and hiring activity for June. Applicant flow is typically high, with candidates attracted through conventional newspaper advertisements and job fairs as well as through outplacement firms. As with her peers in other industries, she prefers brevity and a bulleted format for resumes. "This allows me to get a quick overview about what the candidate is about. If I'm interested, *then* I'll talk to you." Here are June Walker's caveats with regard to presentation.

- "I don't like to see personal information on a resume—I don't want to know if you are married or have two children."

- With regard to use of a summary statement on the resume, June states: "For highly technical positions, this can be a plus. For example, I can quickly pull whether or not the applicant has LAN or wide-area network experience if it is included in the summary portion of the resume. However, for a position such as a senior financial analyst's slot, I don't think the summary is valuable."

- "A two-page resume is fine, if well written, concise, and necessary," says June. Conservative paper colors should be used in our industry (white or ivory preferred, light gray acceptable). I don't like the 'creative' resume papers," June adds, "and find them very distracting." She also notes that a booklet resume (11" x 17" with a fold) is not effective. "It's hard to work with, difficult to copy, and makes it appear as though the candidate has money to throw away."

- June's suggestion for crafting cover letters: "Include in the closing paragraph information that says, 'You can leave a message at . . . ' and provide a voice mail or answering machine telephone number. That's very effective, because I can leave a brief message and ask a candidate to get back to me at his or her convenience."

- A strategy for mailing, according to June, is to time a response so that if an ad appears on Sunday, the resume is not mailed until Wednesday or Thursday. "I don't refer to these as stragglers. Rather, it gives me the opportunity to spend a little bit more time reviewing the paperwork when it's one of five or ten resumes (instead of one of a hundred on Tuesday or Wednesday!)."

- June Walker's advice with regard to follow-up letters is that they "always should be handwritten and definitely *not* typed. Regardless of the level of the position, it tells me that this person has given a little of themselves; they're serious about the opportunity and really appreciated coming in for the interview. They're not just banging out form letters on a PC."

CAREER COUNSELING

A strategy similar to that used to break into corporate human resources departments can be employed when contacting the career counseling centers of colleges and universities in your area. I'd recommend starting within a 50-mile radius of your location. Don't overlook the technical community colleges as well as graduate centers of universities. In these cases, you would do well to promote the professionalism and effectiveness of your packages for new graduates. Specific to this market, you might wish to develop pricing incentives or, as a minimum, discuss the value and cost-effectiveness of "resume materials that make a difference." Knowledge of the competitive job market and environment in which new graduates will find themselves is key when stressing your expertise. Most new graduates have had little professional interview experience—often none. Your ability to stylize a training package for entry-level candidates could be marketed very effectively with attractive resume-package offerings.

Professional Career Counseling Expertise

David J. Denino is the associate director of counseling and career services at Southern Connecticut State University in New Haven, Connecticut; he is also adjunct professor of counseling and school psychology for that institution. His professional background includes more than fourteen years providing career, academic, and personal counseling as well as career testing and placement. Having worked with thousands of students (new graduates, soon-to-be-graduates, and adults at the postgraduate level), Dave has formulated strategies that have proved effective for job searches at a number of levels. Here are his recommendations.

How students can best prepare for the job search.

Dave Denino offers—"a repeated theme for students to subscribe to: in order to do an effective job search, they should conduct one or more *while in school.* This can be done by looking for internships, cooperative education experiences, and student teaching placements."

The specific job search strategies presented to students in one- and two-hour workshops focus on three broad categories: "Know Your Plan," "Target Your Information," and "Develop Your Plan of Action." You might consider blending this information and these recommendations into a package you market to your student client population, especially if you are located near a university.

The first strategy, "Know Your Plan," asks students to consider where their talents and education can best be developed. Students are encouraged to contemplate as many work environments relevant to their major as possible, and then to relate specific expertise to these different environments. Sources of career information for students include university career services centers, local libraries, community adult education programs, and state job service centers.

The second job search strategy is "Target Your Information." Essentially, this exercise requires students to collect data about specific companies, institutions, agencies, or school systems. As a minimum, full address information, as well as contact names/titles and telephone numbers, should be acquired. Reference librarians can assist with obtaining details about publicly held companies.

The last job search strategy suggested is "Develop Your Plan of Action," which is a threefold program.

1. In developing *contacts,* students are encouraged to communicate with employers directly by mail or telephone to inquire about present openings or anticipated hiring plans. Students are also advised to send letters to people who hire or may influence the hiring of new or replacement personnel. Potential networking contacts for students include people they meet during internships, co-op programs, or student teaching experiences, community members, relatives, friends, former full- or part-time employers, colleagues, recent graduates, and professors.

2. Preparation is important for all job hunters, including new graduates. Students are reminded to include all the essential steps in their job search process: developing a resume and cover letter, creating lists of contacts and records of job leads, learning (and practicing, many times) effective interviewing techniques, and structuring a timetable.

3. The last element of the "Plan of Action" is *review and follow-up.* Students are encouraged to assess their job search frequently, with an eye toward evaluating how effective their approach is and whether or not their initial strategies might need to be modified.

How students can develop effective resumes and cover letters.

Dave Denino indicated that workshops provide students with some of the skills needed to develop their resumes effectively. "The resume workshop is specific to the field of work students are seeking to enter," he notes. "We tend to divide the world of work in half—with, of course, times when these overlap. Essentially, business and industry touches on the for-profit sector, comprising big and small business; social services and education focus on the not-for-profit side of business and the educating/ caring/helping professions."

Resume length for students is generally not disputed: One page should be more than adequate for presenting the qualifications and experience of a new graduate. Dave did say that "one rule we have found is that personnel who review resumes from a social services/education viewpoint will read more than one page (but no more than two!), while business/industry views one page as the recognized standard. For very experienced personnel, this may go beyond one page."

How a job search should transpire: techniques for opening doors.

Dave Denino advises students "to conduct a job search using all avenues possible. The mechanical steps include resume and cover letter preparation, contact development (both informational interviewing and networking), interview preparation, interviewing, and the closing. We emphasize that students should use the college career services office to begin this procedure. Naturally, checking the want ads is part of the search process; we remind students that approximately 30 percent of all jobs at any given time are advertised. That leaves 70 percent of what we term the 'hidden job market.' Accessing this portion of the market becomes the challenge."

Key to tapping the hidden job market are the functions of networking and informational interviews. With networking, Dave reminds students "that everyone you know becomes a potential contact for a referral. Friends, relatives, neighbors, professional associates, civic organizations, church groups, past employers, teachers, and professors become your network for information. As a rule, most people are willing to extend themselves when asked to provide a name of an individual in the occupation you would like to explore. Get it and make contact immediately." As a further suggestion, Dave recommends: "Don't be shy. Ask [for a lead], for each time you do not pursue a possible lead, someone else does."

Maintaining good records throughout a job search is important. Especially with regard to networking, maintaining a perpetual log of contacts, address information, and telephone numbers can prove useful throughout a person's career. "Once you have networked and landed potential leads," Dave explains, "the groundwork is laid for an informational interview."

The first step for a client to use in securing an informational interview is to telephone the contact, always noting the name of the person who has made the referral. Dave advises: "Ask if you can have an appointment to speak with the individual for fifteen or thirty minutes about the person's job and career. This gains *access* to the business, school, or agency. Most people are very willing to extend themselves to talk about their work. Practice interviewing skills as much as possible prior to an informational interview. Prepare questions for this session. Keep in mind that a contact is being made that could lead to employment at that site or a related site. While your premise is to 'gather information,' you are really making a contact for future employment: Put your best foot forward, in terms of poise, appearance, and knowledge."

On many levels, the information provided to students through the career-counseling services at colleges and universities is universally applicable to nearly all job seekers. Coupled with the pointers provided by Dave Denino in chapter 12, students and nonstudents alike will find some very useful strategies. Professional resume writers should capitalize on this information when counseling their clients.

OTHER NICHE TARGETS

Another audience for targeted direct mail marketing is printers. Most professional printers are not interested in anything related to resumes except, possibly, straightforward typesetting of these documents. Once aware of your existence, they will usually happily refer clientele to you. As you develop a relationship with a printer (especially if this is who you use for printing your promotional materials), you may wish to establish a reciprocal arrangement whereby clients who want a large number of copies (which you may not wish to provide) are referred to the printing company.

Also contact secretarial and word-processing services in your area to determine if consultation or editorial services relative to resume preparation are provided. In many cases, these companies are not engaged in counseling their clientele and have no desire to write resumes from scratch. Especially in the start-up period (and even more so if you are not interested in developing keyboard skills to typeset the resumes you will be writing), building a relationship with a good secretarial service in your area can be an asset in building a good business on a long-term basis. Even if some of these firms offer full resume consultation services, you may wish to inform them about any specialized services you offer or particular expertise you have (if, for example, you intend to specialize in military-to-civilian conversions, you might market this particular service to a secretarial service that offers resume services).

Lastly, never overlook an opportunity to get your brochures and business cards into the hands of the public. Supply the libraries in your community and the surrounding towns with your promotional materials. Library users frequently ask reference librarians to help them find a "good resume writer" in the community.

QUOTABLE INSPIRATION

"I would advise anyone, new or seasoned, to join our professional association for the wealth of information and support offered to its members, to network as much as possible, to be confident in your ability to provide a professional service, and to not be concerned with those who feel your services are priced too high." —*Joann Milazzo, Joann Milazzo Secretarial Services (Hammonton, New Jersey)*

CHAPTER TEN

CULTIVATING STRONG CLIENT RELATIONSHIPS

TELEPHONE TECHNIQUES

First Impressions: Capturing the Business

It is critically important to establish, from the onset of your business, how you will interact with your clients. Excellence in "customer relations" should be priority number one for you and your business—and regardless of how successful you become, your clients should *always* be considered a top priority. The primary way in which 99 percent of your clients will first meet you is by telephone—truly the bloodline of most any service business, but without exception for a professional resume service! The way in which clients are first greeted—from the very first words out of your mouth (or on your answering machine or voice mail message)—will help to establish the tone and build the all-important ongoing relationship with prospective clients.

When first starting out, attempt to answer personally as many of your telephone calls as you possibly can manage—especially those received before hours, after hours, and on weekends. You can nearly always be certain that calls received outside traditional office hours are from clients in urgent need of speaking with a resume service provider. Oftentimes these prospective clients have just learned that their positions are threatened; they may even have recently received the ominous pink slip. While some prospective clients will attempt to reach you after hours because making such a telephone call during the day from their office would be uncomfortable for them, most callers have a more pressing reason. They have either found you in the Yellow Pages or been referred to you by a satisfied client; they have a definite need for a resume, and *they are ready to buy.*

People in the resume service industry are fortunate in that it is probably one of the few professions in which you don't have to do any cold-calling to build a successful business. I have *never* made (and will never make!) a cold call in my fourteen-plus years in the business, yet I have been busy from almost the very beginning through cultivating positive client relationships with callers who find me in the Yellow Pages or are referred by existing clients. When I ask my clients how they found me (and you *always* want to verify the source of each and every piece of business—no matter how established your resume service becomes), a high percentage tell me that they found me in the Yellow Pages and that it was my telephone presence, confidence, and ability to put them at ease that convinced them I was the right person to handle their all-important career materials—*oftentimes without calling a single competitor!* And I've heard repeatedly from my clients over the years that one phrase I interject in every discussion with a prospective resume client absolutely clinches the booking of an appointment: "I make the consultation process absolutely *painless.*"

One piece of advice I regularly offer to clients after completing their resume is to role-play—use their resume to practice interviewing as often as possible before going in front of a recruiter or hiring manager. The same advice is sound for professional resume writers: role-play. Practice as much as you can, focusing on how you will establish a dialogue with prospective clients and how you will close the sale. Some people are uncomfortable with scripting and believe that working with a script might cause them to become stilted or unnatural. Over my years in business, I have found scripts to be very useful to *refer* to (not read verbatim from) when promoting a new service offering, implementing a new pricing structure, or introducing a new concept. Especially in my first few years in the resume business, I worked diligently to master the spiel I would deliver to each and every resume caller. Far from sounding unnatural, the language became second nature to me (after all, I had written the script the way I would speak). And if you wish to glean ideas from the proposed phrases I present below, I'd caution you to use them only as an *outline* for developing the language that you would like to deliver to your prospective clients. You may prefer a more casual tone, you may wish to ask more questions first—whatever is comfortable, easy for you to deliver, and effective is most important—the key being to engage the caller in a dialogue.

The information presented here reflects a typical call from a first-time prospect who has found me through the Yellow Pages. Sometimes the order varies, depending upon the questions asked by the client. I prefer to lead the discussion and cover the key points I believe will help to sell the caller on my professionalism and ability to work cooperatively to address his or her needs.

The first question out of nearly every prospective client's mouth, is "Do you do resumes?" My classic response (in some form or another) is, "Yes, absolutely! We're specialists in creating distinctive resumes and complete job search materials for our clients. How can we help you?" Very early into the conversation, I like to give callers an opportunity to tell me why they are calling and what they *think* they need. It's not in anyone's best interest (unless you have lots of time to spare) to spend ten minutes in a monologue describing the full range of your services only to discover, when the client gets a moment to inject a word, that he or she was simply looking for a copy shop to mass-produce an already completed resume! Usually, when the question is thrown back to the caller, "How can we help you?" responses fall along one of two lines: The caller either says, "Well, I don't have a resume, but [for whatever reason] I need one," or "I have a resume I like that just needs a little updating." There are certainly variations on these responses, with some clients very clear on what their perceived requirements are. I take great pride, however, in knowing that I could probably count on one hand the clients I've served for whom I did exactly what they thought they wanted. In other words, nearly all the time, resume clients are amenable and, in fact, highly appreciative of any recommendations you may offer and enhancements you may make—with their approval—to a preexisting resume they thought was perfectly satisfactory.

With tact, discretion, and professionalism, you will find that it is *easy* to help clients improve the content of their materials and enhance the appearance and presentation of their background—and make money for your efforts.

QUOTABLE INSPIRATION

"Members of this field should try to upgrade their skills and be aware of what is going on, that is, how to write computer-readable resumes, know who the reader will be, and learn about the jobs and their requirements rather than fancy action words. Besides being an adept resume writer, I am a senior citizen with a profound hearing loss. This should be an inspiration to other mature adults who are considering working from home. When I work with a client, we sit facing each other so I can lip-read, and my phones have hearing amplifiers. Many people are not even aware that I have difficulty hearing."—*Anne G. Kramer, CPRW, Alpha Bits (Virginia Beach, Virginia)*

Let's get back to the first-time caller. Once you've ascertained the nature of the call, it's then the appropriate time to begin to present the service options available to meet the individual's "every need." By the way, unless it's literally the first or second call you are receiving—and you have tons of time to invest in learning the techniques of interviewing prospective clients—I recommend that you avoid having a protracted discussion with the client about every facet of his or her recent layoff or work history. A few minutes should be enough time to elicit the caller's profession or field and find out why a resume is needed—then move into *why the prospect needs you*. While it's important to spend sufficient time cultivating the lead and conveying your confidence, background, experience, and ability to help the person, you don't want to engage in offering professional advice until the caller has agreed on payment terms and booked an appointment with you. You certainly don't want to get into the habit of giving free advice by telephone to strangers who aren't yet committed to doing business with you. But you do need to lure them into "the web" by providing responses of a nature specific enough to demonstrate your knowledge in their field or profession ("Yes, I've worked with a number of professionals in your field . . .") without "giving away the store."

The strategy I have developed that allows me to keep the initial call to about ten minutes (including providing directions to my office—that takes three or four minutes in my case because of my very rural location!) is a smooth way of politely interrupting specific queries with, "Those are exactly the points we will discuss in a full consultation . . . your responses to those questions will facilitate my gaining a very clear grasp of your career objective . . . blah-blah-blah . . . ," and then easily moving into, "When is the most convenient day for you to meet? Tuesday or Wednesday? Would you prefer a morning or afternoon appointment? I have an opening on . . . 3:00 p.m.." This keeps the conversation focused and moving. There are always going to be a certain group of prospective clients with whom what I term "hand-holding" will be required. And it's to be expected that in the course of doing business, you will invest more time in cultivating some first-time callers—and that's fine, especially in the beginning, as you are building your business. A lot of what determines successful cultivation of relationships with first-time callers—and scheduling of the critical first appointment—is your ability to put callers at ease and make them feel confident that they are making the right decision by selecting you as their professional resume writer.

When describing your service offerings to a prospective client, you will need to take into account the way in which you've decided to structure your pricing and services. Depending upon the caller and your impressions of his or her requirements, you might wish to start by describing your top-of-the-line package or service offering; highlight the benefits and components first, then state the price. For someone who indicates that a basic retype with minor editing is all that is wanted, you could first quote a price for doing this, then describe how other services you offer would "truly help you to portray your accomplishments and position yourself for success in achieving interviews." Some professionals in the resume industry prefer *not* to quote prices on the telephone and, rather, schedule an appointment first with the client: Once the prospect is in the door, they are then able to book the appropriate level of service. In my years of doing business, however, I have found that price is a consideration to virtually every prospective client. I have also learned that pricing considerations are secondary to the confidence a caller puts in the professionalism and competence of the service provider. When prices are quoted without apology and with absolute confidence, I don't believe they are ever a crucial consideration for the serious caller!

A final recommendation when speaking with prospective clients inquiring about your services: Don't hang up the telephone without asking for an appointment. After describing your services and reiterating your understanding of their needs, ask either when they would like to meet or if a specific date and time would be convenient for you both to get together. I advise against suggesting to a prospective client that you "will be happy to mail them additional information about the company." This gives them an easy out. Furthermore, my unscientific research suggests that those callers to whom you have promised to send information will probably continue to call other resume services—and may even book an appointment with someone more aggressive than you in asking for the appointment. In my early years I experimented with sending out my company brochure and business card to "casual callers." Not one of these ever resulted in a later booked appointment. But since I began asking for the appointment (as I've done now for many years), I "close" nearly 99 percent of all first-time callers! Some of my colleagues have also reported poor results from mailing information to prospective resume clientele. I believe that the prospects are hottest when they first call you—your ability to seize the moment and book the appointment, right then, is key!

Turning Typical Objections into "Wins"

Over the recent years, I've used, along with a number of my successful colleagues, a variation of the phrase "Oh, I didn't realize price was your *only* concern" when speaking with prospective clients who focus solely on price. If the caller seems totally uninterested in any value-added services and is even grumbling about the price of a basic retype, you can add to the above comment, "In that case, you might try the quick-stop copy shop—they'll add no value to your resume, but they'll do it for a very low price if that's your primary concern." Fortunately, with a handful of exceptions, most prospective callers are either seriously interested in obtaining a quality product for their investment (after all, this is their *career* and their *image* we're talking about!) or willing to be "educated" about how important it is that they project the right image in their career search. Once you've described the benefits that your service can provide in helping to give them the competitive edge—and open the door to interviews—most prospective clients will believe they "are worth it" and happily invest in your services.

Beyond price shoppers, you'll encounter clients who raise other types of potential "objections." Here are four examples, along with recommended strategies for responding to them.

1. Clients who lack confidence in their own background (as in, "Oh, I don't think I've done enough to warrant a real resume.").

    Solution/Response: "Well, just in the little you've shared with me over the telephone, I'm confident we can develop a resume that will play up your years of experience in the field, highlight your achievements, and really work to sell your background positively to the prospective employer." If the prospective client is a woman who has spent a number of years in unpaid pursuits while raising children, for instance, years of civic involvement, community leadership positions, and so on, should be stressed as important accomplishments that warrant space on the resume.

2. Clients who are unsure about your ability to understand their background and accurately develop their resume (as with specialists in highly technical fields, for instance).

    Solution/Response: This is where it is often useful to mention the number of years you have spent helping people to define their accomplishments and develop their resumes. If you are brand-new to the business (and even if not!), consider all the years you may have worked professionally before starting your company and situations where you may have helped colleagues, family members, or coworkers to develop their resumes, recruited or interviewed in a human resources capacity or as a hiring manager within a company, and so on—essentially any experience you may have had in assessing or writing resumes. If this type of experience is completely new to you, then stress that the reason for conducting an in-depth consultation is so that the client can fully describe and discuss background and accomplishments. And mention that you have worked with a number of clients (you don't have to say how many—or few!) in structuring highly individualized, and successful, resumes.

    Also state that you "guarantee" satisfaction. Explain that in the second appointment (when the resume you have written is presented and reviewed—a process discussed in chapter 12), the client will "fully approve the resume" and you will make any and all changes necessary, while the client is in your office, to ensure a completely satisfactory product. If you are just starting out, I suggest that you request letters of recommendation from your first few "very satisfied" clients. You'll know them instantly—they'll rave when they review the completed resume, they'll promise to send other clients to you, they'll profusely thank you. That's the time to ask if they'd be willing to jot a few remarks down by way of recommendation. In fact, offer to type their remarks on the spot to make it easier—and have them sign the letter right in your office! Because of confidentiality and individual circumstances, some clients, while loving your work, may not be in a position to have their name used in a recommendation—those clients currently employed in your geographic area, for example, who haven't given notice to their employer. But you will have the opportunity to work with many clients who are already in transition, unemployed, or leaving a company openly and they will have no reservations about personally vouching for you.

3.   Clients who are overwhelmed by the entire process, possibly intimidated, and have no clue about where to begin (your opening for making the process "seamless and painless"!).

Solution/Response: Such clients typically require—and respond well to—"hand-holding." They want to be assured that you will do all the work—ask all the questions and take care of everything professionally, smoothly, and easily for them. Just reiterate the completeness of your service, how comprehensive the package you offer is, and so forth. Mention that this is an attribute of your company, and perhaps support this by adding, "Many of my clients tell me at the conclusion of the process how surprised they were at how easy it was to have an effective, distinctive, and professional resume and cover letter materials prepared."

4.   Clients with incredibly tight turnaround times, who need full services ("I have a very important interview this afternoon at four and *must* have a resume . . . can you help me?" and it's now 10:00 A.M.!).

Solution/Response: Actually, for the brand-new service provider (with a flexible schedule), these clients are tailor-made! Unlike someone in my position, who is frequently booked up ten days or more in advance (and could not *possibly* see someone the same day, never mind the same week), the person just beginning in this business is beautifully equipped to handle rush work. The recommended key is *not* to reveal that you are sitting by the phone, doing nothing, just waiting for it to ring! You instead want to appear to check your schedule to see if you can accommodate the project—and then, with complete confidence (once you've ascertained that you can, in fact, squeeze in both the morning consultation, the writing time [early afternoon], and the return review [midafternoon]), state that there is a charge for rush service equal to 50 percent of the package price (or whatever you've decided to charge for rush service).

Here is where there's considerable leeway—depending upon your own circumstances, your own price schedule, and how eager (read: hungry!) you are to obtain work in the very beginning. Someone so desperate for a professional resume is probably not going to find many professional resume writers able to accommodate the ridiculously last-minute nature of the request; an individual racing against the clock is not in a position to bargain and you are fully entitled to assess a rush charge. Should you nevertheless feel that it's in your best interest not to charge for express service (if it's your second project, say, and you are very eager to begin attracting loyal clients), at least remember to mention that there is "typically a rush service charge of 50 percent" but that you are waiving it in this instance. In other words, it's your business: You are free to establish whatever rates and policies you wish—and to waive them when it suits you.

Just remember a key principle: Never give clients something for nothing without advising them of what they are receiving! Whenever you waive a charge, for whatever reason, your invoice should say so. I use the phrase "courtesy discount" in many instances, usually followed with a descriptor: "in acknowledgment of the recent hospital project referral," "in appreciation of our years of doing business together," and so forth. Sometimes I will discount an invoice by a percentage; in other instances, as with a straight resume referral, I'll deduct $5 off a client's next invoice for cover letter services when the individual refers someone to me for a basic resume retype, or $10 or $20 off the client's next invoice when they've referred someone for a full consultation. These credits are immediately keyed into the client's computer file for billing purposes, along with a cross-reference to the client who was referred ("$10 credit—thank you for referring John Smith!").

When You Can't Speak with Clients

In spite of my recommendation that you attempt to answer each and every prospective client call in the first year or so of building your business, there will certainly be times when you can't or shouldn't. (Beyond time that you elect to be "out of the office," I firmly believe that you should not answer the telephone while you are in a consultation with a client. Others in the field may disagree, but I believe that each client deserves your undivided attention when you are conducting a prescheduled consultation.)

Therefore, it is important that you arrange for backup coverage of your business telephone. The most common and inexpensive solution is a traditional telephone answering machine. I've upgraded my equipment a number of times and only recently converted from an answering machine to voice mail service. Because my company, Absolute Advantage, provides both desktop publishing services and professional resume services to a wide range of clientele, my message reflects the company image and doesn't describe specific services. In 1994, I decided it was worthwhile (for the first time since starting my business in 1983) to add my name to the message so that callers who might have been referred to me by my name (and not the business name) would clearly know they had reached me.

My voice mail message says: "You've reached the offices of Absolute Advantage and the editorial offices of Jan Melnik and *The Word Advantage* [a quarterly subscriber newsletter I publish—see the Appendix for more information]. We're not available to take your call at this time, but if you will leave a message after the tone, we'd be happy to get back to you as quickly as possible. If you'd like to send a fax, our twenty-four-hour fax number is (860) 349-1343. Thank you for calling Absolute Advantage."

My primary reason for implementing voice mail service was the flexibility of adding mailboxes, thus giving callers the ability to select the appropriate choice (for clients, selecting "1" to inquire about services; for individuals ordering my books or newsletters, selecting "2"; and for individuals responding to articles appearing in *Woman's Day* magazine, *USA Today,* and other publications, selecting "3").

Prior to implementing voice mail service, I used a top-of-the-line Panasonic auto-logic answering machine with all the bells and whistles. It features a portable telephone, (which I continue to happily use), three outgoing message options (which could all be prerecorded so as to enable switching on an after-hours message each day at the push of the button, if desired), and unlimited time for accepting incoming messages. An advantage to a traditional answering machine is the ability to leave the volume up and monitor incoming calls, when desired. Although I recommend that the new service provider answer the telephone directly as much of the time as possible, there are times (when in the middle of writing a resume or meeting with a client) when it isn't possible to answer, yet screening is desirable.

QUOTABLE INSPIRATION

"Never, never give up; determination will always win out. Never let anyone discourage you. Always follow your dreams."—*Cathy Cousear, Institute on Human Service Resources (Fresh Meadows, New York)*

CULTIVATING A STRONG REFERRAL NETWORK

OK, your business is up and running—perhaps not exactly flourishing yet, but at least you are seeing clients now on a sporadic but increasingly regular basis. From your first day in business, you should always be keeping an eye toward building referrals from each and every client that passes through your doors. Business cards should be readily available in the area you use to meet with your clients. Not only should you present each client with a business card in the first consultation with you, but each folder of completed work you give a client should also include at least two business cards. I make it a practice to provide clients with five of my business cards at the appointment where they return to approve and pick up their completed resume or other material. I always invite clients to help themselves to as many business cards as they wish when they are in my office. And I'm not hesitant about telling my clients how much I enjoyed working with them—and that I'd be pleased to work with any family members, colleagues, or friends they might wish to refer in the future. I also mention that I make it worth their while to refer new clients to me: They earn credit for each client referred who subsequently books an appointment. I tell them these credits build up in their account and that some of my more enterprising (and well-connected!) clients have fully funded their continuing cover letter services, just by referring a regular flow of candidates to me!

There are lots of creative and fun ways to build incentives around referrals beyond simply asking for the business (which you should *always* be doing!). Consider offering "in-office" promotions; you can advertise specials in a weekly newspaper, but if dollars are tight, you can simply make a poster and place it visibly in your office area. Some ideas include:

- Special—through February only—save 20 percent on a full resume package!

- Classic "Two-Fer"—we'll discount the second full resume package by 25 percent when both are completed by November 30. (Note: *A two-fer offering is vastly preferred to a 50 percent discount on a single client's purchase. The reason? The doubled referral and repeat business potential from two clients versus just the one!*)

- Book a full resume package and we'll throw in ten personalized cover letters and envelopes for free—good through May 31.

- Upgrade from a basic resume retype to a miniconsultation (at least forty-five minutes in length) and we'll provide you with twenty extra original laser prints of your resume—your choice of paper.

Other industry professionals suggest the following creative strategies:

- Deliver presentations to community groups and provide a free resume consultation as a door prize. *(Vivian Belen, CPRW)*

- Ask clients to make referrals, and during satisfaction surveys, ask, "Would you refer us to others?" ("to help reinforce the idea that they *should*"). *(Barbie Dallmann, CPRW)*

- "For all new resume clients, I place their resume, copies, my business card, and my business brochure in a bright yellow folder with my company name, address, telephone, and fax numbers on a label on the tab. I have repeat clients this way, or they will refer someone because the folder is easy to see and it has all of the information directly on it." *(Jo Hammonds)*
- Offer "bonus bucks" to a client who refers a client. *(Carrie Kuntz)*
- "Provide the original client with free cover letter/fax service for each referral." *(Shelley Newman, CPRW)*
- Offer a free resume set—including existing resume (no free updating), cover letter, and reference list—for each referral made within six months. *(Penni Schratz)*
- "I enclose a $3.00 or $5.00 gift certificate in the thank-you card that I mail after preparing a client's resume. The amount depends upon how much the client spent with me. The gift certificate can be used by the client for any service we offer—*if* the client refers someone to us who subsequently has us prepare his or her resume. There is no expiration date on the gift certificate." *(Connie Stevens)*

The possibilities are endless! You can feature a different promotion each month and really keep the interest level high among clients you may be seeing regularly in their job search cycle. (This can be as short as a month, but, more typically, I find that I work with my local clients a good six months at the executive level in generating individualized cover letters.) While you may not see an actual thread running back to the existing clients, chances are, while they are waiting for you to print the final batch of resumes, prepare envelopes for cover letters, and so on, they'll be noticing your promotional message—especially if you change it at least monthly—and use a *different,* eye-catching paper color each time. Referrals will happen gradually, over time, *but I absolutely can assure you—they will happen!*

Communication Tools for the Resume Professional

My two favorite ways of communicating with clients are through thank-you and follow-up letters and a client newsletter.

Follow-up letters. I write a personalized thank-you note—handwritten, on professional business note stationery—to each client upon conclusion of a full consultation. For new service providers, I'd recommend writing to *every* client in the beginning (why not?). Enclose a business card or two and perhaps a coupon equivalent to $5 or $10 off the next resume update for clients who make a referral. Alternatively, you could offer referring clients ten extra originals of their resume the next time they have it updated. Keep the note short, simple, and individually targeted to the particular client. Here's an example:

> Dear Steve,
>
> It was a pleasure working with you recently in developing your personal marketing materials and CV. I enjoyed the opportunity to collaborate with you in defining your objectives and selecting the appropriate accomplishments from your very impressive career history. I wish you every success in your search and look forward to being of service to you in the future. Please feel free to contact me at any time if I can provide additional assistance. Thanks again for the opportunity to work with you.
>
> Sincerely,
>
> Jan

Depending upon the services you provided to a given client, you might also market additional services by including something such as, "If you decide to pursue the interview training techniques program I have developed, I would be pleased to offer you a Saturday appointment."

I strongly recommend that new service providers touch base with clients six months after completing their resume (if they are immediately commencing a job search—not *every* client you work with will be). Build a tickler system into your computer that will prompt you once a month with the names of those clients with whom you worked six months earlier (and update this every month). A postcard works ideally for contacting them, but if you prefer note card stationery or a full letter, the option is yours. Simply express interest in how the client's search is proceeding, add that you look forward to hearing a report of the success they are experiencing, and close with an expression of your desire to have the opportunity to work with them when an update is warranted—as well as to work with anyone they might wish to refer to your service.

Client postcard mailings. Probably the easiest to implement and least costly form of direct mail is the tried-and-true postcard mailing. There are a variety of ways to handle this, from using traditional-size postcards (four to an 8 ½" x 11" page) to using oversize "jumbo" cards (which you either produce yourself or print on preprinted postcard stock, laser-compatible paper made available by such companies as PaperDirect). Based upon planned volume, you can also arrange to have specialty stock paper printed and cut up by your printer; for most start-up services, handling the small runs yourself gives you maximum flexibility and desired cost savings.

My recommendation would be to develop a year-long direct mail marketing plan (and then update it each year thereafter). I would build such a plan around the use of a quarterly client newsletter (covered in the next section of this chapter) issued in the following months for these respective seasons: spring issue (March), summer issue (June), fall issue (September), and winter issue (December). Interspersed throughout the rest of the year would be your choice of either two postcard mailings per quarter (hence, you'd have a campaign of eight postcard mailings per year—integrated with the quarterly newsletter, you'd be reaching clients and "suspects" monthly) or, for a more modest plan, a postcard mailing once per quarter (six weeks after publication of each quarter's newsletter), producing a total of eight client outreaches per year.

An annual schedule with twelve pieces could look like this (possible topical areas for postcard mailers are noted):

January 15—first postcard campaign. *(New Year's balloons theme for art*—Keeping your New Year's resolution to jump-start your career search . . . develop your resume . . . write a dynamite cover letter? Call us for some proven tips on reenergizing your campaign!)

February 15—second postcard campaign. *(Valentine's hearts theme for art*—Now's the perfect time to declare your intention . . . to get a new job! Get ready with the right resume, cover letter, and personal marketing materials! Call us today to schedule a confidential appointment.

March 15—spring issue, first client newsletter.

April 15—third postcard campaign. *(Tax forms and dollar signs for art—* The taxman cometh . . . and as you review your federal return for the previous year, does it remind you that you'd hoped to enact a job change resulting in a higher salary? Is your resume ready to meet this challenge? If not, give us a call to help get your career materials ready!)

May 15—fourth postcard campaign. *(Laurels/lazy-looking person stretched across a desk for art—*Spring's almost over . . . don't let your employment history rest on its laurels. Take action today to get your career in gear!)

June 15—summer issue, second client newsletter.

July 15—fifth postcard campaign. *(Vacation/suitcase theme for art—* Before packing for vacation, be sure your resume/job package is fully up to date and ready to go. Call us—we're *not* on vacation!)

August 15—sixth postcard campaign. *(Hot weather, droopy dog, sun for art—*Those dog days of summer are no time to relax your career search! Get back on track with help from the career professionals. Call today!)

September 15—fall issue, third client newsletter.

October 15—seventh postcard campaign. *(Halloween; witch theme for art—*Don't be bewitched over your career search progress . . . we'll help you to cast the *right* spell on your quest for the right job! Contact us today.)

November 15—eighth postcard campaign. *(Toolbox, carpenter theme for art—*Gear up, gather the right tools, and motivate *all* your resources for a successful career search! We'll help.)

December 15—winter issue, fourth client newsletter.

An annual schedule with eight pieces could look like this:
February 1—first postcard campaign
March 15—spring issue, first client newsletter
May 1—second postcard campaign
June 15—summer issue, second client newsletter
August 1—third postcard campaign
September 15—fall issue, third client newsletter
November 1—fourth postcard campaign
December 15—winter issue, fourth client newsletter

Client newsletters. For the past six years, I have used a quarterly newsletter (a single sheet, 8 ½" x 11", printed on both sides) entitled *Quips & Clips* to stay in touch with my clients (see sample). I include nuggets of information that might be useful to job searchers, reminders of the importance of maintaining an up-to-date resume or CV, and regularly run minifeatures on the benefits of a well-written, individualized cover letter. I also include a coupon or offer good for the current quarter, usually a percentage or dollar amount off a given service that I might be promoting. I talk about innovative ways my resume clients are conducting their job searches (including the recent surge in generating individualized business plans, especially among general manager, sales, and marketing executives).

Newsletters are mailed first class and are available in my office for clients to pick up if desired. I include on my mailing list the names of all clients with whom I've conducted full consultations or complete development of resumes, plus select clients for whom I may have done only a miniconsultation or basic retype (if I know them to be well connected and a possible source of excellent referrals). I produce the newsletter myself using a desktop publishing program (Aldus PageMaker on the Macintosh) and print it with a 600-dpi laser printer onto specialty paper I order from PaperDirect (see the Appendix for a complete listing of specialty paper companies). The entire cost of the project, including first-class postage, is usually under $400 per quarter—and it *more* than covers itself in terms of valuable client feedback and referrals. I also use my newsletter to communicate notice of upcoming events, periods when the office may be closed (while I'm on vacation or attending a professional conference), and the like.

Regardless of how you prefer to communicate with clients, I strongly urge you to use a regular vehicle. If you keep it simple and straightforward (as my one-pager has proved to be!), you will communicate consistently. *That's* what is most important in building your image. Never mind that you may not, in the beginning, have more than a handful of clients. The reader doesn't know this—and the image you create while generating goodwill with a client newsletter or similar tool will inure benefits to you tenfold, I can nearly guarantee!

Quips & Clips

a publication of Absolute Advantage

Spring 1997   P.O. Box 718, Durham, CT 06422 • 860.349.0256 • e-mail: CompSPJan@aol.com   Vol. 6, No. 1

Greetings!

Happy spring (well, almost … I can dream, can't I?)! With the change in seasons only weeks away, I find many of my clients more ready than ever to invest some extra energy into their business planning. In fact, for my resume and business clientele alike, **business planning** is the operative phrase these days. More and more, I'm seeing the development of business plans by clients seeking to start their own businesses. Sometimes these are individuals who have been impacted by corporate reengineering; they find themselves unemployed and have a unique opportunity to pursue a long-standing desire to start their own company. In a number of instances, small but thriving companies want to expand into new areas and need financial backing. Lastly, I'm seeing a resurgence in the creative presentation of business plans as part of the professional job search process. Highly qualified semi-finalists are developing and presenting distinctive, carefully developed business plans in the interview cycle—and not just senior-level sales and marketing executives, but candidates for general manager opportunities, CEO/presidential slots, and top healthcare and accounting/finance positions.

After some 14 years in business, I recently had an opportunity to develop *my* own business plan for Absolute Advantage's next five years … and deliver it for professional review to a class in the RPI/Hartford Graduate School's MBA program. *That* took courage: opening myself to criticism from some 28 or so management professionals! But the experience was incredibly insightful—and positive. If we can be of help in assisting *you* with creation of a dynamic and thorough business plan, do give us a call to discuss your objectives. And watch for those daffodils … and business … to bloom!

— *Jan Melnik*

Jazz Up <u>Your</u> Notes!

If your documents need some jazzing up, check out the latest additions to our growing library of clipart. We've just added more than 65,000 pieces of clever and imaginative art … sure to be something for every purpose!

- • **Cover Letter Special** — Through March 1, 1997, receive a complimentary cover letter with complete development of a resume ($40 value) … Discover a distinctive and effective way of marketing yourself!

Looking for Some Fresh Personal Marketing Ideas?

Your resume is all set (and if it isn't, you know who to call!) … but you haven't been out there interviewing in years. Headhunters are calling, but you're unsure of the best path to follow. You've decided that '97 is the year you'll "test the waters"—but really wish you had a guide as to how to best present yourself. Well, we can accomplish all of these things in a private consultation –*or*– you can benefit from the synergy that typically results when you pool together the ideas and energies of a small group of professionals … as I will be doing in a workshop through District 13's adult education program in May! If you're interested in attending or would like additional details, give me a call. You just may find you've got everything to gain. (Who *knows* what connections you might make!)

Schedule Alert … Professional Update … On the Road … Again!

Through the spring, **Absolute Advantage** will be closed on Fridays … I'm under contract with my publisher to write another book in the business series and will be conducting interviews of profile candidates on Fridays. Do leave a message, use the 24-hour fax (860.349.1343), or e-mail me (CompSPJan@aol.com) and I'll get back to you promptly.

Please also note that the offices of **Absolute Advantange** will be closed between April 17 and 21 … I will be attending an annual professional conference in Florida. This year, I'll be delivering an address on getting "free" publicity ("Pump Up the Volume In Your P.R. Plans!") as well as moderating a session for newcomers to my industry (topics both "near and dear" to my heart, as they say). Please mark your calendars accordingly and stay in touch so that we can plan any major projects in advance. As always, I'm sure I will learn a few new techniques to enhance my ability to provide top-notch service to my valued clients.

Quips & Clips© is designed, written, and published by Jan Melnik, CPRW, Absolute Advantage.

CHAPTER ELEVEN

CONSULTING AND WRITING RESUMES

A STEP-BY-STEP PRIMER FOR CREATING RESUMES

A book entitled *How to Start a Home-Based Resume Service* should concentrate on the myriad fundamental aspects of building a business, and that is what I have attempted to do throughout this text. I would be remiss, however, if I failed to provide some details about the *craft* of writing resumes. Although it would be nearly impossible for a single text, no matter how expansive, to teach the untrained reader "how to write a perfect resume," I am confident that some of the insights I provide in this chapter will help the practitioner with solid writing skills and a good grasp of the English language to "get up to speed" quickly with regard to conducting effective consultations and writing distinctive resumes and personal marketing materials.

The Whole Process

The timeline below provides an overview of how the resume process works from inception to completion. Obviously, depending upon your own schedule, preferred work style, and client requirements, each component is subject to change. This outline, however, reflects how my service has operated, most of the time, for the past fourteen years (each "entry" in this hypothetical schedule includes a component of time for that day's expenditure on behalf of a fictitious client).

Monday (10 minutes)

- The prospective client telephones the office.
- After discussion, you book the appointment for that Friday morning at 10:00 A.M. (advising the client to bring a calendar to the appointment in order to schedule the return visit). You then complete a consultation work order form (the importance of this document is discussed in chapter 7, particularly as it relates to responsibilities and payment).

Friday (75 minutes)

- The client arrives on time for the appointment at 10:00 A.M. You offer beverages and begin with the question-and-answer process.
- You conduct the consultation, which lasts until 11:15 A.M.
- You schedule the return appointment for the following Wednesday afternoon at four (the client's preferred date and time). You note this information on the consultation work order form, along with a record of the client's deposit, which you collect at this time; the client is asked to sign the work order and a copy is provided for his or her records.

Between Friday and Wednesday (105 minutes)

- You spend an hour and a quarter writing, typesetting, editing, and proofreading the client's resume; because this order was for a complete package, you spend an additional half-hour writing, typesetting, editing, and proofreading a pro forma cover letter.

As an aside, I will tell you something based on my own experience and echoed by many of my colleagues: When "under the gun" of time constraints, it is very possible for an experienced professional to completely write, typeset, edit, and proofread a resume *and* cover letter for presentation to a client in under thirty minutes.

I can almost assure you that you won't be doing this your first year in business; nor am I suggesting that this is a reasonable goal. I'm merely pointing out that the seasoned resume-writing professional, when faced with a critical client need (such as the earlier hypothetical client who needed the document the same day and was willing to pay the extra service charge), can deliver in this short a time frame in some instances—and thus tremendously add to the overall profitability of the business.

Wednesday (30 minutes)

- The client returns to the office at the appointed time; you offer a beverage.

- You present the proposed resume and cover letter in a file folder for the client's perusal. (A pen is also provided.)

- You encourage the client to read carefully and check or circle any item that is inaccurate, questionable, or discomforting. You also remind the client of the importance of careful proofreading (as noted on the consultation work order form, "final proofreading is the responsibility of the client").

- You then instruct the client to take plenty of time reviewing the documents and ask the individual to interrupt you upon completing the review. This allows you to work at your desk on other projects and not engage in a lengthy line-by-line inspection of the resume materials while the client is reading. This practice has *greatly* enhanced my efficiency over the years. Some clients will quickly peruse their materials and be ready for "discussion" in just five minutes; others might spend fifteen minutes, twenty minutes, or even longer thoroughly reviewing their documents. This is fine, but you don't need to spend your time sitting there while clients are doing their review. I get a lot of work done throughout the day during these review periods.

  I find, overall, that the average amount of time a client spends reviewing a resume and cover letter that I've prepared completely from scratch is about ten minutes. But if you have three, four, or more of these *per day,* the extra productive time can really add up— even if you are accomplishing nothing more than simply reorganizing your desktop (literally or on the computer!), invoicing a client, or setting up a format to write the next resume. Plus, I learned the hard way that when you sit beside a client and read the resume along with him or her, discussions frequently become protracted.

- Once the client is "ready to talk," you spend ten minutes discussing any questions he or she may have, clarifying any dates, and so on. (Occasionally, in the original consultation a client will be uncertain of a year, for instance, or the actual name of a professional organization. This information should be verified and confirmation provided during the return appointment.) An additional fifteen minutes is spent keying and checking any revisions, presenting the client with choices of paper for the final resume, and printing the correct number of originals the client is to receive with purchase of the resume/consultation package.

- For record-keeping and pricing purposes, I plan on thirty minutes for the return visit: five minutes for presentation of the folder (I don't include the time the client uses to review the resume, because I'm working on other client projects), ten minutes for discussion, and fifteen minutes for revisions and final printing of the resume.

- One caution: Time spent writing the resume and cover letter and time devoted to the return visit are the areas where the most deviations, in my experience, are likely to exist. In the beginning months of your business, you will undoubtedly spend more time than what I'm proposing is the norm, and that's to be expected (it's part of the learning curve). But in order to maintain profitability, you should strive toward something along the lines of what I have proposed unless you can develop your price structure in some other way to compensate you fairly for the hours you put in.

Total time invested? About 3.7 hours.

When you go back to chapter 5 and really try to understand the implications of package pricing and how you intend to structure the fees for your business, you can clearly see the ramifications of undercharging. As a "for instance," any service that quotes a "complete resume and cover letter from an interview for $50" is receiving about $13.50 per hour (if you follow my scenario based on a typical client above and also presume that the provider is putting together something that's at least halfway decent). If you look at the hypothetical numbers presented in my sample price list (also in chapter 5) and take the package price of $300 and divide it by the 3.7 hours calculated in the example presented above, the "hourly rate" breaks out at about $81. Sound high? Well, this is only an example—appropriate hourly rates in your area may be higher *or* lower.

Keep in mind that the time factored in to the above does not include other overhead time (beyond what was spent on the telephone initially booking the client) and that this cost must yield you with enough to cover such expenses as equipment, paper, advertising, and utilities. If your goal is to work forty hours per week and you look at a conservative billable figure of 50 percent (that is, twenty of those forty hours per week represent billable hours and twenty represent overhead/administrative hours), you need to cover, in your hourly fee, *all* the time you devote to your business (more information on this, including a profitability equation, appears in chapter 7).

To emphasize the importance of establishing outside parameters on any package offerings you may develop and market, I'll share my one consultation horror story. I was not new to this business by any means: This occurred only about three years ago. To protect client confidentiality, I have altered some descriptive facts about this client; the scenario is exact, however. A midlevel manager booked a full consultation with me; she was preparing herself for possible corporate downsizing. She had spent her fifteen-year career with the same company, holding positions of increased responsibility. Although she possessed no formal college degree, she had successfully completed numerous management courses offered by her company.

The consultation filled the hour and a half and was relatively uneventful (that is, it proceeded smoothly and I obtained all of the details I believed I needed to write a dynamic resume for this client). The return visit was scheduled, and a week later the client returned to my office as expected. I presented the package in the manner that I have previously described and worked at my desk, awaiting her "interruption" to advise that she was ready to discuss and finalize the resume materials. Well, she spent almost *an hour* reading. (The resume was one and a half pages in length; one pro forma cover letter was created—about four paragraphs, as I recall—for her review as well.) Then she was ready to talk. This particular day was highly unusual for me in that I did not have appointments scheduled immediately after this one (normally I would allow an hour for a return appointment, though thirty minutes is the typical time required).

To make this long story slightly shorter: The client wanted to discuss literally every phrase, every line, and nearly every *word* of the entire resume. Essentially, her overriding concern stemmed from the insecurity she apparently felt about not possessing a college degree. Her comments were peppered with such phrases as, "Does this make me look important enough? Can we say that even stronger?" She was truly a client in need of services that go beyond what I am qualified to offer; in fact, she would have benefited from the professional services of a psychologist equipped to help her with her self-esteem. We spent *two hours* in discussion and modification of this client's resume (and, unfortunately—although it was a valuable lesson—at that time I had no provision structured into my agreement about charging for overtime in the return visit: She had purchased a flat-fee package). I would change several sections of her resume at her request, she would reread them, and then she'd ask to have things changed *back* to the way I had initially presented them! To say that she was indecisive is an understatement.

This process repeated itself several times before I finally, tactfully and professionally, indicated that I was pleased to make whatever modifications she desired, once she was certain of what she wanted; at this point, she was really not concerned with any professional recommendations I had to offer. I even suggested that she might wish to take the resume home with her (after paying the balance) so she could "fully digest" its contents; then she could contact me for final revisions once she was absolutely certain of what she desired. Having stretched the return visit to three hours, she now decided that this was a good strategy. She paid in full, took one original with her—and it was nearly *a year* before I heard from her regarding the changes she wished to make. By this time, she had changed positions again and wanted to work in this information. We started with a fresh miniconsultation; I apprised her of my rates and told her she would receive twenty originals of the final resume "on credit" (from the original package, which had never been redeemed). As I say, this was certainly a lesson! I have since made it known that the resume package includes a return appointment of *up to thirty minutes* to discuss any modifications or revisions that might be necessary; I am flexible here—I don't charge if the whole return visit goes to forty minutes, for instance. The time limit is simply to protect against the kind of extreme case just described.

CONDUCTING A CONSULTATION: THE QUESTIONS TO ASK

Here are the highlights of a full consultation conducted at 10:00 A.M. on Monday with my pseudoclient, Ed Jones. The "transcript" touches upon all of the key points and questions used to elicit the salient information I need to write an effective resume.

QUOTABLE INSPIRATION

"Keep on learning, whether it be new software, business methods, and so on. Join professional associations for the information, resources, and contacts. Network with others doing the same thing you do. Read a lot—relevant as well as relaxing. Subscribe to appropriate newsletters."—*Jacqueline K. Herter, Professional Word Processing (Kodiak, Alaska)*

Jan: *(Small talk—to establish rapport, make the client comfortable, and put him in a good position to participate in discussion of background, accomplishments, and so on)* Hello, Ed. I'm Jan Melnik. It's a pleasure to meet you. Come on in. I see you had no difficulty in finding my office. *(Because I'm in a very rural section, I'm especially careful with directions, but occasionally, a client will "get lost.")*

Ed: Hi, Jan. It's nice to meet you. No, your directions were perfect.

Jan: Let me take your jacket. May I offer you a cup of coffee? *(Usually the response is affirmative; I find out how he likes his coffee, ask him to make himself comfortable, and quickly get his drink)* Here we go. *(I present the coffee. Then, depending upon how comfortable Ed appears—body language becomes very easy to read in this business—I might engage in a little more small talk about the weather, how long he has been a resident of the area, or whatever, just to "warm up")*

   (Once small talk is complete) Let's start with the logistical information on your resume. How do you like your name to appear? Edward or Edwin? *(He responds)* Do you use a middle initial or any special designation after your name? *(Jr., III, IV, etc.)* What is your home address? Do you have a different

mailing address? *(For a student, for instance, it is typical to show a permanent address and a collegiate address)* What is your home telephone number, pager number, home fax number and/or E-mail address? *(I then ask if there is an office number that he would like to use. Most clients are not in a position to show an office number because of confidentiality, but in some circumstances an office number is appropriate)*

(Once logistics are out of the way)* Ed, in our initial phone conversation, you mentioned you found me in the Yellow Pages. *(Or, "You mentioned Ann Davis referred you. I like to express my appreciation to my clients who refer others; she will be receiving a credit on her account redeemable toward future services." Then, I might add, "How are you acquainted with Ann?")* Was mine the only resume service you contacted?

Ed:　　No, as a matter of fact I did talk with several other services. I was impressed with your professionalism and your ability to put me at ease with your understanding of my field. I thought you could best help me present myself. *(Or, "I appreciated the fact that you offer after-hour appointments" . . . or "accept credit cards" . . . or "are a Certified Professional Resume Writer" . . . or "were actually available to answer my call—none of the other places I tried answered their phones directly, I got answering machines" . . . key point to remember when starting out!)*

Jan:　　Well, thank you for sharing that. It is truly helpful to me from a marketing standpoint to understand what a prospective client is seeking—and to know whether or not I convey the answers they are seeking in our initial phone conversation. *(Sometimes it becomes evident that a client has more to tell me. If so, I'll push a little more to unearth additional information about my advertising, especially relative to what my competitors may be doing)*

Before we get into a discussion of your background and accomplishments, Ed, I'd like to understand your objective in having a resume developed. *(This information may already be known—for instance, Ed may have told me he was just laid off or that he's a candidate for an internal promotion who needs to dust off an old resume and give it a fresh perspective. But the reason for having a resume developed doesn't always come out initially. If I don't know by now, this is the time to ask)*

This helps me to focus my questions appropriately and understand the direction in which we are proceeding.

Ed: Quite honestly, at this point my career with ABC is very secure. As I'll be describing shortly, I've been there nearly twenty years and have moved steadily through the managerial ranks to my current position as Senior Vice President, Domestic Sales. I completed my MBA a few years back and have continued to grow professionally over the years through in-service programs and by attending external seminars. But I'm in a position to know that the company is going to be implementing a fairly aggressive consolidation in the next eighteen to twenty-four months; staff at my level will be susceptible to some cuts, I am certain. I may be in a position to be offered a golden handshake. With two children now in college, however, I am definitely not ready for retirement. Therefore, I'd like to hedge my bets by being ready ahead of the curve—I'd just like to begin testing the waters to explore potential opportunities. One thing I'd like to avoid at this point in my career is a relocation, so I recognize jobs at my level may be somewhat scarce. The last resume I had was written when I left the military—it was so old that I didn't even bother to bring it with me.

Jan: *(Keep in mind, not all clients are this articulate! Most of my mid- and upper-level executive clients, however, do have a clear understanding of their needs, the overall job market, and where they are positioned. What many lack, however, is the knowledge and ability to present themselves effectively to the "outside world." Oftentimes their experience is extensive but limited to just one company. They have not interviewed or searched the open market for employment in several decades! They keenly need a professional resume writer to help them break out of their very narrow corporate mind-set, step outside the*

acronym-filled company they've worked with so long, and present
their very transferable skills to industries possibly outside their cus-
tomary area)

With those points in mind, Ed, I'd like to follow up with
a few additional questions. By the way, as I mentioned on the
telephone, I have blocked until eleven-thirty *(an hour and a*
half) for our appointment. Is it your plan to seek a comparable sales management position in the cosmetics industry? Or,
have you considered taking the breadth of your experience
into another consumer goods industry?

Ed: Initially, I'd like to target some of our competitors. Yes, I do
want to remain in sales management. However, I wouldn't
close the door to considering other industries.

Jan: That's a good approach. As our discussion moves along, I may
wish to recommend various options for presenting two versions of your resume. I'll be in a better position to assess this
once I have actually begun to write your materials. Let's begin
now with your current title and some of your responsibilities,
accomplishments, and results. First, can you clarify the actual
name of the company. *(If there is a holding or parent company, I*
would clarify the exact way this should appear on the resume)

Ed: *(He responds with appropriate details)*

Jan: How many direct reports are you at present managing? Indirect reports? Is the company structured as a matrix organization? What are the lines of responsibility and authority?

Ed: *(This serves as a springboard for discussion of what Ed is handling for*
the company. As he describes responsibilities, I will push for details
about actual accomplishments: programs implemented for which he
can take credit; quantifiable numbers pointing to sales results, per-
formance-to-goal that exceeded quotas and objectives; number of his
managers or sales representatives achieving excellence; types of recog-

nition and awards received—both individually and for his people; short- and long-range planning and implementation of major events; unique and innovative ways of building business; successful incentive programs developed; and so forth. This current experience is the most relevant—and it will consume the largest amount of space on the resume, hence the need for focusing extensively on it. It's also the easiest for Ed to talk about, since it is what he is doing currently. Throughout the question-and-answer process, I ensure that I ask about dates for each position—both month and year at this point; I'll probably drop months once writing, but this way I have a clear picture of when he assumed each new position)

Jan: *(After following up with specific queries about any key programs and accomplishments Ed has mentioned)* Now, before your promotion to Senior Vice President, Domestic Sales, what position did you hold for ABC?

Ed: *(Ed then begins describing his four years as National Sales Manager, the job he held before moving up to the senior veep's job in 1993. I probe for details of his achievements, factors pointing to his selection for promotion, and so on)*

Jan: Before you were named National Sales Manager, you were . . .

Ed: *(This process extends back along the timeline. We spend considerably less time on each position as we move backward, but I always ask Ed to focus on what he believes were the two key accomplishments within each position)*

Jan: Super. I think we've about covered ABC! *(We've probably been talking for nearly an hour at this point)* Please tell me about your military career.

Ed: *(This generally takes about five minutes for a successful military conversion that took place long ago. Obviously, for a client with an extensive, recent military background, we'd focus on the experience just as we did with Ed's current position)*

Jan: Now, where did you earn your MBA? Your undergraduate degree? Any major sales training programs? *(Such as Xerox)*

Ed: *(Ed provides appropriate responses, including location of university or college, type of undergraduate degree and major, and years in which degrees were earned. He also provides some details about a number of management training programs he completed)*

Jan: Ed, in terms of personal background, I recommend leaving out personal details such as age, marital status, and number of children. But I do believe that civic involvement, particularly with regard to positions of leadership, are important and favorably reflect another dimension of your background. Is there any current involvement that you'd like to share with me? *(This phrasing allows clients who are not involved with civic organizations or active within their community to save face)*

Ed: Well, I'm vice president of the Exchange Club. I've been a member of that organization for about fifteen years. I also serve on my town's Conservation Commission. . . . (etc.)

Jan: *(I obtain actual years of involvement, details of elected or appointed positions, and any other salient points that might work into the writing)* Excellent. I believe we've covered the breadth of material I need as far as constructing the resume is concerned. Now, let's move on to how you will market yourself, once you are ready to start the outreach. We talked a little in our phone conversation about developing tailored cover letters to a series of contacts you have within some of the competing industries in your field. In order for me to develop a pro forma cover letter for your consideration, I need to ask you a series of additional questions.

What would you select as your key distinguishing attributes, Ed? When you consider the success you have enjoyed in sales management over the past ten years, in particular, what factors do you believe have played a key role? In what areas do you see the most opportunity for growth and challenge?

What personal attributes would you say describe your style? What kind of manager are you? Can you describe what you believe would be a perfect fit for you in terms of your next position? *(The ways in which I use the responses to these questions will become evident in the writing of the resume later in this chapter)*

Ed: *(Ed provides appropriate responses in a comfortable give-and-take scenario)*

Jan: *(We've just about used our hour and a half. I pull out my appointment book)* Well, I think that about sums it up, Ed. Do you have any additional questions or comments you'd like to share? *(If none)* Certainly, if anything should occur to you before we get together again, please jot down your queries or ideas—we can review them when we meet to go over the resume and cover letter. How does next week look for you?

Ed: *(We schedule the appointment)*

Jan: *(I then complete the financial information)* As I mentioned on the phone, the complete package cost is $XX. I believe we also discussed a deposit of $XX; that can be by check, cash, or credit card—which is your preference? *(He provides payment)*

Would you please review this consultation work order and sign here at the bottom? It explains your responsibility in the resume generation process and details the balance of $XX that will be due when you return on *(the date we have scheduled)*. I'll then make you a copy of this document. *(He signs)*

Thank you very much, Ed. I have enjoyed working with you and will look forward to meeting with you next week. Should you have any questions, please feel free to give me a call.

That's it!

If you are new to conducting full consultations for writing resumes, you may wish to consult the sample resume questionnaire provided in the Appendix. This tool can be tailored for your own use so as to prompt you in all key topical areas for questioning. As with the advice you will provide to your clients with regard to developing their interviewing skills ("practice . . . practice . . . practice!"), the new resume writer develops his or her craft through practice. During your start-up weeks (or before you officially "open"), you might want to consider offering complimentary resumes with consultations for several family members or close friends (ideally in different professions). This will enable you to learn the tools of the trade more quickly and refine your question-and-answer technique so that it's efficient, smooth-flowing, and not overly time-consuming.

QUOTABLE INSPIRATION

"Be prepared to invest the majority of the money you make during the first year back into the business—for advertising, professional memberships, upgrading equipment, and so on. During that first year you need to have the name of your business everywhere that anyone would look for your services in order to obtain the 'share of the mind' you want [Jay Conrad Levinson's quote, whose marketing books she highly recommends]. Network by joining your chamber of commerce or small-business organization. Be prepared to work harder than you've ever worked before, and be prepared to take credit when things go right and the blame when things go wrong. Don't lose sight of the reasons that you started your own business—whether it was to spend more time with your family or for the personal satisfaction that you never received from working for someone else."

Connie delivers high praise regarding some of my materials with the following comment: "Read anything and everything ever written by Jan Melnik. She seems to understand, better than anyone else, the problems that a small secretarial or resume service encounters and is able to offer valuable, viable advice to the beginner or to the old pro."

Connie concludes her recommendations with, "And, finally, you only go around once . . . so you might as well enjoy it!"—*Connie S. Stevens A+ Secretarial Office Support Services (Radcliff, Kentucky)*

WRITING A DISTINCTIVE RESUME

Using the example of Ed Jones from above, I will now present the developmental stages of creating a resume to illustrate how various components of the consultation work themselves into the writing. All of my notes are recorded in handwriting on legal-size tablets. As I write, I cross off the applicable sections in my notes. In terms of process, I key in the name and address header information first, followed by an outline of categories I plan to include in their proper order, along with initial formatting (subject to revision as the writing proceeds). At the initial stage, I plug in whatever information is readily known without laboring over my notes. I attempt to determine if I think I'm looking at a one-page or a two-page resume project. The accompanying sample shows the "first pass" of the resume outline; as you will note, I am anticipating a two-page resume for the subject client, Ed Jones.

I write resumes using a word-processing program: Microsoft Word on the Macintosh; I begin each and every resume with a blank screen. Once the outline has been created, my practice is to work from the bottom up. In other words, I attempt to put together those components that require the least amount of effort and also build in the direction of where I believe the focus is heading. In Ed's case, I write in the information for his educational background, his military career experience, and his civic involvement. These items, which all appear on my proposed page two, might look the way they appear below.

EDUCATION

HARVARD UNIVERSITY • Cambridge, MA
- MBA (1991)

BROWN UNIVERSITY • Providence, RI
- B.S., Political Science (1977; summa cum laude)

Successfully completed numerous management courses with ABC, including
- Executive Sales TQM Program
- Xerox Selling Skills
- Management by Objectives

SAMPLE RESUME—FIRST STAGE

EDWARD D. JONES
123 Main Street
Your Town, USA 66666
(222) 666–3333

SUMMARY
- xxxx
  xxxx
- xxxx
  xxxx

PROFESSIONAL EXPERIENCE
1977–Present   COMPANY • City, State

1993–Present   *Title*
                 description
                 - Bulleted points
                   xxxx
                 - xxxx
                   xxxx
                 Accomplishments
                 - xxxx
                   xxxx
                 - xxxx
                   xxxx

19xx–xx   *Title*
                 description
                 - Bulleted points
                   xxxx
                 - xxxx
                   xxxx
                 Accomplishments
                 - xxxx
                   xxxx
                 - xxxx
                   xxxx

PROFESSIONAL EXPERIENCE

COMPANY (cont.)

19xx–xx   *Title*
                 description
                 • Bulleted points
                   xxxx
                 Accomplishments
                 • xxxx
                 • xxxx

19xx–xx   *Title*
                 description
                 • Bulleted points
                   xxxx

EDUCATION

UNIVERSITY • City, State
• MBA (19xx)

UNIVERSITY • City, State
• B.__ (19xx)
*Successfully completed numerous management
courses with ABC, including*
          • xxxx
          • xxxx
          • xxxx

MILITARY

UNITED STATES AIR FORCE • Various
locations throughout the world
•*Title* (19xx–xx); Honorable Discharge, 19xx

CIVIC

•Member, xxx (19xx–xx)
•Member, xxx (19xx–xx)
•Member, xxx (19xx–xx)

MILITARY

UNITED STATES AIR FORCE ■ Various
locations throughout the world

■ First Sergeant (1969–72); Honorable Discharge,
1972

CIVIC

■ Vice President, The Your Town Exchange Club
(Member, 1981–Present)

■ Member, The Your Town Conservation Commission
(Elected, 1990–Present)

■ Coach/Volunteer, The Your Town Little League
Association (1986–Present)

With those elements in place, I next concentrate on the professional experience, starting with the oldest information first. Although I have found that I am most efficient, once again, proceeding from the foundation up, you should certainly experiment and use whatever method of writing works best for you. I always save the writing of the summary (when used) as the last element of the resume, and I never begin writing the cover letter until the resume is completely written. The sample that follows shows Ed Jones's resume after it has been fully developed.

Dos and Don'ts to Make Your Resumes Sizzle

There are probably as many good books on typography, layout, design, and desktop publishing as there are on writing resumes. (There is a clear distinction between books that show hundreds of "actual" resumes, books that help the reader write resumes, and this book, which describes how to build a business out of writing resumes; the Appendix provides a listing of excellent resources to give you ideas and acquaint you with the wide variety of resume presentations that are possible.) I'll provide what I consider to be the key points to remember in creating resumes that, once the content is superb, really present themselves distinctively.

The listing below has been compiled through my work with thousands of clients—and interviews with hundreds of hiring managers—over

EDWARD D. JONES
123 Main Street Your Town, USA 66666
(222) 666–3333

SUMMARY

■ Accomplished executive sales management professional with 20-year career characterized by successful experience in all facets of management and sales leadership.

■ Dynamic and effective communications skills complemented by demonstrated abilities to mobilize global efforts and establish clearly defined objectives.

■ Motivated team player with commitment to excellence in customer service, achievement of bottom-line performance goals, and optimum positioning of organization for future goal achievement.

PROFESSIONAL EXPERIENCE

1977–Present   ABC Company • New York, NY

1993–Present   *Senior Vice President, Domestic Sales*

Manage 8 direct and 29 indirect reports; oversee a sales organization comprising 500+ personnel throughout the country. Develop and execute strategic sales plans across 9 domestic divisions comprising health, personal care, fragrance, and beauty lines for largest cosmetics company in the world.

Accomplishments

■ Sales have grown from $12 billion in 1993 to $18 billion for the year ending 1997; account penetration has increased tenfold across the same timeline as a result of implementing major planning initiatives and incentive programs at regional levels.

■ Analyzed and successfully implemented quarterly event program unique to industry in which every account has an individually developed plan to boost sell-through; with additional implementation of automated store-level planogramming, order writing across all accounts has increased more than 85% from 1994 to present.

1989–93   *National Sales Manager*

Acquired responsibility for two divisions with business throughout all 50 states ($44 million in sales annually).

Accomplishments

■ Developed aggressive recruitment program to identify top sales personnel and heavy producers; hired/trained 8 Executive Account Managers.

■ Between 1989 and 1993, 63 Sales Representatives within the two divisions were recognized as top performers and were recipients of ABC's Corporate Excellence Recognition (highest number ever to be recognized from this area).

■ Maintained growth of business between 20% and 45% per year between 1989 and 1993.

■ Through development and implementation of cost containment programs, reduced spending and enhanced both manpower budgeting and sales forecasting.

PROFESSIONAL EXPERIENCE

ABC COMPANY (cont.)

1982–88   *Executive Account Manager*

Managed all sales activity for New England, Mid-Atlantic, Atlantic Seaboard, and South-Central United States

Accomplishments

- Acquired region that had not met sales objectives for five years running; successfully implemented training program, identified new business opportunities, and established aggressive sales objectives. Within one year, region made goal.

- Achieved an average annual sales volume varying between 125% and 200% over quota each of 6 consecutive years after 1982; tripled account based between 1982 and 1984; doubled base every two years thereafter.

1979–82   *Senior Sales Representative*

Recognized as "Sales Representative of the Year," Domestic Sales, for three consecutive years (1979, 1980, and 1981); promoted (1982) to Executive Account Manager's position.

EDUCATION

HARVARD UNIVERSITY • Cambridge, MA

- MBA (1991)

BROWN UNIVERSITY • Providence, RI

- B.S., Political Science (1977; summa cum laude)

Successfully completed numerous management courses with ABC, including

- Executive Sales TQM Program
- Xerox Selling Skills
- Management by Objectives

MILITARY

UNITED STATES AIR FORCE • Various locations throughout the world

- First Sergeant (1969–72); Honorable Discharge, 1972

CIVIC

- Vice President, The Your Town Exchange Club (Member, 1981–Present)

- Member, The Your Town Conservation Commission (Elected, 1990–Present)

- Coach/Volunteer, The Your Town Little League Association (1986–Present) the years. It has been supplemented through the contributions of David J. Denino, Associate Director of Counseling and Career Services and Adjunct Professor of Counseling and School Psychology at Southern Connecticut State University in New Haven, Connecticut (he was also quoted in chapter 9).

- Lead with the strengths of your client. If experience speaks louder than education, lead with that. If the client's degree (as with a new graduate) is the best card, lead with that. The client must sell the reader in the top half of the resume (as Dave Denino states, "The first chapter of a book can convince you to keep reading or put it down!").

- Ensure good use of "white space" on your resume—don't crowd too much onto one page—and remember the golden rule of brevity.

- Don't use too small a type font—and I recommend against using a sans serif typeface (such as Helvetica or Geneva) for an entire resume; if you like the look of your subheads being cast in a different font and like sans serif for that purpose, fine.

- Don't skimp on paper quality: Present at least several choices of good stock from which your clients can choose (refer to the guidelines in chapter 6 for additional information).

- Don't overuse special features, such as **boldface** and *italics*. Except for using an underscore (actually, a line from the border feature in formatting) to separate the header information from the body of the resume, resist the urge to use underscores (underlining) altogether.

- Don't mix more than two typefaces in a resume. Even better, stick to one font throughout—just vary size (but consistently!). In other words, depending upon the font you select, you might cast the client's name in 14-point boldface small caps, all subheadings in 12-point boldface small caps, and all text in 11 point (all the same font). Company names might be bold caps (but 11 point), with titles in bold italics, upper- and lowercase. Experiment, but remember that the design you develop is to complement the client's background and make information easy to read and allow it to be clearly presented: You are not trying to win awards for unique design in the resume field. Keep it conservative, understated, elegant, *clean*.

- Avoid nonpertinent information (particularly personal details).

- Write the resume with a keen eye toward what the prospective employer or hiring manager will be seeking. This may require customized tailoring for a variety of unique applications ("Not everyone likes the same book," as Dave Denino points out).

- While clients are ultimately responsible for final proofreading, always carefully proofread your work before presenting it to a client. Ensure that there are no errors in grammar or punctuation. And double-check for consistency in font selection and formatting.

- Use "action words" to begin sentences; never use the word *I* or *me* in a resume. ("Directed, organized, planned, and motivated people and resumes move quicker and further than those who aren't," notes Dave Denino.)

- Remind your clients of the objective of a well-written resume: to get an interview (resumes, themselves, do *not* get job offers). Encourage clients to use their resumes as the first step in the job search process. Once it is mailed (with a distinctive cover letter—as discussed later in this chapter), the job seeker should use follow-up telephone calls to insure optimum chances for success in landing an interview.

- Advise your clients to mail their materials flat in a 9" x 12" envelope (a matching one, if costs will allow); for the extra postage (about a quarter), it is well worth it!

By the way, the very first suggestion Dave Denino provides to under-graduates and graduates alike is: "Do prepare your resume in a professional manner. *Pay* for it to be done if you don't have the means to produce a professional-looking product. This is a reflection of you." (And my favorite line of Dave's: "Your competition is doing it right the first time!")

CHAPTER TWELVE

WHAT THE HIRING EXPERTS SAY

HELPING YOUR CLIENTS TO BEST PRESENT THEMSELVES

In chapter 9, I discussed what executive recruiters, personnel consultants, and career counselors look for in resumes and cover letters. In this section I will provide commentary gleaned from interviews with some of the final hiring authorities. As a resume writer advising clients in undoubtedly numerous professions, you are wise to educate your clients that they can't possibly be "all things to all people." Nonetheless, by following as many of the general guidelines as possible, including the "Dos and Don'ts" provided throughout this chapter (note that some overlap key suggestions from recruiters provided in chapter 9), you create the likelihood for the best possible positioning of your clients.

As general manager for Asea Brown Boveri (ABB Service Inc., Eastern Division), Chuck Embree oversees the operations of eleven facilities that provide electrical energy equipment and services to customers along the Eastern Seaboard. With twenty years' experience in the electrical engineering profession, including six years with Westinghouse before joining ABB, Chuck has interviewed hundreds of candidates for entry-, middle-, and senior-level technical and management positions. As with many hiring managers I interviewed, Chuck vastly prefers resumes organized methodically in a chronological format. "Two pages are fine," he notes. "If it goes to three pages or more, I start getting nervous. I like to see an objective and a summary, and candidates must definitely convey their knowledge of terminology reflective of this industry. It's key, in this field, to use the right buzzwords."

Chuck Embree shared an excellent example of how a well-written, well-researched cover letter "made all the difference." This particular candidate (a military-to-civilian convert) used the alumni directory of his alma mater to locate graduates employed in the field of electrical engineering. He identified Chuck as a fellow alum of Worcester Polytechnic Institute and used that fact in his cover letter opening. "His taking the time to research the alumni records, identify me, and then write with a strong letter and resume made an impression. Although I wasn't hiring at the time, I did make sure the resume was forwarded to some key players in the organization with a recommendation that he be interviewed."

In terms of newspaper advertisements, Chuck advises candidates to answer immediately ("We're looking to fill a job, we want a timely response") and clearly link the cover letter to the ad. "Show me that you've read the ad and have the necessary qualifications. If I don't see that link in the cover letter, I don't look further [at the resume]." Chuck adds that presentation is critical and "says a lot about the candidate." He vastly prefers reading materials that have been mailed flat (not folded into number 10 business envelopes). This point, by the way, was echoed by nearly everyone with whom I spoke. An interesting comment by Chuck: "I'm more likely to open an oversize envelope which has been hand-addressed than [one that's] typed."

With regard to follow-up telephone calls, Chuck Embree recommends that candidates "work the clock" and try calling early in the morning and late in the afternoon, "up to perhaps three times. If after two or three messages you are not having any success, chances are there is no interest." Chuck appreciates the effort of a well-written thank-you letter after an interview and says "it carries a lot of weight if done immediately, professionally, and if enthusiasm for the position and the responsibilities is conveyed." He adds that "it can be a factor in the hiring decision. When everything is on equal footing, a letter is really important and demonstrates not only desire, but the sign of a true self-starter." A final point:

"Pay to have [materials] word-processed professionally if you are unable to do it yourself." Chuck recommends communicating in writing with both the interviewer and the director of human resources (by carbon copy of the letter to the interviewer, if you are not interviewed directly by the director of human resources).

George M. Eames IV, president of W. A. Parsons Company, Inc., in Durham, Connecticut, is involved with the interviewing and hiring of both professional staff and blue-collar employees at the forty-five-year-old company, which specializes in sheet metal fabrication. Beyond demonstrated professionalism, George looks for candidates who "show me their versatility and their ability to wear multiple hats." He points out that this is extremely important in a small company. "I want to see that, regardless of position or assigned responsibility, a candidate is not one-dimensional. Candidates should illustrate, in their cover letters, why we should hire them, why they are critical to our business." Sloppy presentation, functional formatting ("especially with obvious gaps"), and poor or missing references all serve as cause for rejection. Based upon his experience, which also includes a ten-year career in commercial banking, George states that a two-page resume is fine, "provided that it is well organized and delivers succinct and meaningful information."

As purchasing manager for Dow-United Technologies, Inc., in Wallingford, Connecticut, Robert E. Francis oversees a staff of nineteen individuals responsible for procuring $26 million in materials and parts to support the aerospace subcontractor's business. His staff of eighteen is evenly divided between facilities in Wallingford and Tallassee, Alabama. As an aviation professional with more than fifteen years' experience in aerospace, purchasing, and materials management, Bob has done extensive recruiting, interviewing, and hiring.

In his current capacity Bob Francis interviews many applicants who have been initially screened by the three or four temporary services that Dow uses. The practice of engaging staff through temporary channels affords candidates an opportunity to test "fit" at the same time that Dow is able to evaluate performance before making a long-term commitment (the trial period usually lasts two to four months). The three factors Bob looks for in candidates' paperwork:

- "Quantitative results—I want to see that [candidates have] achieved quantitative results in what they have done and then have them demonstrate how those achievements helped the business to grow or maintain position in whatever their particular industry or market is."

- "Second, I look for managerial strengths and accomplishments—again, relating this to quantifiable results. A candidate should show, for example, how he or she was able to organize a department and align the organization toward a particular quantifiable objective."

- "The last key is leadership. I want to see how a given candidate has successfully utilized leadership qualities in, for instance, bringing people together under adverse conditions, used motivational techniques to build teamwork, and progressed—both the candidates themselves and the people under their direction."

With regard to style, Bob Francis prefers a mix between bulleted statements detailing quantitative accomplishments and short narrative conveying overall responsibilities. He also looks for ongoing training and growth, as illustrated by the candidate's continuing participation in professional development programs. Cover letters should always accompany resumes, Bob advises, but he cautions applicants "to avoid redundancy in the letter. It should not be a repetition of what is presented in the resume. Also, while it is important to draw parallels between experience or qualifications and what the employer may be seeking as stated in a newspaper ad, for instance, the letter shouldn't match, item for item, everything stated in the ad."

Within academic circles, different criteria sometimes apply to prospective employee paperwork. While rules concerning perfect spelling, grammar, and a professional presentation apply to every field, there are specific strategies for clients who seek professional opportunities as teachers or administrators within the field of education. Among the many candidates in this area I work with in my business are

- prospective first-time teachers just out of school, with an undergraduate or graduate degree in education;

- individuals with a number of years' teaching experience followed by a break (often related to raising young children), who now wish to return to the classroom;

- experienced classroom educators ready to move into the administrative ranks; and

- existing building administrators who are preparing to assume a superintendency.

Depending upon the unique requirements in a given geographic area and the background of the resume writer, there are conceivably any number of specialty fields a resume business could incorporate in its service offerings. I believe that education represents a prime field for specialization for the resume writer—one that has the unique potential of becoming a top-producing niche segment in nearly every location throughout the country. Unlike high tech or engineering (in which there are pockets of the country where this market has exploded—and then seen downturns), schools operate in every county and most towns throughout the entire United States. There is always turnover—through relocation, retirement, and other attrition—and hence the ability of a professional resume writer to cultivate experience and talent working within this area of specialty cannot be overemphasized. This section of the text, then, focuses on that market segment: on what educators seek in preliminary paperwork and in interviews with prospective teaching and administrative candidates.

Donald J. McCarthy began his thirty-year career in education as an elementary school teacher and moved progressively toward his current position as superintendent of schools in North Branford, Connecticut. Exhibiting both insight and commitment, he shared in-depth information with me about every facet in the process of hiring a building administrator—from recruitment and multiple levels of interviewing through to the offer. His insight regarding the efficacy of the interview process (both for the school district and in terms of establishing fit for the candidate) reflects well upon his commitment to ensuring not only the best-qualified applicant for a given position but also the long-term cultivation of a satisfied, contributing team member.

Don characterized the candidate interview and selection process as "more of an art than a science." An underlying premise he has always subscribed to is that "the cream will rise to the top." This theme pervades the entire hiring process, and Don communicates it freely to his school board; with due diligence and a well-thought-out recruitment and interview program, the best candidate for the job will become evident. When choosing principals, Don encourages the hiring committee that's formulated for each position vacancy (and that typically includes two teachers, two parents, a member of the board of education, the outgoing principal, the assistant superintendent, and himself) to "have the courage and the confidence to make their selection. Once they've followed the very detailed process we have in place, I recommend that they step back from that process to see if it works. It always does."

While all hiring within a given school system is likely to reflect the district's philosophy and mission statement, there are also unique needs that depend upon grade level. In no area is this more true than for middle school principals. In touching upon a number of specifics (and, by the way, these points can be integrated effectively into the planning for teacher candidates who wish to instruct in the middle school grades), Don highlighted some of the characteristics desired of a middle school principal. The best candidate has these attributes:

- Possesses strong and effective leadership qualities ("One who understands the change process and will 'walk lightly' and not rush or push too quickly")
- Places a high value on mutual respect
- Has the ability to get others to assume leadership roles without their "knowing" it
- Knows the lingo and is comfortable with middle-school-age children (as well as clearly embraces the differences between the former junior high school concept and a true middle school)
- Understands adolescent age groups
- Demonstrates support for teaming, a child-centered approach, and the middle school concept (for example, scheduling skills, curriculum)
- Can effectively handle criticism
- Respects individuality
- Respects the ability to teach
- Can relate well to classroom instruction and learning and is not a stranger to the classroom
- Possesses strong communication skills (written and verbal)
- Especially evidences good listening skills

- Has good interpersonal abilities
- Is highly supportive of building cooperative teams ("Is versed in new approaches in implementing teaming but sensitive to the fact that he or she will be with experienced staff")
- Effectively manages staff and staff concerns
- Promotes high expectations and excellence in performance
- Displays management skills in budgeting, scheduling, and so on
- Is a good disciplinarian who is consistent and clear in action
- Possesses sound computer knowledge and skills ("In this era of dependence upon technology, everyone must be technologically literate—able to access information and keep up with the rapid growth in this area")
- Interfaces effectively with peers, teachers, parents, and students
- Is community-minded
- Maintains professional involvement, including state and national organizations
- Remains current on important and relevant issues
- Presents positive references from the community
- Has a range of personal accomplishments and interests

The challenge when developing a resume for a client in this field is to demonstrate these points concisely and accurately. Proper presentation includes not only the resume (or curriculum vitae) but the cover letter. Don McCarthy advises: "Use the cover letter to make me want to see you. Demonstrate you know something about our district. Be unique, but present a professional-looking package. Show knowledge of the community and the town. Always verify spelling of names, the school, the town. Be certain to individually tailor the letter—don't let it scream 'mass mailing.' Present your awards, your accomplishments, your involvement in the community."

For first-time administrators, according to Don, it is imperative that the candidate "indicate why he or she wants to leave the safety of the classroom and take on the challenge of administration. Equally important, for teacher candidates, is presenting their reasons for wanting to teach." Candidates are advised, however, to temper their written presentation with the idea of saving something for the interview. Specific interview recommendations from Don: "A candidate shouldn't be too casual. Appearance and dress should always reflect the professional, and, especially for administrators, language should not be too 'me' or 'I' focused—instead, state things such as, 'My staff and I implemented . . .'." A key part of the candidate search, according to Don, is site visits, wherein candidates can be assessed "on the job."

Don further suggests, for teacher candidates, that transcripts and student teacher evaluations be incorporated in the initial inquiry package—"present as professional and comprehensive a package as possible." It is important for all candidates, regardless of position desired, to demonstrate competencies in technology. Creative thinking and problem-solving abilities are equally key. Not surprising, Don notes that for administrators and teachers alike, it is relevant to demonstrate "how that individual can help market the budget in the community." Finally—although it almost goes without saying for any position—Don McCarthy reiterates that candidates must demonstrate "enthusiasm and energy—and a sincere desire to become a contributing team member. We're looking for creative thinkers and people who can work together collaboratively and cooperatively, pooling their knowledge and experience."

William D. Breck, Ed.D., is superintendent of schools for Regional School District 13, Durham/Middlefield, Connecticut. A seasoned professional with more than twenty-five years' experience in education as both an administrator and a classroom teacher, Bill is widely published in the academic community and has provided consulting services in a variety of capacities. Bill's comments with regard to candidate preparation paralleled many of the ideas shared by Don McCarthy. A key point for teacher candidates to convey—in their resume and cover letter materials as well as in interviews—is "what they can do to contribute to student achievement," Bill notes. "Diversity in experience is important, particularly work in the private sector. Those teachers with a variety of other experiences bring to their teaching a much broader perspective of the world."

Bill Breck emphasizes that successful candidates display "enthusiasm, excitement, energy, and commitment. Oftentimes, the difference between two qualified candidates is the level of energy that they would bring to the job. We want someone willing to give a hundred and ten percent. I look for the enthusiasm behind a candidate's response in the interview. When we interview candidates who demonstrate a high level of enthusiasm and their desire to contribute to a team, it's contagious." Another important factor for candidates to display is a demonstrated commitment to the continuous pursuit of learning.

When he interviews finalists for a teaching position in his capacity as superintendent, Bill Breck explains, he is essentially looking for candidates to demonstrate their overall sense of the district and their expectations. He frames questions broadly enough to allow candidates the opportunity to elaborate. If he senses any resistance, he will push a point. "I try to gain a sense of the type of person—and determining a candidate's degree of flexibility and inflexibility is important. The successful candidate needs to be able to grow with the organization."

With regard to a candidate's paper presentation, Bill Breck looks for several things "beyond the obvious of being well written, clearly presented, easy to read, and just long enough to pique my interest [but not too long]. Of course I look for a match between an individual's background and experience and what we are seeking—but I spend as much time looking at what the candidate *doesn't* say as what he or she does say. And, concerning accomplishments, I am much more interested in *how* candidates achieved what they did than in what precisely was accomplished."

Offering further advice with regard to developing a resume and cover letter as well as preparing for the interview, Bill advises that candidates "show how they have overcome diversity, difficulty, and challenge. They should demonstrate problem-solving ability and be prepared to share specifics." A key point for position finalists: "Understand the community and district in which you are interviewing and match your interview appearance and style appropriately." Bill strongly favors use of well-written follow-up letters that reiterate important points discussed in the interview and highlight strengths. For candidates for administrative positions, all follow-up correspondence should be professionally typed; for teacher candidates, while typing is preferred, handwritten notes are acceptable.

To gain additional insight, I interviewed two principals in Regional School District 13. Robert A. Esposito is principal of Brewster School (grades K–2) in Durham; Robert Wolfe is principal of Korn School (grades 3 and 4) in Durham.

Bob Esposito—whose twenty-eight years in education include elementary school teaching as well as counseling at the elementary, middle, and high school levels before moving into administration—strongly advocates that candidates present professional and thorough materials. For the typical teaching position that becomes available, there are generally 200 applicants. In order to distinguish one's paperwork in a pool of candidates this large, Bob recommends that individuals "reflect upon the district's mission statement [and match it to their own philosophy] in the personalized cover letter. That says a lot to me about how serious this applicant is." He adds, "I use my name in all advertising and I anticipate that applicants will also use my name in their cover letters (spelled properly)."

Materials should, of course, be professionally prepared. "Mailing materials flat is effective," Bob Esposito observes. "Provide original materials that can be photocopied (we circulate copies before the interview process)." Bob states that spelling, grammar, and presentation should be "perfect" and encourages applicants to get their materials in "first and perfect," noting that it is totally acceptable to indicate in a cover letter that letters of reference have been requested and will be forwarded separately.

Bob pointed out that applicants would be well served to ensure the quality of the references they have requested. "Be certain that the people you have asked to write on your behalf are, in fact, willing to write supportive recommendations." What constitutes irrelevant paperwork? "Copies of CEUs [continuing education units]—we don't need to see these; rather, a professional, single-page listing of CEUs earned is appropriate. Especially for candidates who may have been out of the classroom for a period of time, CEUs can demonstrate that they are current and 'always learning.' It's critically important to demonstrate a commitment to lifelong learning."

Bob Esposito appreciates seeing volunteer experience on a resume. As far as format is concerned, he—like all other educators I spoke with—prefers a traditional style with dates at the left-hand margin.

Bob Wolfe, principal at Korn School, reflected upon his twenty-seven years in education (from elementary classroom teaching to administration, complemented by teaching at the graduate level as an adjunct professor at Southern Connecticut State University). "No resource is more important than my people," he states, with regard to the candidate review process. Applicant paperwork weighs heavily in Bob's opinion. "I read everything—about twenty percent of what I receive is discarded." What makes the reject pile? "Typographical errors, misspelling, and sloppy appearance, including messy use of Wite-Out; a poorly written cover letter." In Bob's view, "Resumes can be up to two pages in length, but should be crisply written and in a chronological format. Concrete facts should be presented in the applicant's summary at the beginning of the resume."

Bob Wolfe recommends that applicants who have been out of the classroom for a period of time clearly demonstrate that they have been "active in child-related activities, be it involvement in scouting, sports, a parent-teacher organization, church, or school: Show experiences that demonstrate you love kids. Also present what you have been doing to remain current—show me you understand literature-based reading programs, use of hands-on science activities, flexible grouping."

In summary, Bob Wolfe's recommendation to applicants is universal in its application: "Attitude is the number one criterion—an expressed willingness to try and learn. I look for enthusiasm . . . [and for prospective teachers expressly] we want candidates who live, eat, and breathe kids and are committed to making the learning environment exciting."

Resume writers can benefit greatly from *regularly* surveying experts in their own market areas, much as I did for this book. Interview hiring authorities in businesses that are representative of your clients' community to learn where job opportunities are anticipated and what these professionals want to see from prospective employees. Push for details. Ask what does and does not work in candidate paperwork and in the interview. Find out what strategies are effective for getting the door to open for interviews—during times when there is active recruiting as well as when only an informational interview is sought. What distinguishes, in the minds of these experts, the truly exceptional job candidate? What factors are deal-killers?

Ask for enumerated "short lists" of the absolutes ("the three things you absolutely must see in a candidate's resume or cover letter," "the mistake that will convince you to reject a qualified candidate without even scheduling an interview," and so on). Ask, too, for specifics with regard to the presentation of paperwork. If you can schedule an in-person meeting (as opposed to a brief telephone interview), present samples of your work—using fictitious names!—and ask, "Is this style of resume effective? What do you like—and not like—about this resume? How about color?

Number of pages?"

Research of this type distinguishes top resume-writing professionals. Savvy individuals need to know what is going on in the marketplace. Resume professionals must be in a position to counsel their clientele appropriately. It goes beyond simply keeping up with local and national business periodicals; as I like to say, you need to have your finger on the pulse of the hiring process. What better way than to conduct interviews of human resource professionals and hiring managers on a methodical basis? (In this same vein, chapter 13 discusses the benefits of membership in professional associations and regular collaboration with colleagues.)

QUOTABLE INSPIRATION

"The sky is indeed the limit in this profession. Hard work, high quality, and good business sense will take your wherever you want to go. I recommend to newcomers to join a professional association; make contacts who understand precisely what you're going through in your business. Attend conferences and meetings to keep current in the field and develop a network. These sources will be your biggest help and inspiration."—*Louise Kursmark, CPRW, Best Impression (Cincinnati, Ohio)*

HOW TO MARKET PROFITABLE ADD-ON SERVICES

Creating Cover Letters

There's not a resume in existence that can't be enhanced through an effective and distinctive cover letter. Likewise, the likelihood of job search success is immeasurably improved with a strong cover letter. The best cover letters are individually tailored (or *appear* so) and specific to the opportunity at hand. Since well-written cover letters are the ultimate in effective personal marketing tools, the resume professional is wise to develop cover letter writing skills fully and market the importance of this tool to each and every resume client.

A cover letter serves as the door opener that subjectively presents a candidate's strengths and qualifications. Accompanying a well-written resume, a cover letter serves to link background and experience objectively highlighted on a resume to the specific hiring needs of a company. A good cover letter should invite further interest and compel the reader to review the resume. A cover letter can be used in various ways:

- To respond to advertisements
- To contact recruiters and search firms
- To market a candidate to a target person or organization
- To thank someone for information or referrals

David Denino, the career services expert at Southern Connecticut State University who was quoted earlier, states: "You cannot get to an interview unless your resume is read—and you cannot get your resume read unless your cover letter inspires the reader to read on!" Here's how he summarizes the three components of a cover letter: The opening paragraph: why you are writing to the employer, using specifics; the name of the position for which you are applying; and how you learned of the opportunity.

The second paragraph: *You.* Talk about your ability to do the job and how your education and experience make you a valuable asset to the employer. Use action words to describe accomplishments. What differentiates you from—or makes you more appealing than—all other applicants?

The closing paragraph: Thank the reader for his or her time and consideration. Always request a response or an interview—your cover letter is designed to obtain an interview, so ask for one!

Cover Letter Dos and Don'ts

With credit for some of these points to Dave Denino, I provide the following dos and don'ts to be considered when developing cover letters.

COVER LETTER DOS

- Address the letter to a specific individual if at all possible (double-check the spelling and correct title).
- Keep the cover letter to one page.
- Ensure that the letter is perfect—free of any typographical or grammatical errors.

- Tailor the cover letter to the specific opportunity and company, organization, or institution.
- Use stationery that matches the resume.
- Mention the candidate's willingness to relocate, if applicable, and specify any geographic areas of interest.
- Research the company and include salient points about it in the letter.
- If the candidate is a recent graduate, reflect any relevant internship experience.
- When the candidate is referred by an individual, mention the name of that person in the opening paragraph of the cover letter to draw the reader's interest and attention to the purpose and content of the letter.
- Use the core of the letter—two paragraphs at most—to describe the candidate's qualifications, accomplishments, and suitability for the position. Stimulate the reader's interest by connecting the candidate's desire for the job and qualifications to the needs and problems of the company. Motivate the reader to want to read more in the resume and set up an interview.
- Close a cover letter with a strong reinforcement of interest in the company, an expression of confidence that the candidate "can make a contribution," a thank-you for the courtesy of the consideration, and a "call to action."
- If responding to an ad, draw parallels between the requirements of the company and a candidate's background.
- Be concise and honest.
- If asked for salary requirement, there are basically two choices of approach: "I would be pleased to discuss compensation if it is determined that I am a viable candidate" or "I am considering opportunities in the $XX range."
- If salary history is requested (and this, as Walt Truscinski previously suggested, is "fair game"), and if the current or most recent salary is the highest, use a statement such as "My total compensation package is in the midseventies." To cover instances where there may have been substantial cuts recently, as with a candidate

who goes from a fully salaried position of $65,000 to unemployment, then accepts a position with estimated earnings of $45,000 in the first year, this is appropriate: "Over the past five years, my annual salary has ranged between $45,000 and $65,000." A formal salary history document can also be prepared (as discussed later in this chapter).

COVER LETTER DON'TS

- Don't use "Dear Sir or Madam" (unless responding to a blind ad where the identity of the recipient is unknown).
- Don't exceed one page.
- Don't use a "shotgun, one-size-fits-all" approach.
- Don't exaggerate or inflate information presented.
- Don't use paper of an inferior quality.
- In responding to an ad, don't mention any shortcomings or areas where the candidate's background is not a match for the position.

Leave-Behind Documents and Follow-Up Letters

Examples of leave-behind documents include a formalized sheet of references, salary history information, and a concise, one-page biography format of a resume for a client with a two-page format. Follow-up letters are traditionally the thank-you letters that should immediately follow every interview. I recommend that all ancillary personal marketing materials be printed on the exact same stationery selected for the resume itself (the Appendix features a listing of recommended paper vendors, including some specialty houses for distinctive applications).

References

Encourage clients to provide you with a listing of three to five professional contacts; for students, names of professors, a student adviser, and one or two employers is appropriate. A reference sheet should use the header information extracted from the resume itself and then list the items below, usually in a column centered horizontally on the page, with the entries aligned flush left.

- Individual's name
- Title
- Place of employment
- Business address (note if this is a residence)
- City, state, zip
- Business telephone
- Home telephone (so identified)
- Relationship (if not obvious—for example, Manager, 1989-93)

Recommended fee: Typically a flat fee, anywhere from $7 to $30, is charged.

SAMPLE REFERENCES

SARAH V. THOMPKINS
123 Main Street
Anytown, USA 66666
(333) 666-3333

Professional References

Jane Smith
General Manager
ABC Company
123 Main Street
Your City, USA 55555
(888) 222-5555 (office)
(888) 555-3333 (residence)

Don Adams (*manager, 1988–90*)
President
XYZ Corporation
667 North Street
The City, USA 44444
(666) 222-4444

Peter Lee (*manager, 1979–88*)
Chief Executive Officer
LMN Company, Inc.
666 South Avenue
Your Town, USA 99999
(222) 666-3333

Salary History

Preparing a formal salary history is a straightforward matter of taking an identical copy of the completed resume on the computer and cutting out the descriptive information to leave just the company name, time frame, and position titles, and then adding in the ending salary—as shown in the sample.

Recommended fee: Typically a flat fee, anywhere from $10 to $40, is charged unless consultation is necessary.

SAMPLE SALARY HISTORY

SARAH V. THOMPKINS
123 Main Street
Anytown, USA 66666
(333) 666–3333

Confidential Salary History

CBS COMPANY
General Manager
1990–Present   current salary: $72.5K plus annual bonus
Office Manager
1986–90   ending salary: $50K

THE FULLER GROUP
Lead Office Administrator
1984–86   ending salary $36K
Executive Secretary
1981–84   ending salary $25K

One-Page Biography

A one-page biography is useful for clients with resumes and CVs two pages in length (or longer, as with a number of CV clients). It serves as a "snapshot" representation of your client when presented after an interview. To create a one-page leave-behind document, start with an identical copy of the final resume on the computer. Essentially your job will be to edit down the document to fit cleanly on one page. If a summary has been used on the resume itself, this should also appear (usually verbatim) on the one-page biography. Also include educational background, but show only degrees held, universities where studies were completed, years, and major (any other information that might be relevant to the resume is deleted for this purpose).

As demonstrated in the accompanying samples, professional experience and employment background are presented in one of two ways: either as a "functional" presentation or as a very abbreviated listing of companies and titles, with one or two lines reflecting overall responsibilities. For a functional presentation (the more common approach), experience is usually excerpted and placed into common categories—typically two, three, or four subject areas, such as "Management/Operations Experience," "Sales/Marketing Background," and "Financial/Accounting Expertise."

Recommended fee: This varies widely. Most often the fee is not a flat one because of the editorial time (and, occasionally, consultation time) required. Most typically a biography could be completed in as short a period as perhaps half an hour, but it could take up to two hours or more. Compute the fee using your hourly editorial rate.

Follow-Up Thank-You Letter

Advise your clients to write a follow-up letter immediately (*the same day!*) after any interview—even to a company in which they *think* they have no interest—and send it by first-class mail. Reflect upon key points in the interview, show appreciation for the interviewer's interest and time, and demonstrate enthusiasm.

> Dear_____ :
>
> I enjoyed speaking with you earlier today and appreciate your time. After reviewing the requirements of the position and my qualifications, I'd like to reiterate my strong interest in the ABC Company and the [title] position. I believe I would be an asset to your team and look forward to participating in the next stage of the interview process. Please do not hesitate to contact me with any additional questions. I will look forward to talking with you again.
>
> Sincerely,

Recommended fee: To create a template follow-up letter (which the client may opt to handwrite or *hire* you to word-process), most services charge a flat fee, ranging anywhere from $15 to $40, or more.

Posting Resumes on the Internet

The advent of the Internet and World Wide Web has opened up many new avenues for job seekers and prospective employers alike. Used first by primarily the computer crowd, the Internet is now used by everyone from corporate executive to general laborer.

The Employer's Perspective

From the employer's perspective, using the Internet to advertise available positions can be extremely beneficial. For a cost comparable to that of newspaper advertising, an employer can post vacancies in well-established databases accessible by job seekers throughout the world. Many companies choose to add employment listings to their existing World Wide Web sites. Companies today recognize the value of advertising on-line—not only are they using their advertising dollars wisely; they're reaching a pool of candidates they would never have been able to pinpoint by advertising in the local newspaper or employment journal, or even in larger, regional newspapers.

Sample Functional One-Page Leave-Behind Biography

EDWARD D. JONES
123 Main Street
Your Town, USA 66666
(222) 666–3333

EXECUTIVE SUMMARY

Management

- Accomplished executive sales professional/MBA with 20-year career characterized by successful experience in all facets of management and sales leadership.
- Track record of performance demonstrates consistency of growth within profession to highest sales management position with ABC Company, the world's largest cosmetics company.
- Excellent human resources skills. Developed aggressive recruitment program to identify top sales personnel and heavy producers; hired/trained 8 Executive Account Managers.
- Motivated team player with commitment to excellence in customer service, achievement of bottom-line performance goals, and optimum positioning of organization for future goal achievement.
- Through development and implementation of cost containment programs, reduced spending and enhanced both manpower budgeting and sales forecasting.

Sales

- Dynamic and effective communications skills complemented by demonstrated abilities to mobilize global efforts and establish clearly defined objectives.
- Developed and executed strategic sales plans with outstanding results in each of

five positions with company over a 20-year period. Between 1993 and 1995, grew sales from $12 billion to $14 billion and increased account penetration tenfold throughout domestic organization (9 divisions).

- Implemented major planning initiatives and incentive programs at regional levels.
- Analyzed and successfully implemented quarterly event program unique to industry in which every account has an individually developed plan to boost sell-through; with additional implementation of automated store-level planogramming, order writing across all accounts has increased more than 85% from 1994 to present.
- Managed national sales growth of business between 20% and 45% each year, 1989–1993.
- Directly managed regional sales activities; achieved between 125% and 200% of quota each year, 1982–88; tripled account base between 1982 and 1984; and doubled base every two years thereafter.

ABC COMPANY • New York, NY (1977–Present)

Current Position: Senior Vice President, Domestic Sales

Previous Positions: National Sales Manager, Executive Account Manager, Senior Sales Representative, and Sales Representative

EDUCATION

HARVARD UNIVERSITY • Cambridge, MA

- MBA (1991)

BROWN UNIVERSITY · Providence, RI

- B.S., Political Science (1977, summa cum laude)

The Job Seeker's Perspective

Job seekers themselves look to the Internet to seek out available positions that may not be advertised locally. The Internet can play a key role in a job search for someone planning to relocate to another part of the country. Job seekers can post their resumes in databases for employers to access, and they can actively search classified advertising for many of the country's largest newspapers.

Internet Career Services as a Profit Center

As with any service, job search assistance can be a highly profitable avenue for those in our field. René Hart, president of First Impressions Résumé and Career Development Services in Lakeland, Florida, charges clients a lesser fee for providing Internet job search assistance as opposed to what she terms "local" job search assistance. "In essence, clients are saving me time and energy by taking advantage of what the Internet has to offer. I don't have to spend my time running all over town collecting newspapers or faxing resumes to personnel agencies. Instead, I can sit at my computer and point and click my way through various job sites."

There are many aspects to using the Internet to assist clients in their job searches. You can actively search job databases and employment listings, utilizing the specifications your client has set forth. You can also post your client's resume on-line, or E-mail the resume in response to a particular employment listing.

Locating Job Openings Through On-line Sources

It's really very simple to job search on the Internet. Search engines such as Yahoo! or Alta Vista can be a vital part of navigating a path to various employment sites. By simply plugging in the key word *employment*, job seekers will find more than 650 resources to which they can connect. Using different search word combinations may increase the number of resources found (for instance, jobs + aviation). Job seekers who wish to pursue specific companies can use search engines to determine if the company has a Web site, then check for employment vacancies at each individual site. For the resume service owner, offering Internet career services to those clients without Internet access of their own (or without the time to perform the search on their own) can be a profitable ancillary service.

There are many avenues that you can use to search for employment openings on the Internet for your clients.

Company Sites

Companies large and small are using the Internet to sell their products and services, and many of them are also discovering the advantage of advertising job vacancies on-line. Advertising open positions on the Internet enlarges the company's pool of prospective candidates. Columbia/HCA Healthcare (www.columbia.net) advertises its vacancies on its Web site and even provides an on-line resume form that candidates can complete and submit for immediate consideration. Sonoco Products Company (www.sonoco.com), headquartered in Hartsville, South Carolina, also advertises available positions on-line, as does The Watson Clinic (www.watsonclinic.com). Even company sites not advertising vacancies on-line can be a great help to job seekers, because they often provide valuable information about the company itself. While not all companies maintain Web sites, and not all that have Web sites list their job announcements on-line, finding the ones that do provide these services can be an invaluable resource to your clients. The easiest way to check to see if a particular company has a Web site is to search for the company name using one of the Internet search engines such as Yahoo! (http://www.yahoo.com), Excite (http://www.excite.com), or Web Crawler (http://www.webcrawler.com). Once at a company Web site, look for a link to Human Resources, Job Openings, or Employment Opportunities.

On-Line Newspaper Classifieds

Many of the country's largest newspapers have moved into the Internet community and have made their classified advertising available to everyone. North Carolina's largest newspaper, the *News and Observer,* offers job seekers a wealth of information about available positions statewide. Its site, located at http://www.nando.net/classads/employment, gives visitors the option of choosing from approximately twenty employment categories. Other newspapers, such as the *Chicago Tribune* (http://www.chicago.tribune.net) and the *New York Times* (http://www.nytimes.com), work much the same way. The advantage of utilizing on-line newspaper classifieds over other Internet-based employment listings is that they can provide leads for the types of jobs that aren't typically found in great numbers on the Internet, such as positions in publishing, insurance, and retail.

Internet Job Banks

Internet job banks are World Wide Web sites devoted entirely to matching employers with potential employees. In addition to job vacancy listings, they frequently contain many other resources. Access to job openings are usually free, although sometimes registration is required, and the openings can be searched by using key words (e.g. *healthcare + management + $75K*). A few of the major Internet job banks include Career Mosaic (www.careermosaic.com), the Online Career Center (www.occ.com), The Job Network (www.conquestprod.com/resume.html), and The Monster Board (www.monster.com). Other resources often available at Internet job banks include the ability to post resumes to an on-line database that can be searched by employers, articles on career development and job searching, job fair announcements, and lists of recruiting firms. In some cases, these on-line databases are more appropriate for locating technical jobs (the computing industry, engineers, and so on), but there are those out there devoted to specific career areas, such as healthcare or entertainment.

Internet Newsgroups

Subscribing to Internet newsgroups can also be an effective way to assist clients in their searches. Internet newsgroups are much like an electronic version of a bulletin board. That is, a message left by one person can be viewed by anyone who subsequently visits that newsgroup. There are career-related newsgroups both for posting resumes to be viewed by employers and for viewing job openings posted by employers. The real advantage to career-related Internet newsgroups is that many of them are designed for specific metropolitan areas, thus allowing you to search for jobs for your clients in a particular geographic area. Some of the larger regional newsgroups include atl.jobs (job listings for Atlanta, Georgia), atl.resumes (where you would post a resume if you were looking for work in Atlanta), and nyc.jobs.offered (job openings in New York City).

Using the Internet to Distribute Your Client's Resume

Once you've located a job opening for your client on the Internet, you will most likely need to forward that resume to the employer electronically. Or, you may simply wish to upload your client's resume to a resume bank (usually located at the same site as Internet job banks) so that it can be accessed by the employers subscribing to its service. In either case, you will need to prepare an Internet-compatible version of your client's resume and should charge an additional fee for both preparation time and the actual resume posting.

Preparing an Internet-Compatible Resume

Because there are so many word processors and computer platforms being used by people on the Net, your first concern is that it can be viewed by anyone, regardless of his or her software or computer system. Thus, the first step in creating an Internet-compatible resume is to convert it into ASCII text format. Lisa Freeman of Advanced Office and Resume Services in Florence, South Carolina, offers this advice: "I've found that the easiest way to convert a client's resume to ASCII is to select and copy the entire document, then paste it into a text editor such as Windows Notepad. This is to make sure that I don't accidentally let my word processor throw in some noncompatible codes like curly quotes, em dashes, and bullets." Below are several other key points to keep in mind:

- Delete all tabs and indents. Tabs are recognized by ASCII text, but some Internet databases are confused by them. You can replace each tab with four or five spaces to maintain some of the document's layout.

- Remove all bullets. If you've used bullets in your original resume document, you may notice that the ASCII version has replaced it with very tiny bullets. Again, some databases are confused by them. You can instead use an asterisk or a dash followed by a space to replace them.

- Shorten all line lengths to sixty characters. Some E-mail readers won't display more than sixty characters on a screen.

- Make all information flush left. For example, if you've formatted your resume so that the dates of employment are flush right, you will need to enter a carriage return and place the dates on the left.

- Make sure that the client's name appears on the first line; the street address on the second line; city, state, and zip code on the third line; and telephone number on the fourth line. If not already present, place an E-mail address on the last line of identifying information. The following pages depict an example of an Internet-compatible resume.

Maintaining Your Clients' Anonymity

There is one critically important aspect of distributing your clients' resumes across the Internet that you should be sure to convey to them. Anyone can access the Internet, including your clients' present employers. If your clients are attempting to conceal their job searches from their employers, they need to take appropriate measures to maintain their anonymity. This means that you should strip their resumes of all identifying information: their names, addresses, phone numbers, names of companies for which they've worked, and, of course, any reference names they may have included. Once all of the identifying information has been removed from the resume, you obviously need to include a method by which the prospective employer can reach your client. This can be as simple as a nonidentifying E-mail address or an unlisted fax number. Post office boxes can also be used to maintain your clients' anonymity; however, it is a little-known fact that post office boxes used for business purposes *can* be identified to the general public. For instance, if in the course of your business, you have request a post office box number to receive both personal and business mail, anyone who has that box number can call the post office and find out to whom that box is registered (a valuable hint to job seekers faced with responding to a "blind" newspaper advertisement!).

Jan Melnik
P.O. Box 718
Durham, CT 06422
(860) 349-0256
E-mail: CompSPJan@aol.com

PROFESSIONAL SUMMARY

* Highly Motivated Data Processing Professional with
  career background reflecting continued professional
  growth and advancement.
* Expert project management skills complemented by effective
  negotiation and communication abilities.
* Demonstrated expertise in effective relationship management
  complemented by strong interpersonal skills.
* Talented in successfully managing all aspects of complex,
  multi-vendor/multi-site project implementations.
* Keen analytical and assessment skills.

TECHNOLOGICAL EXPERTISE
  - OS/2
  - Windows
  - CICS/OS/2
  - Informix
  - Power Builder
  - LAN Distance
  - CID Distribution
  - PC/LAN Installation
  - Dialogue Systems
  - SAS
  - DB2
  - CICS
  - LU62

PROFESSIONAL EXPERIENCE

January 1991 - Present
JOHNSON HEALTHCARE, INC., Center City, CA

Director, Applications - Managed Care Systems
May 1994 - Present

  Manage Medical Management Information System (MMIS)
  which provides network, hospital, and physician profiling
  capability to 20 nationwide healthplans. Application spans
  mainframe, distributed environment, and PCs. Manage complex
  multi-vendor relationships. Oversee 12 direct internal
  reports with new development, operational, production, and
  distributed environment responsibility. Manage technical
  budget of $13 million.
    * Implemented remote on-line distance learning program;
      full-feature system provides numerous in-field benefits
      including tutorials and support services. Anticipate
      training 500 users by the end of FY98.

* Created personnel job descriptions, hired/trained staff, and developed solid team of key professionals to successfully support and implement MMIS.

Senior Systems Consultant - Managed Care Systems
January 1991 - May 1994

Charged as work group leader to orchestrate and manage major Boston conversion, integrating two separate Health Services models into one highly effective referral/ authorization system for Johnson's largest healthplan (15 sites throughout Northeast). Healthplan goal was to provide 24x7 on-line accessibility as well as PC remote access to all locations. Managed 15 direct/indirect reports as well as interfaced with technical liaisons from corporate technical division.
* Complex project management included establishment of a LAN or remote access in each of 39 sites, provision of technical and application-specific training to 300+ PC users (for many, this was first exposure to a PC), and delivery of comprehensive training concurrently throughout 15 sites. Collaborated with technical and business resources to establish post-implementation hotline support center.
* Project scope entailed extensive effort in delivering comprehensive LAN Distance OS/2 remote access capability, a completely new technology product for Johnson.

June 1987 - January 1991
ABC COMPUTER SYSTEMS, San Diego, CA

Lead Systems Designer/Programmer - Special Risk Operations

As Lead Systems Designer, was responsible for developing and coding a system for long- and short-term disabilities, life, and AD&D group products.
* As team leader, oversaw system enhancements and conversions; developed thorough documentation and training materials for implementing smooth transition of entire system to Santa Fe.
* Staffed organization to deliver high level of support and ensure seamless operation throughout transition process.

EDUCATION

Bachelor of Arts, 1987 - Magna Cum Laude
TUFTS UNIVERSITY, Boston, MA
Major: Computer Science, Minor: Programming

Extensive continuing professional education with emphasis on technical training, project management, and personnel management programs and seminars.

INTERVIEW TRAINING TECHNIQUES

For many resume-writing professionals, preparing your clients for what to do after the resume is complete is as much a part of the business as the resume writing itself. Consulting with clients about effective interview strategies can be formalized (and become a separate profit center) or it can be done more loosely, as a component of the resume consultation process. In any event, the expertise a resume writer gains over the years can clearly benefit clients; explore this area of knowledge for ways it can benefit your clients while enhancing your bottom line. Many of the suggestions below were provided by the professionals quoted throughout this book. Their comments in this section relate specifically to interviewing techniques.

Hiring Managers' Expertise

Walter S. Truscinski, CPC, the president of Professional Staffing Services of Shelton, Connecticut, is quoted extensively in chapter 9 with regard to preparation of client paperwork. He adds to his "resume remarks" these pointers about effective interviewing:

According to George Eames, president of W. A. Parsons Company, Inc., the following concerns typify the interview (and, ultimately, hiring) process at his firm: "At the initial stage of the interview, we look for 'fit' and push for details regarding the salient points of the accomplishments presented in the resume. We want to know *how* candidates accomplished what they did." Particularly interesting for resume writers to note, George states that "it is especially important for us to assess communication skills [including written ones] when we believe a resume may have been professionally written." He adds that he can generally detect a professionally written resume, typically by its format and "perfect" appearance. "I'll directly ask candidates if they have had their resume professionally prepared. This is not a 'negative,' but I may then ask for samples of business correspondence so as to see their written communications capability. This is to insure that a candidate can communicate concisely and articulately—skills critical in business."

George explains that there are concerns when the verbal communication skills of the interviewee do not match the presentation in the cover letter or resume. This point bears repeating for professional resume writers:

While a resume writer should make the client "look good" in the most professional fashion possible, it is essential that the "voice" in the resume and cover letter appropriately reflect the style of the client. Some "dressing up," of course, is correct—but if the client is *in no way* able to communicate as you, the professional resume writer, have suggested in the paperwork, there could be a break-

- A client still in the early stages of the interview cycle might be presented with this "sometimes innocent question": "George, what is it going to take for you to join our organization?" Walt's recommended response is something along the lines of, "Well, my current salary is $64,000 a year. I'm up for a bonus review in another thirty days. My understanding is that our purpose in getting together is for me to get to know you and better understand your organization and how I might make a potential contribution to your objectives. If you have an interest in that contribution, I'm confident you will want to make me a fair and equitable compensation offer."

- For overqualified candidates or those recently reengineered out of a highly paid position after many years' experience, the question often becomes one of how to present for an opportunity that pays well below the level of compensation previously earned (and how to structure the presentation positively so that the prospective employer doesn't immediately presume that the candidate will "jump ship" for a higher comp package at the first opportunity). Walt recommends that if a candidate was previously earning $85,000 to $90,000 and is applying for a position that has a likely salary of $60,000 (and this knowledge is confirmed "going in"), the matter should be addressed up front in the cover letter accompanying the resume. Suggested language: "First, you should know that while my most recent salary was $90,000, I understand the parameters of this particular position. I want to express my commitment to this opportunity and the professional challenge it represents. These are the types of activities that are important to me and that I want to become involved with. Second, I have reconciled and justified reorganization of my lifestyle so that the salary within the prescribed range will not be an issue on my end."

- If there seem to be concerns about age and possible overqualification, Walt also suggests that "candidates, as an important sales technique, stress to the prospective employer how much they are getting for the money: 'Yes, I have commanded a salary of $90,000 and previously managed a department of twenty individuals. But look at the breadth of experience I can bring in a hands-on management capacity to a small group.'" Walt recommends "selling the *benefit* of the experience and not the negative aspect of being overqualified. Attempt to diffuse any issues with regard to overqualification and age so that you don't give the 'gatekeeper' an opportunity to lock you out of the interview process. Instead, give the hiring manager reasons for *including* you in the process."

down in the subsequent interview process.

In George Eames's opinion, there are several key elements sought in the interview. "We look for a team-oriented approach at our company. If a candidate is responding to every question with, 'Well, I did such-and-such' and 'Yes, I implemented . . . ,' it begs the question: 'Well, did you have support staff or accomplish any of this through collaborating or working with others?' In other words, can this candidate offer more than a one-dimensional viewpoint; does this person have the ability to be cross-trained if hired?" George notes that the biggest favor a candidate can do for him- or herself is to "be yourself. The interview is a two-way process and it should go both ways. A candidate should be interviewing to determine his or her own fit and the appropriateness of the position to personal career goals just as the company is attempting to find out if the candidate would complement the existing organization and bring key attributes to the table." Two of the primary mistakes candidates make: "Talking too much. And not researching any background about the company." Beyond these suggestions, George notes that "keen listening skills and good eye contact" are important skills for any candidate.

As a private consultant and a former employee relations manager for Bristol-Myers Squibb, Cynthia B. Cannon has special insight about what comprises an effective interview. "A lot of what happens involves body language, eye contact, and direct answering of questions," she says. "Some people will go on and on without responding to specific questions that you [as the recruiter] are targeting. This can be time-consuming, and most recruiters simply don't have much time to interview someone." Cindy adds that "candor and honesty are very important. When candidates attempt to duck answers or choose not to offer reasonable explanations to questions, the situation becomes problematic."

Cindy understandably frowns on candidates who fail to show for a scheduled interview without calling to cancel the appointment. "There's no excuse for not making contact. I recall a candidate I interviewed for a professional position who had called in advance of the meeting time to indicate that she was being detained and would be arriving a little late. At the conclusion of the interview—which was successful, by the way—she related to me that the reason she was late in arriving for the interview was that she had been involved in a serious automobile accident and needed to arrange for a cab to get to the interview!"

According to Cindy, "interviewing is all about excavating for what you need to find [as a recruiter], confirming facts, and making sure there is a fit. I call it doing a 'culture' check. There isn't a formula, but once a candidate has been screened by telephone and is scheduled for an interview, we've already ensured that there is presumably a skill set match. Now, the important thing is to determine that there is a fit for both parties."

Robert E. Francis, purchasing manager for Dow-United Technologies, Inc., of Wallingford, Connecticut, reflected upon several faux pas committed in interviews by applicants. Caution your clients to be careful not to repeat these behaviors:

- "Becoming too casual or too friendly too quickly. It's better to have a bit of an edge and be aware that the entire interview process is an evaluation."
- "Making negative remarks about previous positions or employers."
- "Exaggerating or assuming credit for grandiose accomplishments." Bob Francis adds: "What people go through in their normal business lives is generally a series of negotiations and steps toward objectives that are not easily attained. Applicants should be realistic in describing their contributions and careful not to overstate results."

With regard to follow-up activities, Bob was very clear on his bottom line: "It is almost an automatic 'no' if I don't receive a follow-up letter thanking me for an interview; I presume the candidate is not serious or not interested in the opportunity." Bob adds that it is important for applicants "to express their enthusiasm and their assertiveness in following up after an interview."

Peter V. Ferris is the director of marketing and co-general manager for the Automotive Materials Division of The Dexter Corporation, which is headquartered in Windsor Locks, Connecticut (Peter's division is located in Seabrook, New Hampshire). Before joining Dexter in 1991, Peter was the president and general manager of the Natural Juice Companies (with locations in Boston, New York, and Connecticut). His thirteen-year managerial career has included significant recruiting and hiring experience in areas ranging from sales and marketing to highly technical and midlevel management positions.

In discussing the formal interview process, Peter offered particularly insightful recommendations, in part based upon his own experiences. "The most important thing a candidate can do is to thoroughly prepare for the interview process. A personal experience I can share which demonstrates what can happen when not prepared is an interview a recruiter had arranged for me while I was traveling on business from Connecticut to Florida some years ago. The interview was with a contact within the regional office of Pizza Hut in Orlando, Florida; I was under the impression that the position I was interviewing for was to manage several different pizza restaurants. The interview was squeezed in on my way to the airport and I didn't have the opportunity, nor did I *make* the opportunity, to research the company and learn any background information.

"Upon meeting with the person interviewing me, I quickly realized I had made a major mistake. This human resources manager was a Harvard graduate seeking a candidate for a fast-track position within the *parent* corporation; as it turned out, Pizza Hut is part of PepsiCo. The ultimate insult during the interview process was when this manager asked me if I would like to have a Pepsi. My response (before knowing Pizza Hut's affiliation with PepsiCo)? I said, 'No, I'd prefer a Coke instead.'" A valuable learning experience.

"When I interviewed with The Dexter Corporation," Peter notes, "I had already studied several years' worth of annual reports and could quote chapter and verse the mission statement for the corporation. I'd learned from my painful experience with Pizza Hut/PepsiCo the importance of fully preparing before interviewing for a position that really meant something to me—and ultimately I succeeded."

Peter offers these preinterview recommendations: "Ask questions before going into the interview to learn as much as possible about the company, the position, and, most importantly, who the players are that are participating in the interview process. When I was interviewing with Dexter, I initially had two rounds of preliminary interviews. The final interview day extended from 8:00 A.M. until 5:45 P.M., with eight or nine interviews scheduled across the day. I was interviewing with probably the most senior people in the corporation worldwide—culminating with an interview with the CEO himself. The way the process worked, I'm very glad I did *not* know until after the fact that throughout this entire process, if any one player in the interview schedule felt strongly that you were not a viable candidate for the position, the interview process would have immediately ceased—and you would have been politely excused for the balance of the day. A strategy I successfully used? Before going on to each subsequent interview, I would ask the person I'd just interviewed with a little about the *next* person I would be meeting—what his or her position was, area of responsibility, and so on. People like to be asked for their advice."

Peter Ferris favors innovative but professional approaches from prospective employees and appreciates creativity in candidates who are trying to "get in the door." He cites a successful strategy he employed to land an interview at Dannon before making his career transition from Natural Juice to The Dexter Corporation.

As an aside, by way of sharing a little background about the relationship I developed with Peter: We worked together for a number of years when he was president of the Natural Juice Companies. Among a variety of other responsibilities, I handled recruitment and candidate screening activities for sales/management positions throughout the Northeast for Natural Juice. In addition, when Peter was implementing his career change, we worked sporadically (around his busy schedule) for nearly eleven months in developing his personal marketing materials, defining his search approach, and tailoring his highly customized packages. Peter's particularly innovative approach, methodical and professional techniques, and demonstrated expertise allowed him to position himself for a number of fine employment opportunities. One such opportunity that he cultivated (before joining Dexter) was with a company in a similar industry as his Natural Juice Companies: Dannon.

"There were many people interested in Dannon. What I did to distinguish myself as a potential candidate was take some of the products that my company manufactured at the time—several varieties of fresh-squeezed juices—and package a few quarts in a Styrofoam cooler (we used cold-packing material stored in my freezer and assembled the package at midnight in the garage adjacent to my home office!). To this package, I added serving cups and napkins, plus a description of the products and my involvement in the marketing of them. I also enclosed a television videoclip of a business profile about me that had recently run on the evening news. I hired my nephew (navy blazer, tie, and all) to personally drive the package from our Connecticut office to Dannon's corporate headquarters in Westchester, New York. There, he had strict orders not to leave the package at the front desk—he had to hand-deliver it to the person in charge of marketing (I had previously researched and found his name). The package was, in fact, delivered to this individual—and I got an interview immediately. *That's* success—and that's what prospective candidates should be trying to do: get the door open for the interview."

Peter Ferris further recommends that candidates use all possible means to learn as much as they can about a company. "Companies like to hire from similar type molds. A company such as Dexter is technology driven based on product innovation and leadership—and will ideally seek candidates with experience at companies in the same vein. It's important to match the company profile, the company philosophy. For publicly traded companies, candidates should get copies of the annual report and read the CEO's statement on the first two pages; that's the focus and thrust of the business, and the goal should be to demonstrate a match. If the company isn't publicly traded, a candidate should pull a Dun & Bradstreet and find out as much as possible about the company. Use CD-ROMs at a large public library to research a company. Bottom line? Do your homework prior to the interview."

William D. Breck, Ed. D., the superintendent of schools in Durham/Middlefield, Connecticut, describes a number of problems that can occur in candidate interviews. "Probably one of the biggest pitfalls for interviewing is the tendency to talk too much. In responding to specific queries, briefer is better. Candidates are advised to pay close attention to cues—verbal and physical—and to balance their responses." Reiterating a point shared about the writing of a resume, Bill states: "Answer within the context of the question, and be certain to provide enough detail regarding *how* something was accomplished, not simply *what* was achieved. Show that you are a good problem solver, that you can work *with* and *through* people to accomplish goals." Other potential areas for risk in interviewing include appearing self-centered or arrogant, not gearing style to the level of formality—or informality—of the environment, being insensitive to verbal and physical cues, and wanting a position so badly that you lose sight of your own self, strengths, and style. Applicants are encouraged to present themselves as interesting—as well as inspiring—school leaders who are multidimensional.

In describing attributes of the "successful interviewee," Bob Esposito, principal of Brewster School in Durham, Connecticut, notes that "a firm handshake is important, as are good eye contact, an assertive, forthcoming style, and, if possible, demonstrated calmness and competence. Rather than bringing out folders of materials before requested, it is more appropriate to ask if samples can be left behind for review. A sense of humor is always a plus (occasionally candidates are asked to recite their favorite joke—certainly an area of risk for nearly any applicant, and one where advance planning could be a big advantage!)." Bob also reports that, in the interview, questions are framed to draw out candidate interests that extend beyond the classroom—those that might relate to family, reading material, cultural interests, and so forth. Most of the question-and-answer session is open-ended, providing applicants with an opportunity to elaborate as they deem appropriate. It is likely that applicants will be asked questions about their impressions of their own weaknesses and strengths.

Follow-up to an interview provides candidates with a final opportunity to distinguish themselves. "A thank-you letter which is carefully written and conveys enthusiasm, shows forward thinking, reflects upon the interview, and perhaps discusses work ethic is a plus," according to Bob Esposito.

Bob Wolfe, principal at Korn School in Durham, Connecticut, notes that while there are certain key areas that questioning follows during an interview, it is "shaped directly to the applicant. I attempt to do role-playing with regard to situations that are challenging. I want to see how resourceful this candidate is." Of the literally hundreds of questions teaching candidates are likely to be asked, the following were suggested by Bob Wolfe as representative of key areas. The resume professional can use this information to tailor interview training specifically for prospective teachers among their clientele. As an alternative, the questions could be included in a handout and presented to clients with the full resume upon completion of the consultation.

Sample Interview Questions for Teachers

- Why do you want to teach?
- Why do you want to teach in this district or community?
- Describe your personal background.
- What are your professional plans or goals?
- What are your strongest traits? Your weakest?
- What are your attitudes toward extra-duty activities?
- What information do you have about the district?
- What quality in other people is most important to you?
- What do you believe your role and obligations should be in regard to other faculty members?
- Would you enjoy team teaching?
- What techniques do you use in developing rapport with students?
- How do you handle curricular content in classes with many levels of ability?
- How would you individualize instruction in your classroom?
- What do you consider to be the ideal learning environment?
- What teaching techniques are effective for you?
- How do you expect to motivate students?
- What kinds of experiences have you had that will be of help when you begin teaching here?

- Tell me about your student teaching or previous teaching experience.
- Why are you leaving your present position?
- How would you handle discipline problems?
- What procedures work best for you in maintaining discipline?

Types of Interviews

While most interviews will probably not adhere exactly to one of these formats, it is likely that the general tone will pattern a particular format.

Direct interview. In this style of interview, the interviewer maintains absolute and total control. Factual data are amassed through limited and specific questions, often prepared in advance for all candidates for a given position.

Shotgun interview. The interview consists of a series of short, rapidly asked questions, with little or no pattern, jumping from subject matter to subject matter. The concept seems to be fire away and eventually you might hit something.

Indirect interview. This most frequently follows the pattern, "OK, tell me all about yourself." The responsibility for the interview is almost completely turned over to the job candidate. If unlimited time is available, valuable territory might eventually be covered. For the strong, well-prepared candidate, this is the perfect interview format for showcasing his or her experience and talent.

Stress interview. This type of interview (quite rarely conducted, actually) is what applicants most often fear. The interviewee is literally asked to react to an array of stress-producing stimuli—often openly hostile or belligerent in nature. The greater the stress, the lower the trust level and the more difficult it becomes for a candidate, solid or otherwise, to assess the opportunity and fit accurately or give any useful information about his or her background.

Patterned or structured interview. The conversation is guided by the interviewer, yet the interviewee is encouraged and given the opportunity to speak freely and at length about relevant topics. Even though the format is controlled, information is gathered in a spontaneous manner that prompts most candidates to react favorably and perform well.

It is impossible for candidates to know in advance the style of interview they will be facing (and within the same company, different interviewers are likely to use different styles). The best advice? Ensure that your clients are well acquainted with the differing interview styles and are well prepared for them all. You may also wish to "arm" your clients with copies of the following few pages, which detail typical questions interviewers ask and the attributes or characteristics most interviewers will be looking for in the course of the thirty or sixty minutes scheduled for the interview.

CANDIDATE ATTRIBUTES

- Appearance
- Mannerisms
- Ease of expression
- Responsiveness
- Ability to communicate
- Flexibility
- Demonstrated leadership
- Self-motivation
- Productivity
- Skill level
- Required training
- Relevant work experience
- Educational background
- Intelligence
- Knowledge level
- Team player
- Reaction to authority
- Attitudes about work and people
- Sincerity
- Honesty
- Perseverance

- Self-opinion
- Outside interests
- Emotional stability
- Personal values
- Job expectations
- Energy level
- Time management skills
- Maturity of judgment
- Independence
- Future wants
- Decision-making ability
- Ability to handle pressure
- Listening skills
- Importance of success
- Self-confidence
- Sense of humor
- Warmth
- Sensitivity to feedback
- Integrity
- Motivation
- Determination

SAMPLE GENERAL INTERVIEW QUESTIONS

JOB-RELATED

- Tell me about your job with [name of firm].

- What aspects of the position did you find most satisfying and stimulating—and why?

- What aspects did you care for least—and why?

- What were some problem situations or challenges you encountered while performing that job? How did you end up handling them?

- Was your assignment a one-person operation or did it call for a team effort? How did you feel about operating in that way?

- How did your starting salary on your new assignment compare with what you were earning on the previous one?

- What would you say were your major accomplishments in that job?

- What were some of the things that you may have done less well, things that perhaps pointed to the need for further development?

- What are some of the things you look for in any job assignment? Things that give you satisfaction?

- If you could choose any job, what would you pick? Why?

- What type of work can you see yourself doing five years from now?

- What was the most difficult assignment you ever had? What made it so?

- How could your present job be made more meaningful? Have you discussed this with anyone? What were the results?

- What were the circumstances leading up to your decision to leave that job?

- You've been unemployed for a period of time . . . what activities have you been participating in to remain current in your field?

- When the process of reengineering transpired at your former company, how was it determined that your position would be eliminated?

- What kind of people do you like to work with?

- What kind of people do you find it most difficult to work with?

- What do you need from your manager in order to be as successful as you can be?

- What are some of the things your previous supervisor did that you particularly liked or disliked? Why did you feel that way?

- How do you feel your boss rated your work performance? What were some of the things he or she indicated you could improve upon?

JOB- AND COMPANY-RELATED

- How do you evaluate our company as a place to build your future?

- I know you don't have a good perspective on this job yet—not being in it—but from your present vantage point, what would you say there is about the job that is particularly appealing to you?

- What is it that you are looking for in a company?

- What do you see in this job that makes it appealing to you that you do not have in your present [or last] job?

- What kinds of things do you feel most confident doing?

- What are some of the things you are either doing now or have thought about doing that are self-development activities?

- In what ways do you feel you have grown most in the past two to three years?

EDUCATION-RELATED

- What do you believe is the basic meaning of a college education?

- What do you believe is the most valuable contribution it will make or has made to your life?

- How did you choose the school you attended?

- What type of program did you take? How did you decide to concentrate on that field?

- If you could choose again, would you major in the same thing? Why?

- In what areas were you most interested? In what areas did you do the best work?
- Which classes did you care for least? In which classes did you have the most difficulty with the work?
- What were your grades like?
- How large was your class? Where, approximately, did you rank in the class?
- In what extracurricular activities did you participate? Why did you select these?
- What did you learn from those activities that serves you well today?
- What went into your decision not to finish your formal education?
- Did you ever consider continuing or extending your education? What happened?
- What advice would you give someone just starting school today?
- How did you finance your education?
- What would you say is the most important thing you learned from your college career?
- Have you had any specialized training or courses since leaving school?
- What would you consider to be your special achievements during school?
- How do you feel your education has prepared you to achieve your career aspirations?

EXTERNAL INTERESTS AND CIVIC INVOLVEMENT
- What do you do with your spare time?
- What are your hobbies or special interests?
- In what ways does your use of spare time help you in your position?
- If you had more spare time, what would you do that you can't do now?

- Are there skills you possess that are used during your leisure time that you have been able to employ in a work situation?

- What is most important to you about your time off the job?

- What do you do to relax?

- In what civic or community activities are you involved?

- Would relocation be a problem for you to consider?

- Is travel a consideration?

COMPETENCIES, DEVELOPMENT NEEDS, GOALS, AND AMBITION

- How would people who know you describe you?

- What kind of first impression do you feel you make? How does that impression differ once someone gets to know you?

- Looking over all the areas that we've covered, what are your most positive assets?

- Are there any other strengths I should know about?

- At this point in your life and career, what have you achieved?

- Since we all have ways in which we need to develop further, in what areas do you feel you could make some improvement?

- Tell me about a time when you received some "constructive criticism." How did you feel about it? What did you do as a result?

- When you are backed into a corner and have to stand your ground, what type of behavior has worked best for you? Please provide an example.

- How do you go about learning from others?

- Where do you see yourself going from here?

- What is your long-term career objective?

- What would you say has accounted for your fine progress to date?

- What would you say are some of the basic factors that motivate you?

SELF-APPRAISAL QUESTIONS

- What skills do you have that might account for your fine success in [field or profession]?

- Of course, not all things come easily. What was there about this particular position as a [job or title] that made it a bit difficult for you?

- What was there about this particular position that appealed [or did not appeal] to you? Why do you suppose you liked [or disliked] it?

- How would you evaluate yourself as a [job or title]? Good? Fair? Poor? What traits or skills do you have that might have accounted for your success?

- If I were to call up your supervisor and ask what kind of [job or title] you were, what do you suppose he or she would say?

- You said that you have ambitions to become a [job or title]. What is there about yourself that makes you think you would be a good [job or title]? What area do you feel you might still need to develop before you could perform at an excellent level in that position?

CHAPTER THIRTEEN

RUNNING THE BUSINESS— AND EXPANDING IT

PROFESSIONAL ASSOCIATIONS

The Professional Association of Resume Writers

Frank Fox is the executive director of the Professional Association of Resume Writers (PARW), headquartered in St. Petersburg, Florida (information regarding membership appears in the Appendix). He also serves as executive director of the National Association of Secretarial Services (NASS). Frank founded both professional associations, NASS in 1981 and PARW in 1990. According to statistics compiled by PARW, of the approximately 3,200 resume services nationwide, nearly 1,000 are members of PARW; roughly 25 percent of this total (about 285) are home-based. As my research supported, a sizable number of home-based resume professionals also provide adjunct professional services—from career counseling and employment screening to word-processing, secretarial, and desktop publishing services.

Frank Fox describes PARW's mission as follows: "To help every member survive, grow, and succeed (to whatever extent they aspire), and to continually elevate the image, acceptance, and prestige of the resume profession." PARW provides a menu of benefits to members, including the opportunity to earn the credential of CPRW (Certified Professional

Resume Writer) through a study, testing, and certification process.

Membership in this professional association is strongly encouraged (by me, many of my colleagues, and, of course, the executive director). As Frank states, "PARW members, by virtue of their professional interest in joining their industry's association, demonstrate that they are dedicated and committed to serving their clients, staying current with ideas and information that they can use in marketing to their clients more effectively, and so on." The association publishes a monthly newsletter for its members and presents a three-day national convention once each year (the location varies).

In describing some of the benefits that inure to PARW members, Frank Fox notes that "when PARW started in 1990, the first members called after they had placed the 'Member of PARW' logo in their Yellow Pages ads to say that they were booking more and more clients because the affiliation with PARW made them stand out as professionals over competitors listed in the same directory who weren't members." He adds, "Now we're hearing this same reaction to CPRW status."

Frank presents the following four steps as recommendations to home-based resume service professionals who are just starting out:

- "Read and understand everything you can lay your hands on concerning the job placement field. There should be particular emphasis on resume-writing strategies and techniques, but this study should also include interviewing, career search techniques, use of cover letters, occupational titles and job descriptions, trends in your local job market, and so forth. In short, do everything possible to become an expert in the field *before* your first client comes to you for expert help!"

- "Have a talent for writing. An effective resume markets an individual's strengths, credentials, and experience while injecting a sense of enthusiasm and the client's personality. And the principal component a resume writer has to work with is words (design can help draw the reader's attention, but the words sell the candidate). The resume has to answer the question: 'Why should I hire this candidate instead of the fifty, hundred, or five hundred other applicants who have sent their resumes for the same position?'" With regard to writing ability, Frank adds that "the importance of this skill should not be taken lightly, because writing is what a resume is all about. Ideally, a new resume service owner will have paid experience as an advertising copywriter, newspaper reporter, freelance writer who has actually been published and paid for his or her work, and so on. Those who have never done much or any writing before should either get some professional experience (perhaps try to get a job at an established resume service) or start out as a retype service. That allows the aspiring owner to work with lots of resumes, suggest minor changes to a client's text, and then, if these changes are accepted—and as clients begin to report back favorable responses from interviewers—move into the full composition phase of resume writing."

- "Be professional. Join PARW. Earn the CPRW credential. Attend PARW conventions. Network with other PARW members. Network through other local business and professional organizations. Write articles for PARW, your local newspaper, and business magazines. Treat your clients with respect, compassion, fairness, and honesty."

- "Spend the money to do it right! Clients expect you to have not only the expertise to do their resume right, but also the tools. Have the computer, printer, software, and other office equipment necessary to do the job. Have a selection of papers on hand. Spend the money on advertising so people know about you—and keep spending it even when you're booked solid for a few weeks. Spend the money necessary to stay current in your resume profession and to learn how to run aspects of your business you don't know much about: Take a bookkeeping or accounting course at night, for example."

Frank makes a definitive statement that can't be emphasized enough: "Business owners who try to get by spending nickels and dimes too often find they can only charge nickels and dimes for the service they offer. How an owner positions his or her business from the very beginning can define that business forever."

In summarizing some of the additional benefits to PARW membership for the home-based resume-writing professional, Frank Fox notes: "We are here to help every resume writer, at whatever stage of professional and business development he or she may be. Someone just getting started will benefit from the wealth of information and experiences of those members who have dealt with all of the same problems and challenges. The entrepreneur doesn't have to reinvent the wheel or make costly mistakes at the very beginning when he or she can least afford mistakes. And, as the beginner advances in skill and success, PARW is there to introduce other members who have the experience and information needed for the next step, and the next, and the next.

"There's also the PARW benefit of 'not being alone' that applies to any home-based business owner who, perhaps more than those who are out and about in the business community every day, tends to feel isolated and cut off from the real world. PARW and its members become an outside link with others who understand what a resume writer does, what the process is like, what the problems and frustrations are, and who know the answers to these business questions. Sometimes our role is to reaffirm that what an owner is doing is accepted and right; other times, we provide what one member described as 'I didn't know what I didn't know.'"

Frank Fox offers this by way of final inspiration to resume writers: "I think the future of the resume field has never been better. The job market in recent years has made everyone in the workforce aware of the vital importance their resume represents in a successful job search. Ten years ago, for example, it was unusual for clerical applicants, blue-collar workers, and others to have a resume. They expected to fill out a job application on-site, be interviewed, and get a job on that basis. Today it seems that every serious job seeker needs to have a resume, regardless of income or job level.

"As the number of people using resumes increases, the distinguishing factor in this glut of paper then becomes 'Which resumes are best?' And that's where the pro will shine, and the amateur will be left behind. If the resume isn't good, a job seeker might as well not have one at all.

"As more people are exposed to PARW, PARW members, CPRW sta-

QUOTABLE INSPIRATION

"Certify as soon as possible. Join a local service network with members who do what you do . . . or are planning to do; also join PARW. Prepare a well-worded Yellow Pages ad. Attend conferences and other events, plus use other available means to keep your knowledge up to date. Make yourself visible in your community (join local chamber of commerce, and so on)."—*Georgia Adamson, CPRW, Adept Business Services (Campbell, California)*

Running the Business and Expanding It

tus, and so forth, members of our industry will be in increasing demand. Because if a resume is worth having, then it's worth having the best. And PARW, particularly those who are CPRWs, will represent the very best."

National Resume Writer's Association

The National Resume Writer's Association (NRWA) is a new professional organization built on membership-driven goals and needs. It was officially established in February of 1997. The NRWA, a not-for-profit trade association, is dedicated to providing readily available mentoring, education, and support services to the resume-writing community. The NRWA was established to be a democratically run organization with regional, member-elected representation on a national board of directors. The organization, as described by its president, Martin Weitzman, "is, and shall remain, an inclusive organization, actively seeking and welcoming input and active participation from all our members."

Membership benefits include the following:
- Bi-monthly meetings and seminars, open to the membership.
- A professional certification program designed to promote the best resume writers that North America has to offer, while providing legal protection.
- The Ethics and Standards Committee, which will assure that the membership adheres to the organization's Code of Ethics and proper business practices at all times.
- Annual NRWA Conventions to foster the organization's educational goals.
- The NRWA Website that provides a sophisticated interface for all of the organization's members. Private chat rooms and other innovations are presently under development, not the least of which is eventual teleconferencing of the organization's meetings for national membership viewing on the Internet.
- A videotape program that enables members from across the country to observe workshops and meetings without actually attending. Current tapes include telephone techniques, add-on services, office automatation, and pricing strategies for the resume-writing business.

- *The Writer's Resource*, the NRWA newsletter, which provides innovative articles and features to guide the professional resume writer through every nuance of the business,. Some features include the "Critics Corner," an unbiased review of products (books, tapes, etc.), targeted to the resume community; "Techno Talk," which addresses issues relating to ever-changing technologies and related problems; and "Help Wanted," a column designed to answer questions the membership may have on any number of issues, such as "Do you sell clients the disk, and, if so, for how much?" or "Do you provide a free consultation, and, if so, of what does that consist?"
- A cooperative client newsletter, developed by and for the organization's members for distribution to their clients.
- Member discounts on goods and services are a reality. The NRWA has negotiated discounts with a number of vendors including paper suppliers (PM Resource and Metro Paper) and an on-line resume posting service (Wayne Gonyea's On-Line Solutions).

Additional membership information appears in the Appendix.

OPTIONS FOR EXPANDING YOUR BUSINESS

You will quickly note that some of the ideas shared here about expanding your business are equally relevant when starting your business. At this point, you are simply capitalizing on key strengths you may possess in certain areas of the resume profession and building in those directions.

Lecture, Teach—The Sky's the Limit!

Lecturing in your community as well as delivering presentations before your peers at national conferences are two good ways to gain additional credibility and visibility within the resume industry. These ventures may or may not be directly income-producing—but you can nearly always be sure that when you gain visibility and the often accompanying publicity and free advertising, you are building the potential for increased revenue stream in the future for your business. A community lecture may be as simple as a fifteen-minute address delivered to members of the Exchange Club or the chamber of commerce. A likely topic might be "Developing

Effective Personal Marketing Materials"—a quick overview describing techniques that members of the audience can use to refine their resume and cover letter materials.

You might also consider developing a presentation to supplement a local library's series on employment and job search strategies. Thirty to sixty minutes in length is probably the typical program length—and with plenty of opportunity for question-and-answer with the participants, you can easily take the types of materials you draw upon in an individual resume client consultation and build them into an interactive workshop.

If you especially enjoy writing, developing an occasional or regular column for the business section of your local newspaper is a good way to display your creative talent, offer salient career advice, and gain excellent visibility—and status as "the resume expert" in your community. Contact business editors to explore options for creating such a feature. In addition, convey your willingness to share information in the broad field of employment—as in being contacted for "pull quotes" on any stories the business editor might be compiling that touch on your areas of expertise and draw upon the fact that you have your finger on the pulse of what is happening with regard to employment in your area.

Lastly, if you enjoy speaking before a group, you might want to consider building a formal workshop out of your resume, cover letter, and career-marketing materials and delivering this program either independently or through a structured format such as a community adult education program. See the Appendix for details about a complete package I have prepared for entrepreneurs who want to offer resume, cover letter, and personal-marketing workshops through adult education programs; you can use it "as is" or tailor it to your own market. The Appendix also includes information about an excellent guide written by Dawn LaFontaine for marketing yourself to the community at large.

Need Help? Explore Adding Subcontractors or Employees

The entrepreneur's dream-come-true scenario: Your business has grown to the point where it is no longer feasible, or even possible, for you to maintain the high level of service on which you've built your reputation and meet existing client demand—let alone attract new clients. Your options? A good starting strategy is to ensure that your fee structure properly reflects the level of skill and quality you are providing. An old rule of thumb (often quoted by the seasoned "pros" in our industry): If no one is complaining about your fees—that is, if you never lose a prospective resume client because of your rates—you probably aren't charging enough. Look at it this way: If you raise your rates 20 percent and lose the bottom 20 percent tier, you probably will find yourself handling more of the top-end resume work, spending less time at work, and making more money.

After reviewing your rate structure to ensure that it is appropriate for your efforts and your market, there are several directions in which you might wish to proceed. You may opt, as some in this field do, to specialize in certain aspects of the business—such as development and creation of resume materials—and turn away other work, such as preparation of individualized cover letters or basic retypes of existing resumes. Of course, you can simply decline to accept a project in which you are not interested. But your clients, especially those who refer others to you, will be more satisfied and appreciative of your professionalism if you refer them to another professional service that *can* handle their project needs. You can investigate cultivating formalized "referral" services with a secretarial service, for instance, and establish a mechanism for earning a flat fee or a percentage on each referred client (check out Nina Feldman's referral-program documents in the Appendix if this aspect of building business interests you). Or you may decide that an "informal" referral system appeals to you more—one in which you establish a referral relationship with a single secretarial service that does not offer resume services; instead of a "fee-based" relationship, you simply agree to refer to this service all of your cover letter and application-typing work, for example, in exchange for referrals of all resume consultation projects that the secretarial service receives.

The remaining option to consider is whether or not keeping the business "in-house" makes sense and, if it does, how you can accommodate the growing workload. There are basically two ways: hire an employee (full- or part-time) or establish your own subcontractor network (one or more people who handle work for your business from their homes). This is an area where I recommend you proceed very cautiously—and where it definitely will make sense to contact an accounting professional if you lack expertise. The rules regarding employment are somewhat complex—

some would say very complex!—and the distinction between an employee and a subcontractor is a very important one. Guidelines are available through the Internal Revenue Service (address information is provided in the Appendix). By supplementing the information in the IRS publications with advice from a CPA, you should be in a good position to know the best way to proceed in your circumstances.

Essentially, subcontractors do not work for you directly; rather, they perform work according to their own schedule, outside your home, using their own equipment. Also, you are not the only consumer of a subcontractor's services; he or she provides services for other people as well. A subcontractor provides an invoice to you for work performed on a project basis, usually billing at a predetermined hourly rate. Generally, a relationship is established with a subcontractor with some sense of the anticipated number of hours or projects planned on a week-to-week basis. Subcontractors are paid for the total number of hours they bill you; they are then responsible for handling their own payment of taxes, filing of quarterly returns, and so on.

An employee relationship is clearer; the individual works under your direct supervision in your home office according to a fairly fixed schedule (but it can be flexible for a part-time employee). You, as the employer, establish the work to be done, how it is to be performed, and provide the work space and equipment. In computing wages, you are responsible for withholding social security and unemployment taxes and filing the appropriate returns. You must have an employer identification number (separate from your own social security number). You may determine it is worth the incremental expense to engage the services of a payroll processing company to handle payroll, even for one part-time employee; such companies handle filing of all necessary returns, prepare paychecks according to the schedule you stipulate, and provide you with weekly, quarterly, and year-end tax documents—all for a fee. Your accounting professional can provide further information regarding both employee and subcontracting options.

Because this book is written for home-based entrepreneurs, I will devote little space to considering expansion of your business to "the outside world" (such as a private office, retail location, or executive-suite space). As successful as my own business is—to take just one example—I *never* intend to "move out." Some critics say, "Oh, as soon as your children are further along in school or grown, you'll *want* a real office." Well, some-one wise once said, "Never say 'never!'" But I had my home business long before I had my kids—and I plan to have it long after my kids are grown!

Keep in mind a very important fact when reinforcing your desire to operate a home-based business: Experts state that if you move a home-based business to an office- or suite-based location, in order to equal the profits generated in the home-based business, you must *triple* your revenues. In other words, to cover the major increases in overhead and costs (usually related to the one person at minimum you would have to hire, just to provide coverage and reception during regular office hours), your sales will need to be three times what they were for your business when you were home-based—just to stay even!

Ancillary Profit Centers

Once a resume service is fully equipped to offer its clients professional products through state-of-the-art word processing and laser printing, the savvy entrepreneur might not be able to resist the appeal of using such capital investments in other ways to bring in additional revenues. High-lighted below are just some of the ways that the business of providing resume services can be expanded, *if desired,* to generate cash flow. And for those resume professionals in their first year or two, the ability to offer other services using the equipment that has already been purchased for the resume business can be an excellent way to smooth over the cash flow "peaks and valleys" that naturally occur in a start-up endeavor.

Most home-based resume services provide some degree of word pro-cessing and secretarial services to their resume clientele through prepara-tion of the resume documents and tailored cover letters for job searches. If this is an option you are already providing—and in the interest of offer-ing your clients "full service" and "one-stop shopping," I highly recom-mend that you do just this—you may wish to explore ways in which you can expand some of these services to other clients in your market area.

Once you have established a positive working relationship with a resume client and this individual successfully lands his or her next posi-tion, you have a good basis already in place for marketing additional ser-vices. How this frequently transpires is that a satisfied resume client contacts your office to see if you know someone who could handle word processing and editing of an employee orientation manual or some similar project, such as an in-house newsletter or a mailing to shareholders. The options for generating overlapping, add-on business with resume clientele are numerous—and probably limited only by your interest level and ability. You might not be interested in taking on a large project requiring word-processing skills (say, a 200-page policy-and-procedure manual), but after exploring the option of using a subcontractor to do the typing, you may want to consider overseeing the project for a client—and farming out the bulk of the work to a trusted subcontractor. You can reserve final editing or proofreading responsibility, charge a premium for this time, and mark up the subcontractor's fee as well for a reasonable profit on such business.

On the other hand, there may very well be areas in which you *are* interested in channeling some of your energies. For example, working with corporate training departments or individual training consultants in developing materials designed for specific audiences within a company can be especially compatible with a resume service business. Depending upon your background and expertise, you might wish to become involved in writing such materials—or in editing and typesetting companion documents.

Regardless of the new areas you branch into, if expanding the scope of your business is your objective, you would be well served to implement a regular client communiqué (such as a quarterly newsletter, suggested in chapter 10). Using such a device, you can constantly increase your circulation simply by adding the names and addresses of your ever-increasing roster of resume clientele. You can determine which services you most want to provide—and market them accordingly through a newsletter mailing to your regular resume clients. There are numerous ways that resume professionals have effectively parlayed their editorial and design skills into profitable areas that enhance their home-based resume service businesses.

AFTERTHOUGHT

To every resume service entrepreneur and every aspiring resume writer, I salute your courage and motivation. You have embarked on the most rewarding journey of your professional life. I'm confident you'll discover the numerous satisfactions I've enjoyed—and I encourage you to pursue your passion in building your home-based business. In closing, consider G. W. F. Hegel's observation:

We may affirm absolutely that nothing great in the world has been accomplished without passion.

—Georg Wilhelm Friedrich Hegel,
Philosophy of History (1832)

APPENDIX

A questionnaire form like the one on the following pages is especially useful when first beginning resume consultation and writing; some professionals always use similar tools, regardless of level of experience. If you do employ such a form, you should also have a pad of paper to use during the consultation to record additional information.

SAMPLE RESUME QUESTIONNAIRE

Date of Client Consultation _____

Client Name _____

Address, City, State, Zip _____

Telephone Numbers to Use on Resume   (home) _____

(business) _____

(fax) _____

(Pager) _____

(E-mail address) _____

(Before getting into questions about client's background)

Purpose for Developing Resume

_____

_____

_____

_____

Ways in Which Client Will Use Resume for Job Search

_____

_____

_____

_____

Develop Cover Letter   Y / N

Ideas for Cover Letter

_____

_____

_____

Professional Experience

Company _____

City/State _____

Total Time with this Company (in months/years) _____
_____

Title of Most Recent/Current Position _____
_____

Time Frame in this Position _____
_____

Key Responsibilities/Accomplishments _____
_____

Achievement About Which Client Is Most Proud _____
_____

Company City/State _____
_____

Total Time with this Company (in months/years) _____
_____

Title of Position _____
_____

Time Frame in this Position _____
_____

Key Responsibilities/Accomplishments _____
_____

Achievement About Which Client Is Most Proud _____
_____

Areas to address: Number of direct/indirect reports; human resources responsibilities (recruiting? interviewing? hiring? training? supervising? managing? developing? terminating?); any programs developed/implemented? For sales professionals—performance to quota and time period, results, increase by "X" percentage, any cost savings or productivity gains (in dollars, percent), and so on.

Company _____

City/State _____

Total Time with this Company (in months/years) _____

_____

Title of Most Recent/Current Position _____

_____

Time Frame in this Position _____

_____

Key Responsibilities/Accomplishments _____

_____

Achievement About Which Client Is Most Proud _____

_____

Company _____

City/State _____

Total Time with this Company (in months/years) _____

_____

Title of Most Recent/Current Position _____

_____

Time Frame in this Position _____

_____

Key Responsibilities/Accomplishments _____

_____

Achievement About Which Client Is Most Proud _____

_____

Education

College/University

City/State

Degree Held   Year Earned

Major   Minor

GPA (for a recent graduate only)

College/University

City/State

Degree Held   Year Earned

Major   Minor

GPA (for a recent graduate only)

Licenses/Certifications Held

Type   Year

Type   Year

Type   Year

Type   Year

Internships

Institution/Company
_____

City/State
_____

Position Title _____ Months/Years _____

Highlights
_____
_____
_____
_____

Institution/Company
_____

City/State
_____

Position Title _____ Months/Years _____

Highlights
_____
_____
_____
_____

Institution/Company
_____

City/State
_____

Position Title _____ Months/Years _____

Highlights
_____
_____
_____
_____

Military Background

Branch of Service _____

Locations (if relevant) _____

Position/Rank Achieved _____

Years of Service _____

Honorable Discharge? _____

Key Accomplishments/Special Recognition/Awards _____

_____

_____ _____

_____

Special Skills

Computer Proficiency? Hardware _____

Programs/Applications _____

Languages? (fluency—verbal/written) _____

Civic/Community Memberships

Organization Name: _____

Years Involved: _____

Positions Held: _____

_____

_____

Professional Memberships

Organization Name

Years Involved

Positions Held

Recognition/Awards

Publications

Article Title

Publication Name

Coauthor?

Year

Speaking Engagements

Topic of Speech

Organization Addressed

Keynote Speaker?

Year

Ideas for Objective Statement (if used)

(professional/career goals)

_____

_____

_____

_____

_____

_____

Ideas for Summary of Qualifications (if used)

(characteristics, traits, attributes, key accomplishments)

_____

_____

_____

_____

_____

_____

References

Name _____

Title _____

Company _____

Address _____

_____

City/State/Zip _____

Home Telephone _____

Office Telephone _____

Name _____

Title _____

Company _____

Address _____

_____

City/State/Zip _____

Home Telephone _____

Office Telephone _____

ABBREVIATED PROFILES OF COLLEAGUES

One of the fascinating aspects of the field of resume writing is the numerous options that exist for building a highly successful business. Throughout this text I have interspersed recommendations, experiences, and inspirations of colleagues in our industry. I've presented information about the variety of styles and diversity of backgrounds found among professionals in this industry. Some of this information was extracted from extensive questionnaires completed by resume professionals from around the country. More than 250 home-based professional resume writers were contacted; the profiles of the individuals selected for inclusion (whose candid recommendations and motivational messages appear throughout the text) are detailed in alphabetical order in the following section.

Resume Professional:	Georgia Adamson, CPRW
Company:	Adept Business Services
City/State:	Campbell, California
Year Established:	1991
Equipment/Software:	PC 486 and Pentium 90 (custom built); HP LaserJet IV Plus; WordPerfect, Microsoft Word for Windows

Resume Professional:	Vivian Belen, CPRW
Company:	The Job Search Specialist
City/State:	Fair Lawn, New Jersey
Year Established:	1990
Equipment/Software:	IBM compatible; HP LaserJet IIP, WordPerfect

Resume Professional:	Janette M. Campbell
Company:	Business Assistants
City/State:	Washougal, Washington
Year Established:	1988
Equipment/Software:	PC 386 sx; Panasonic XKP-1124, HP LaserJet IIP; WordPerfect, Microsoft Word, Microsoft Excel, Alpha 4, Quickbooks

Resume Professional:	Cathy Cousear
Company:	Institute on Human Service Resources
City/State:	Fresh Meadows, New York
Year Established:	1994
Equipment/Software:	Macintosh 575; laser printer (300 dpi); ClarisWorks, Personal Page

Resume Professional:	Carla L. Culp, CPRW
Company:	Best Impression Resume Writing & Design
City/State:	Edwardsville, Illinois
Year Established:	1982
Equipment/Software:	IBM compatibles (486 dx4 66, 486 sx 25, 386 dx 40); HP LaserJet MV (600 dpi); WordPerfect for Windows, Microsoft Word for Windows

Resume Professional:	Barbie Dallmann, CPRW
Company:	Happy Fingers Word Processing & Resume Service
City/State:	Charleston, West Virginia
Year Established:	1984
Equipment/Software:	IBM compatibles (486 and 386); HP LaserJet IIIP (300 dpi), HP DeskJet; WordPerfect (DOS and Windows), Q&A, Graphic Impact, Dollars & Sense

Resume Professional:	Wendy S. Enelow, CPRW
Company:	The Advantage, Inc.
City/State:	Lynchburg, Virginia
Year Established:	1986
Equipment/Software:	IBM compatibles (486 and 386); HP LaserJet IIIs (300 dpi); PageMaker, Word Star, Quickbooks, Microsoft Excel, Microsoft PowerPoint, Windows

Resume Professional: Alan D. Ferrell
Company: ADF Professional Resumes
City/State: Lafayette, Indiana
Year Established: 1993
Equipment/Software: Macintosh LC475; Apple Laser Writer II (300 dpi), HP LaserJet 4 (600 dpi); Microsoft Word

Resume Professional: Emily Goss-Crona, CPRW
Company: Boulder Valley Secretarial Solutions, Inc.
City/State: Longmont, Colorado
Year Established: 1992
Equipment/Software: IBM compatible; Canon LPB 860 (600 dpi); WordPerfect, WP Presentations, PageMaker, Microsoft Word

Resume Professional: Jo Hammonds
Company: Words Plus Secretarial & Resume Service
City/State: Douglasville, Georgia
Year Established: 1990
Equipment/Software: Compaq Prolinea 4/33 (486); HP LaserJet III (300 dpi), HP 560C, Panasonic 1124K; WordPerfect, Microsoft Word, Microsoft Publisher

Resume Professional: Jacqueline K. Herter
Company: Professional Word Processing
City/State: Kodiak, Alaska
Year Established: 1988
Equipment/Software: IBM compatible (486); laser printer (300 dpi); WordPerfect, MYOB, Quicken, Quickbooks, EZ-DOT, Windows

Resume Professional:	Pat Kendall, CPRW
Company:	Advanced Resume Concepts
City/State:	Aloha, Oregon
Year Established:	1982
Equipment/Software:	IBM PC 486; NEC Postscript laser printer; Ventura Publisher, Word for Windows, Corel Draw

Resume Professional:	Anne G. Kramer, CPRW
Company:	Alpha Bits
City/State:	Virginia Beach, Virginia
Year Established:	1983
Equipment/Software:	IBM compatible (486 dx 33); laser printer (600 dpi); WordPerfect (DOS and Windows)

Resume Professional:	Carrie A. Kuntz
Company:	Professional Typing & Resume Service
City/State:	Ontario, California
Year Established:	1986
Equipment/Software:	IBM compatible; Panasonic laser printer; Microsoft Word, Lotus 1-2-3, Harvard Graphics, dbase III+

Resume Professional:	Louise Kursmark, CPRW
Company:	Best Impression
City/State:	Cincinnati, Ohio
Year Established:	1982
Equipment/Software:	Macintosh Quadra 650; HP LaserJet 4M (600 dpi); Microsoft Word, PageMaker, Freehand, Photoshop, Quicken, Persuasion

Resume Professional: Dawn LaFontaine
Company: The Business Wordsmith
City/State: Ashland, Massachusetts
Year Established: 1993
Equipment/Software: IBM compatible; laser printer (300 dpi); Word for Windows, PageMaker, Microsoft Excel, PowerPoint

Resume Professional: Rhodney LaLand
Company: LaLand Resume and Career Services
Country: Saudi Arabia
Year Established: 1988
Equipment/Software: IBM compatibles (486 dx 99 and 386 dx 33); HP IIIP laser printer (300 dpi), HP 560C inkjet printer; Windows, AmiPro, Quick & Easy Fed Jobs, Accent (multilingual word processor) dbase for Windows, Corel Draw

Resume Professional: Kathy McConnell, CPRW
Company: The Oval Office Resume & Career Services
City/State: St. Clair, Michigan
Year Established: 1985
Equipment/Software: IBM compatible; laser printer; WordPerfect, Windows, Microsoft Works, Quicken

Resume Professional: Jan Melnik, CPRW
Company: Absolute Advantage
City/State: Durham, Connecticut
Year Established: 1983
Equipment/Software: Power Macintosh 7100/66 (PowerPC), Macintosh IIvx, Macintosh PowerBook 100; HP LaserJet 4M Plus (600 dpi); Microsoft Word, PageMaker, Microsoft Excel, Quicken, Dollars & Sense

Resume Professional: Joann Milazzo
Company: Joann Milazzo Secretarial Services
City/State: Hammonton, New Jersey
Year Established: 1989
Equipment/Software: IBM compatible (386); HP LaserJet IIIP
                       (300 dpi); WordPerfect, CAPS

Resume Professional: Shelley Newman, CPRW
Company: Ability Plus
City/State: Winthrop, Massachusetts
Year Established: 1994
Equipment/Software: IBM compatible (486 dx 33); HP LaserJet
                       4P (600 dpi); Microsoft Word for Windows,
                       Microsoft Publisher

Resume Professional: Cindy K. Patton, CPRW
Company: Choice Business Service
City/State: Gulfport, Mississippi
Year Established: 1991
Equipment/Software: Acer Pentium, Positive (486 dx 33); two
                       AST 486 33s; laser printer (300 dpi); Page-
                       Maker, WordPerfect, WinWay for Resumes

Resume Professional: Carol Ribar
Company: Professional Office Services, Inc.
City/State: Island Lake, Illinois
Year Established: 1988
Equipment/Software: IBM compatible; laser printer (300 dpi);
                       WordPerfect, PageMaker, Lotus 1-2-3, PC
                       File, Corel Draw

Resume Professional: Penni D. Schratz
Company: Resume Composition & Design
City/State: Traverse City, Michigan
Year Established: 1994
Equipment/Software: Gateway 2000; HP 4Plus (600 dpi); Microsoft Word, AmiPro, Microsoft Works, Freelance Graphics, Harvard Graphics, WordPerfect, Quark XPress, Lotus 1-2-3, Microsoft Excel, Superpaint

Resume Professional: Connie S. Stevens
Company: A+ Secretarial Office Support Services
City/State: Radcliff, Kentucky
Year Established: 1973
Equipment/Software: IBM 486; laser printer (600 dpi), InkJet (300 dpi); WordPerfect for Windows, Microsoft Publisher for Windows, Microsoft Works for Windows, Quicken for Windows, Lotus 1-2-3, Harvard Graphics, Microsoft Word for Windows, QuickLinkII

Resume Professional: Cheryl Stoycoff
Company: C&C Publications
City/State: Stockton, California
Year Established: 1994
Equipment/Software: Packard Bell PC (486 DX 2); laser printer (600 dpi), color inkjet (300 dpi); WordPerfect, PageMaker, Corel Draw, Photo Styler

MISCELLANEOUS RESOURCES

Government Agencies

Internal Revenue Service
1111 Constitution Avenue NW
Washington, DC 20224

Small Business Administration
P.O. Box 15434
Ft. Worth, TX 76119

Merchant Account Status

Discover Card Services, Inc.
401 Columbus Avenue
Valhalla, NY 10595
(800–347–2000)

Professional Associations

National Resume Writers' Association (NRWA)
8 Croydon Court
Englishtown, NJ 07726
(212–681–0887; fax 212–661–7595)
E-mail: Gilcareer@aol.com

Professional Association of Resume Writers (PARW)
3637 Fourth Street North, Suite 330
St. Petersburg, FL 33704
(800–822–7279; 813–821–2274; fax 813–894–1277)
E-mail: PARWHQ@aol.com

Specialty Paper and Supply Sources

Artmaker Super Sheets (909–626–8065)
BeaverPrints™ (800–923–2837)
Business Envelope Manufacturers (800–275–4400)
Computer Sensations (800–848–9001)
DataCal (800–752–6222)
Edge/UN Communications (800–434–3343)

Flying Paper Works (800–752–6222)
Global Ink Spectrum (714–241–7753)
Idea Art (800–433–2278)
IJ Technologies (800–356–6962)
Kelly Paper (800–675–3559)
Kirk Paper (909–715–3959)
Letraset (800–343–8973)
MEI/MicroCenter (800–634–3478)
Metro Writing & Design (800–607–2737)
NEBS (800–752–5266)
On Paper (800–820–2299)
Paper Access (800–727–3701)
PaperDirect (800–272–7377)
Paper Graphics (313–522–8200)
Penny Wise Office Products (800–942–3311)
PM Resource (800–842–6558) (my personal favorite!)
Power Up! (800–851–2917)
Premier Papers (800–843–0414)
Queblo (800–523–9080)
Quill (800–789–1331)
RapidForms (800–257–8354)
Reliable (800–735–4000)
Stephen Fossler Company (800–762–0030)
Streamliners (800–544–5779)
Viking Office Products (800–421–1222)
Wholesale Supply Company (800–962–9162)

Thanks to Shelley Newman and Connie Stevens for their contributions to this listing.

SPECIALTY PUBLICATIONS

The Word Advantage, published by Jan Melnik, CPRW (yours truly!), author of this book and of the popular *How to Start a Home-Based Secretarial Services Business.* She is president of Absolute Advantage, division / Comprehensive Services Plus of Durham, Connecticut, founded in 1983. This twelve-page quarterly newsletter (with an additional three- to eight-page supplement per issue) features "creative ideas and marketing strategies for those who work with words . . . keys to success that will give your business the advantage!" Contributing editors include some of the professionals cited in this book (Louise Kursmark, Carla Culp, and Dawn LaFontaine). *The Word Advantage* is shipped flat to all subscribers (always first-class mail) and features three-hole punching for convenient binder storage for reference purposes. Features include:

- Great ideas for new profit centers
- Strategies for attracting and retaining clients
- Successful techniques for improving your productivity *and* profitability
- Details on how to expand into broader market areas
- Pricing Q & A
- Sample ads, brochure copy, and marketing/promotional tips
- A forum for subscribers to exchange good ideas and tips for running a successful business
- Resume feature in each issue (frequently an effectively annotated "before/after" example)

To subscribe, send check, money order, or complete credit card information (MasterCard, Visa, Discover/Novus, or American Express, with account number and expiration date) in the amount of $40 for a one-year subscription ($75 for a two-year subscription) to *The Word Advantage;* Department GRB, P.O. 718, Durham, CT 06422. Many back issues, filled with timeless, valuable information, are also available.

Resume/Personal Marketing Workshop Kit, by Jan Melnik, CPRW. This complete workshop was developed and written by Jan Melnik. Take your business "on the road" with classes—teach! Build visibility in your community by instructing classes from your home office, in the public library, or through an adult education of community college program. This complete package (which you can use "as is" or tailor to meet your exact needs) includes everything you'll need; the proposal letter to pitch your program, along with the method for marketing to help ensure success; the materials you'll need for classes (roster, evaluation form); and a comprehensive "how-to" formula for teaching resume writing and cover letter crafting in a two-part workshop. The program is designed to educate individuals who believe they'd like to write their own resumes; nevertheless, in many instances, delivering the training will encourage attendees to *book appointments with you later, instead!*

To order, send $34.95 (check, money order, or MasterCard, Visa, Discover/NOVUS, or American Express information [full account number and expiration date]) to Department GRBT, P.O. Box 718, Durham, CT 06422.

Creative Client Communiques, produced by Jan Melnik, CPRW. This comprehensive package features an extensive collection (forty-plus pages) of effective and innovative communication vehicles for clients . . . from five years' worth of quarterly newsletters (you can copy as many of these ideas/articles as you wish in your own client newsletter) to fee schedules and from handouts for resume clients (which you may copy) to samples of actual ads and effective client follow-up correspondence, plus much more. Your creative energies will be triggered with these proven ideas that Jan has used in successfully building her business. To order the package, send $12.95 (check, money order, or MasterCard, Visa, Discover/NOVUS, or American Express information [full account number and expiration date]) to Department GRB, P.O. Box 718, Durham, CT 06422.

To obtain information about all of the publications and materials that Jan Melnik produces, please send a stamped, self-addressed business envelope to Department GRBI, P.O. Box 718, Durham, CT 06422. To order any materials through the Internet, using a credit card, contact the author at CompSPJan@aol.com.

Bootstrappin' Entrepreneur Resource Collection, published by Kimberly Stanséll. A survival package of special reports and newsletters to help people start and run businesses on a shoestring budget. Published by the author of *Bootstrapper's Success Secrets* (Career Press, 1997). For more information, send a SASE to Research Done Write!, Suite B261–JLM, 8726 South Sepulveda Boulevard, Los Angeles, CA 90045.

Designing Your Web Site: A Blueprint for Success, written by Lisa Freeman, president of Advanced Office and Resume Services in Florence, South Carolina, and René Hart, CPRW, president of First Impression Resume and Career Development Services in Lakeland, Florida. Lisa and René have developed this guide to give you the basic tools you'll need to design and publish a Web site for marketing your resume services to clients across the globe. Building a Web site will enhance your company's image and serve as an additional source of income for existing business. In addition to providing you with the basics of designing your site, Lisa and René give you the resources you can use to promote your site, both locally and on the Internet, as well as furnish tips on how to build effective, long-lasting relationships with your long-distance clients.

To order, send a check or money order for $17.95, plus $3.00 shipping and handling, to Blueprint for Success, Department JLM, 817-G Parker Drive, Florence, SC 29501. Lisa's URL is http://members. aol.com/Resumewin.

How to Make Your Resume and Cover Letter Work for You! Creative Format, Dynamic Content, and Effective Writing Techniques, written and published by Carol Lawrence, CPRW, president of A Better Resume of Savannah, Georgia. This complete seminar (spanning four hours) presents detailed, step-by-step strategies for building a commanding resume and cover letter. Included are fifteen transparencies for illustration, sample worksheets, class handouts, directions to ensure a successful experience for the instructor, and a disk with all materials to allow personalization. It's a proven, powerful marketing tool for your business.

To request additional information and an order form, send a SASE to A Better Resume, P.O. Box 9826, Department JLM2, Savannah, GA 31412. Please include a daytime telephone number. (PARW members will be quoted a discounted price on the package.)

Internet Job Search Guide, written by René Hart, CPRW, president of First Impressions Resume and Career Development Services of Lakeland, Florida, and Lisa Freeman, president of Advanced Office and Resume Services in Florence, South Carolina. Still a little vague about the role the Internet can play in your client's job search? This booklet is a step-by-step guide to conducting your client's job search on-line. From investigating specific companies to searching well-established databases and submitting your client's resume through the Internet, this guide will assist you in formulating a plan of attack that will allow you to quickly and easily transition your client's job search on-line. Resources included in this comprehensive guide:

- Detailed instructions for using Internet job-listing databases.
- Corporate Web site directory
- Tips for finding and using resume submission sites

To order, send check or money order for $17.95, plus $3.00 shipping and handling, to Internet Job Search Guide, Department JLM, 7100 Pebble Pass Loop, Lakeland, FL 33810. René's URL is http://members.aol.com/ResumesFL.

Job Search Mastery, developed by Steven Green, CPRW, president of Careerpath, Northboro, Massachusetts. This two-cassette audio program, created by Steven Green and published by CareerTrack Publications, gives your clients the ultimate advantage. A job hunt shouldn't be a haphazard shot in the dark—it should be a quest for the best. This program will get your client's head in gear and point him or her in the right direction. Some of what your clients (and you!) will learn in this program:

- A new way of looking at the job search: taking charge of your career—and your life

- How to identify the unique strengths, skills, and value that you bring to the table—knowing these at the outset puts you way ahead of the game

- Make sure you pursue work that you really love, rather than settling for "just a job"

- Ways to zero in on the company that's right for you: how culture and environment can make the difference between tedium and stardom

- Three key factors at work in today's job marketplace and how they affect your choice of careers

- Why your education can't stop with your diploma: how to create an edge for yourself in an ever-changing arena

- The global economy and you—how to pursue positions in the expanding international markets

- Ways to put yourself in your employer's shoes: the advantage you gain by identifying your interviewer's hot buttons

- How to be yourself in an interview and still sell your strengths clearly and convincingly

- The SOLER model: five proven techniques that will help you come across as a strong candidate in any interview

This program is available in bookstores nationwide for $15.95, or you may order directly from the author for $10.00, plus $3.50 for shipping and handling. Send check or MasterCard/Visa credit card information to CareerPath, Dept. JanRes, 242 Brewer Street, Northboro, MA 01532; call (800) 393–5548; E-mail Careerpath@gis.net.

The Working Families Newsletter, published by Patricia Schiff Estess. This is an engaging, informative, and upbeat six-page monthly publication that serves as the linchpin for a broad-based work/life program. The focus is on easing the stress of juggling work, family, and personal responsibilities by providing employees with "news to use" and tips for finding more time, energy, and money. Although it is targeted to employees of large corporations, nearly all the tips are equally valuable to someone working at home.

To subscribe, send a check for $24 for a one-year subscription to Working Families, Inc., 40 East Twenty-first Street, Fifth Floor, Department Jan-Res, New York, NY 10010, or call (212) 674–4420.

The Working Smart Newsletter, published by Steven Green, president of CareerPath of Northboro, Massachusetts. This publication is a free newsletter distributed via E-mail. Its mission is threefold: (a) to give small and home-based businesses a road map to ensure their success; (b) to assist the individual to optimize career potential; and (c) to analyze and report on future trends and how they affect the individual, small business, and the workplace. The newsletter's slogan: "Working smart . . . because it's always better to work smart than to work hard."

To subscribe, send an E-mail message to workingsmart-list@webcoach.com. Be sure to put "subscribe" in the subject field. Mention in the body of your E-mail that you learned of this offer in Jan Melnik's resume book.

BIBLIOGRAPHY

The Adams Resume Almanac. Holbrook, Mass.: Adams Publishing, 1994.

Allen, Jeffrey G., J. D., C. P. C. *The Perfect Follow-Up Method to Get the Job.* New York: John Wiley & Sons, 1992.

Beatty, Richard H. *175 High-Impact Cover Letters.* New York: John Wiley & Sons, 1992.

———. *The Perfect Cover Letter.* New York: John Wiley & Sons, 1989.

Bolles, Richard N. *What Color Is Your Parachute?* Berkeley, Calif. Ten Speed Press, 1996.

———. *The Three Boxes of Life, and How to Get Out of Them.* Berkeley, Calif.: Ten Speed Press, 1978.

Corbin, Bill, and Shelbi Wright. *The Edge Resume & Job Search Strategy.* Carmel, Ind.: UN Communications, 1993.

Dun and Bradstreet Million Dollar Directory. New York: Dun and Bradstreet.

Gieseking, Hal, and Paul Plawin. *30 Days to a Good Job.* New York: Fireside, 1994.

Hellman, Paul. *Ready, Aim, You're Hired! How to Job-Interview Successfully, Anytime, Anywhere, with Anyone.* New York: AMACOM, 1986.

Kennedy, Joyce Lain, and Thomas J. Morrow. *Electronic Job Search Revolution: Creating a Winning Resume.* New York: J. Wiley & Sons, 1994.

———. *Electronic Resume Revolution: Creating a Winning Resume.* New York: J. Wiley & Sons, 1994.

Krannich, Ronald L., and William J. Banis. *High Impact Resumes & Letters.* Manassas, Va.: Impact Publications, 1988.

Kursmark, Louise. *How to Own and Operate a Home-based Desktop Publishing Business*. Old Saybrook, Conn.: Globe Pequot Press, 1996.

Lucht, John. *Executive Job-Changing Workbook*. New York: Viceroy Press, 1994.

Marcus, John J. *The Complete Job Interview Handbook*. New York: Harper & Row Publishers, 1985.

Melnik, Jan. *How to Open and Operate a Home-Based Secretarial Services Business*. Old Saybrook, Conn.: Globe Pequot Press, 1994.

Melnik, Jan. *How to Start a Home-based Secretarial Services Business*, 2nd Ed. Old Saybrook, Conn.: Globe Pequot Press, 1996.

Molloy, John T. *New Dress for Success*. New York: Warner Books, 1988.

Moreau, Daniel. *Kiplinger's Survive & Profit from a Mid-Career Change*. Washington, D.C.: Kiplinger Books, 1994.

Parker, Yana. *Resume Pro: The Professional's Guide*. Berkeley, Calif.: Ten Speed Press, 1993.

Petras, Kathryn, and Ross Petras. *The Over-40 Job Guide*. New York: Poseidon Press, 1993.

Poor's Register of Corporations, Directors, & Executives. New York: Standard and Poor's Corporation.

Resumes (National Business Employment Weekly, The Wall Street Journal). New York: John Wiley & Sons, 1994.

Tepper, Ron. *Power Resumes*. New York: John Wiley & Sons, 1992.

Thomas Register of American Manufacturers. New York: Thomas Publishing Co.

Vilas, Donna, and Sandy Vilas. *Power Networking*. Austin, Tex.: MountainHarbour Publications, 1992.

Weinberg, Janice. *How to Win the Job You Really Want*. New York: Henry Holt and Co., 1989.

Yate, Martin John. *Cover Letters That Knock 'em Dead*. Holbrook, Mass.: Bob Adams, 1992.

———. *Knock 'em Dead: The Ultimate Job Seeker's Handbook*. Holbrook, Mass.: Adams Media Corp., 1995.

———. *Knock 'em Dead with Great Answers to Tough Interview Questions*. Holbrook, Mass.: Bob Adams, 1991.

———. *Resumes That Knock 'em Dead*. Holbrook, Mass.: Adams Media Corp., 1995.

INDEX

work order form, 101
aptitude and skills testing, 2
auctions, 7

B

brochures, 6, 85, 107–8, 114, 143, 156
business
    cards, 5, 54, 56, 80, 110, 143, 156, 167
    closing new, 9–11, 162
        objections/solution responses, 162–65
    expansion, 248–53
        ancillary profit centers, 252–53
    lecturing/teaching, 248–49
        subcontractors/employees, 249–52
    name, 39–40, 43, 51–57, 266–72
    organization, 40–41
    slogan, 114–16, 266–72
business plan
    for clients, 60
    for your business, 73–86
        appendix and resources, 86
        company background and industry, 75–76
        contingency planning for areas of potential risk, 77–78
    executive summary, 74
    financial data, 78
    general description of the business, 75–77
    marketing and sales planning, 75–77
    mission statement, 74–75
    projected costs for business start-up, 79–85

C

career changers, 3, 62
career counseling/coaching, 2, 60, 152–55
cash flow, 9–11, 252, 100–102
Certified Professional Resume Writer (CPRW), 15, 243–47
Chamber of Commerce, 108–9
checking account, 5, 83

D

DBA (doing business as), 39

deposit, 31, 100, 176

desktop publishing, 9, 45, 57

direct mail campaigns, 2, 85, 107, 133–34, 144–45, 155

discount offers, 49, 59, 63, 65, 68, 77, 107

disk storage, 4, 15, 65, 70–71

donations, 76, 107, 110

downsizing, 3, 143

E

editorial/writing services, 9, 65, 69

electronic resumes, 111, 136

employees, 4, 249–52

employment applications, 2–3, 6, 51, 60

envelopes, 6, 65, 68, 83, 140, 198

executive resumes, 3, 30–32, 56, 59,

executive suites, 4, 252

expense sheet, 81

F

fax

    machine, 6, 84, 166

    pricing, 65

first-time employment, 3

fonts, 5, 79

furniture, 6, 83–84, 90–93

G

guarantees, 15, 57, 102

H

hiring managers' practices/interview expectations, 134–43, 225–32

home-based business

    benefits/rewards 17–21, 230–38

    challenges, 230–38

    full-time, 7

hours/scheduling, 103–5, 229–42

ideal, 3, 9, 11

part-time/moonlighting, 7, 78

safety and security, 88–90

human resources' expertise, 141–51

I

increasing prices, 62–64, 250

insurance, 41

internships, 3

interviews, 2, 60, 71, 92, 224–32, 234–240

informational interviews, 154–55

interview questions, 237–41

interview training, 2, 9, 56, 60, 69, 158–59, 225

investing in your business, 7

invoicing, 40, 52–53, 94–99

IRS, 251

J

job search techniques, 2, 56–57, 152–55, 225–31

L

laser printing, 4, 5, 15, 65, 79

layoffs, 3, 143

leads clubs, 110

leave-behind materials, 2, 59, 211–15

letters of recommendation, 6, 164, 206

library, 6, 15, 85, 112, 156, 249

licenses, 5, 83

lighting, 6–7, 84

M

marketing to

career counselors, 152–55

hiring managers, 134–43

human resources, 141–51

recruiters and placement specialists, 134–43

S

salary history, 59, 137, 143, 149, 151, 213

sales and use tax permit, 5, 40, 96

scheduling, 102–5

secondhand furniture, 83–84

secretarial services, 2, 156

security, 4, 53, 89

self-employment, 7

service offerings, 15, 43, 53, 58

SF-171 preparation, 2, 51, 60

skills and attributes necessary for resume writing, 13–17, 47–50

slogan, 51, 54–58, 74, 113–116

specialized services, 156, 201

stability, 4

start-up costs, 11, 37, 79–85

stationery, 64–66, 80–83

students
    discounts, 59, 65, 68, 107
    graduate, 3, 46
    job search strategies, 152–55, 192–96
    undergraduate, 3, 46, 59

style analysis, 2, 60

subcontractors, 249–51

summary of qualifications, 2, 135–36, 139, 142, 148, 151, 193

T

tag sales, 7, 83–84

taxes, 40, 95–97, 251

teaching workshops, 96, 107–8, 112, 143–44

telephone, 5, 11, 36, 79
    answering machine, 5, 8, 54, 78, 80, 166–67
    client relationships, 157–62

thank-you letters, 59, 149–51, 169–71, 198, 205, 211, 214–15, 229, 232

time management, 23–36
    answering machine, 24
    colleagues' advice, 26–30

ABOUT THE AUTHOR

Jan Melnik started her resume, office support, and desktop publishing business, Comprehensive Services Plus (CSP), in 1983 from a small room in her basement. As the business (and her family) grew, she moved to a spare bedroom before building her current dedicated office adjacent to her home. Upon the publication of her first book, *How to Start a Home-Based Secretarial Services Business,* she began to expand into business consulting, offering lectures, workshops, and other training programs for home-based professionals.

The subscriber newsletter Jan Melnik edits and publishes, *The Word Advantage,* is about to enter its third year of publication. She has several new book projects in development and continues work on her series of children's stories, whose story line encompasses her three sons: identical twins Weston and Daniel, born in 1987, and Stephen, born in 1990. She enjoys traveling, tries to find time to keep up with her voracious reading appetite, and still builds flower gardens in her spare moments.